BoJACK HORSEMAN

The Art Before the Horse

MISPRINTS

¿Q U E?
Me gusta
XXI
HABL
ESPA
Guapo
I'M A
ZELDA

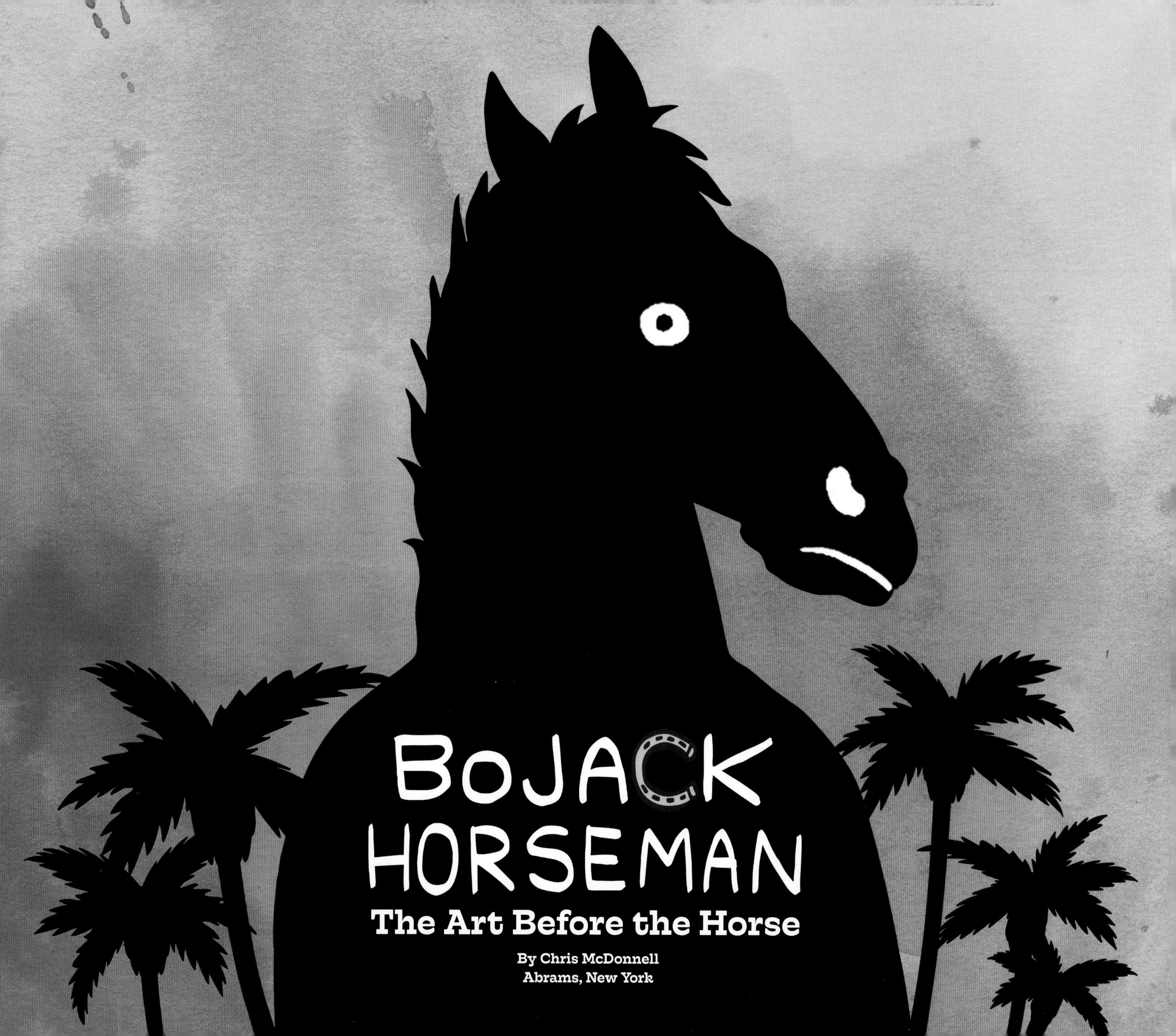
BOJACK
HORSEMAN
The Art Before the Horse
By Chris McDonnell
Abrams, New York

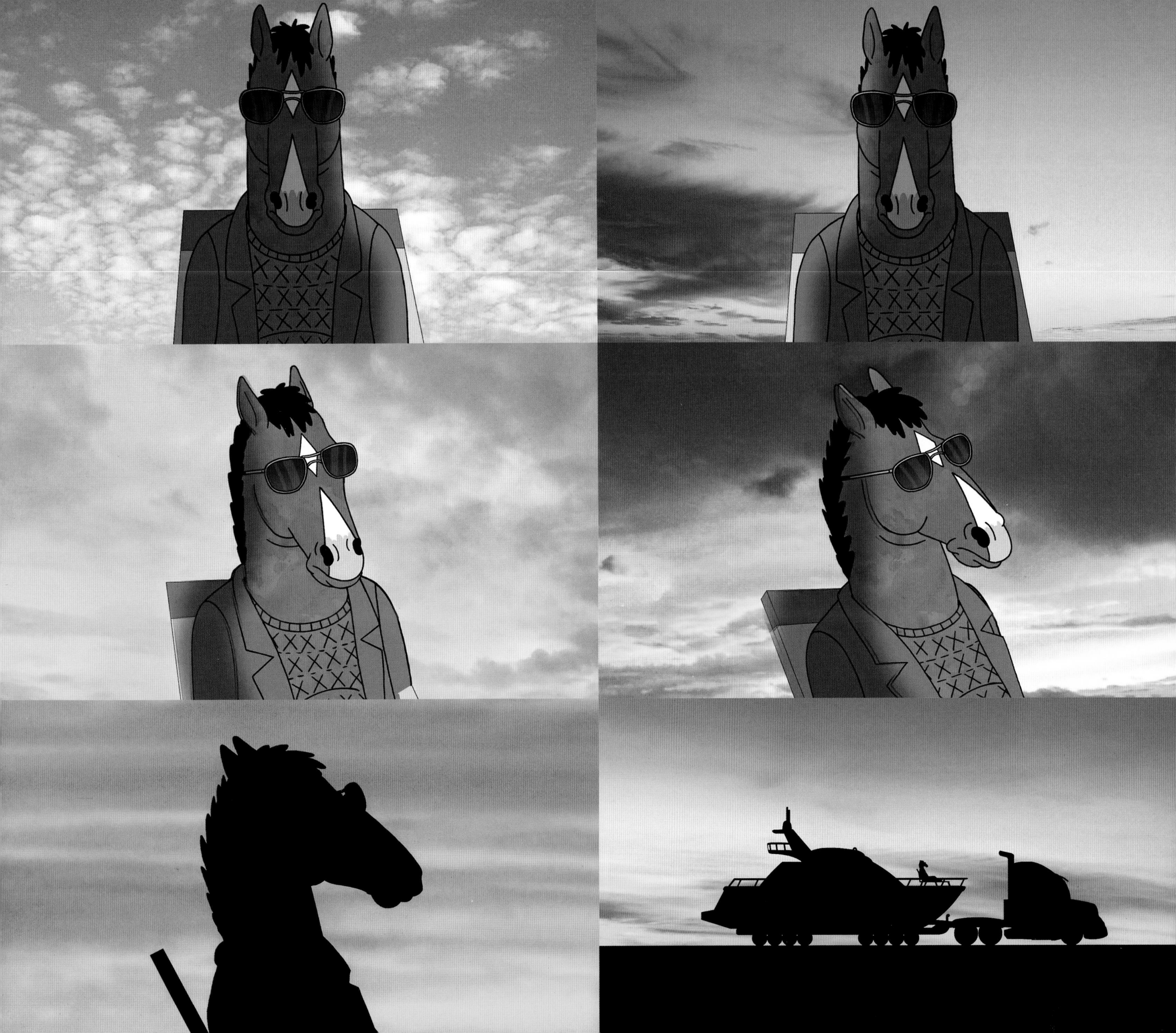

Contents

Foreword

By Lisa Hanawalt

I was terrified when Raphael told me the news that *BoJack* had been picked up. I probably tried to Google "how to design an animated show" and came up with no real answers. My diary from my first month at work has entries like:

- I feel like the new kid at school. I had to sit in on a meeting and I got so bored and anxious I almost threw up!
- I've been trying to communicate the way I think clouds should be drawn so that they aren't boring.
- This job is intensely social in a way that is alien to me. I have to constantly communicate with other people. I like it, but it's also completely exhausting.
- Elizabeth, our prop designer, has been sending me props and it's fun to form an instant opinion about which EKG machine looks better. She draws phone cords really well and I realize this is a thing I'm going to become particular about. Later I ask another designer to redraw a phone cord several times because it isn't quite right and I've been spoiled by Elizabeth's.
- I feel panicked and mute during large meetings, but much more in my element when speaking one-on-one with designers because I can help make choices and bad jokes. Today I told one designer, "This restaurant should have a dumb fountain. What if there was a baby elephant cupid with water coming out of his trunk and dick?" I know these are the least important elements of the show but they give me the greatest feeling of pride.

I'm feeling slightly more confident after four seasons, but I'm still learning new skills (and making new mistakes) every day. This show has such a wild variety of imagery, I relish the excuse to research, form opinions about, and draw specific types of bird, species of rodent, 1940s period costumes, deep-sea anemones, vintage movie posters, advertisements, furniture, etc. It feels like a fun puzzle every time I have to design a comely snake or smarmy rabbit or dentist/clown duck. Every episode comes with unique and wonderful challenges.

I learned it's OK to ask for help and input, and that needing to work together with other people to complete a project is a strength, not a weakness. I'm lucky to work with so many talented individuals who tolerate my approach to things like purple clouds and blue-tongued lizards and are not only cool with me getting my paw prints all over everything, but also add their own unique line, color, shapes, and jokes. My favorite moments of the show are the inside gags, worst puns, made-up words, butt paintings, and the wonky drawings we didn't fix because they just looked funnier that way.

Every artist on this production has contributed something meaningful, and I hope they feel proud when they look through the following pages. I'm so proud of all of us.

PS My apologies to the furry community and all animal-tail enthusiasts for the lack of tails on this show. Please feel free to grab a marker and add tails to all the following pages in your *personal copy* of this book.

Lisa Hanawalt is an artist in Los Angeles. She is also the author of *My Dirty Dumb Eyes*, *Hot Dog Taste Test*, and most recently, *Coyote Doggirl*.

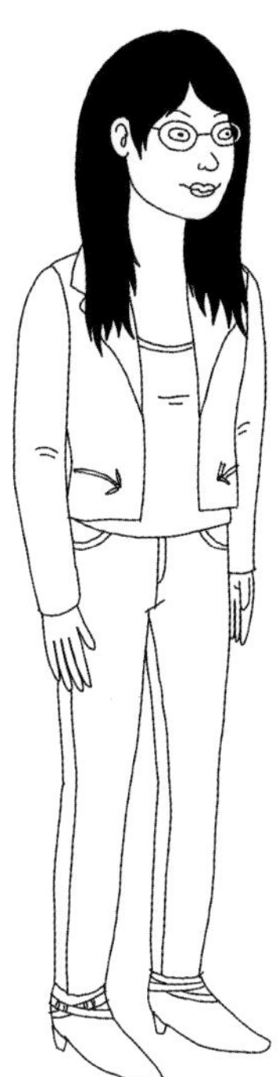

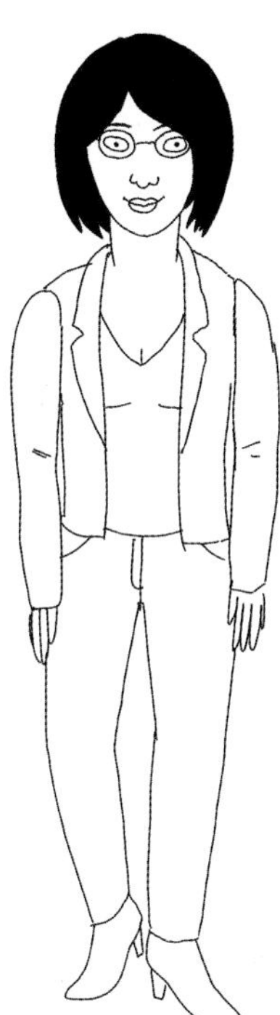

Introduction

By Raphael Bob-Waksberg

THIS IS THE MOST BORING PAGE IN THIS BOOK, and I feel so bad for you that you are reading it right now. Literally every other page is more interesting than this one, and yet here you are, like a sucker, still reading this page.

Every other page in this book is bursting with gorgeous illustrations, meticulous breakdowns, mercurial breakthroughs, history, pre-history, histrionics, animatics, animated panics, frantic fragments, remnants, remembrances, never-before-seen-full-screen-behind-the-scenes ephemera, et cetera—or, as a mouse might say, et cheddara.

And yet here you are, idling in this introduction instead of moving forward. You are a fool, plain and simple, and I do not envy those who have chosen to share their lives with you and are now forced to constantly put up with your foolish insistence on reading the worst pages in books.

It just occurred to me that perhaps you have not purchased this book yet. Perhaps you are just thumbing through it, trying to decide whether or not to buy it and you've somehow stumbled upon this page, in which case:

A. Congratulations, you have by sheer happenstance landed on the very worst page, and even having been informed (vehemently!) how unrepresentative it is of the larger work, instead of exploring the treasure trove of other pages literally at your fingertips, you have chosen to stubbornly park yourself on this page.

B. Maybe it is not so wise of me to call a potential customer "a fool, plain and simple" right at the moment this potential customer is trying to decide whether or not to purchase our wares. (Is a book *wares*? Or just *ware*, singular? A ware? Is that right? I'm not aware of a thing being a ware, but I guess some ware must be, somewhere.)

C. Please forget about the part where I called you a fool. Thank you. That was not appropriate. I'm sorry. Please buy this book.

Wow. This has gone way off the rails. Let's focus on the positive. Again, every other page in this book is better than this one, so you have a lot to look forward to. (And yes, I understand this is now a different page than the one I previously said was the worst page in this book, but I assure you this page is no picnic either.) Chris, the author, has spent the last year and a half tirelessly (well, that might not be accurate; it's possible he got tired) conducting interviews and collecting artifacts, all in the service of telling (and showing!) you everything you could ever want to know about the show *BoJack Horseman*.

This book will take you through the years of development when the show was but a mere inkling of a shadow of a notion of an idea—you can read the many ways I described it to people as I was still figuring out what it was, and see how it bounced around and took shape as we finally pitched it to Netflix and then made the first season.

This book will tell you how an episode gets made, wending you every bend of the way, from the conception through the writing, acting, designing, animation, and post-production, with insight from all the major players and oodles of doodles and index cards and script pages and storyboards and character sheets and lighting passes and all the things that when you put them together in a big pot and stir it all up, it somehow makes a show.

This book has a funny story about my friend Kevin in it—so you have that to look forward to as well.

This book does NOT contain a recipe for a delicious vegan pasta dish with artichokes, walnuts, olives, and sun-dried tomatoes. Sorry, we couldn't find a way to get it in, because it really

just didn't seem relevant. If you would like to try this delicious vegan pasta dish, you'll just have to come to my house and I will make it for you.

OK! Now at this point in the foreword, I'm going to shift gears for a second, so be forewarned. (Side note: *Is* this a foreword? As I was writing this, I couldn't remember if I was supposed to be writing the foreword or the preface or the introduction or the postscript or the table of contents or the blurb on the back where some famous person goes, "Heyyyy man, this is some book, huh? Mostly I don't like books, but this one? Pretty good book," and you, the fan of that famous person, thinks, "Well, gee, if my favorite famous person is telling me to purchase this book, surely then I must!" Anyway, hopefully this doesn't end up being called an introduction as opposed to a foreword so I can keep all my awesome foreword-related wordplay, which we all agree is hilarious and good.)

I would like to talk about Bertolt Brecht for a second. I know the early twentieth-century German playwright might not seem particularly germane, but this is my page and I can do what I want with it and if you wanted to stop reading it, you really should have done that by now and you didn't so now you're stuck with me. Now I'm no Brecht expert (or Brexpert, if you will)—in fact, one time in college my professor told me, "I think you're pretty severely misreading Brecht here," while discussing a paper I wrote—my senior project—about Brecht—but I did see Meryl Streep and Kevin Kline perform *Mother Courage and Her Children* in Central Park once, and that was pretty cool. Anyway, I'll get to back to that later.

When people find out I'm the creator of *BoJack Horseman* (Did I mention I'm the creator of *BoJack Horseman*? I guess I should have made that clear earlier in the foreword. Maybe you already picked that up through context clues? I don't know. I've never done one of these things before.), there are often two things they assume about me which are incorrect, and I would like to use this opportunity to set the record straight.

The first is that I had a rough childhood because I grew up in a bitter broken home like BoJack did. In fact, I come from a large and loving family who taught me how to be funny and taught me how to be compassionate. I am very lucky and I would not be where I am now without their support.

The second thing is that I am a tremendously hopeless individual, because *BoJack Horseman* is such a hopeless show. I will let others decide if I am hopeless or not, but I personally do not believe that *BoJack Horseman* is. Maybe I'm biased because when I watch the show I see all the love that goes into it, all the hard work and care from all the talented people you're about to meet over the next bookful of pages. Maybe when you finish this book, you will see what I see, but I think it's also helpful if you saw Meryl Streep and Kevin Kline in Bertolt Brecht's *Mother Courage and Her Children* in Central Park.

By the end of *Mother Courage and Her Children* in Central Park, Meryl Streep has lost everything, partly to the viciousness of war and partly through her own shortsightedness. But rather than giving in to her grief, the final image of the play is Meryl Streep picking her cart back up and moving forward.

Brecht believed audiences were wrong to sympathize with Mother Courage and in revisions he made efforts to make her less likable, but I still think in those last moments, it's difficult not to feel sorry for her pain or admiration for her fortitude in the face of tremendous loss.

Anyway, that's what I think about when I hear people call *BoJack* hopeless. Because maybe I'm misreading my own show the same way I misread Brecht, but when I look at *BoJack*, I see a lot of hope. I see a world full of characters who suffer tremendously but still always somehow find a way to pick up their cart and keep moving.

Please enjoy the rest of this book. You can read it straight through or just jump to random sections and look at the pictures. There are a thousand wonderful ways to get lost in this beautiful world of a book. I hope you liked this little section from me, but if you didn't, that's OK too, because every other page is so much better.

Raphael Bob-Waksberg is the creator and executive producer of *BoJack Horseman*. For more information on *BoJack Horseman* or Raphael Bob-Waksberg, please read this book.

This spread: Early concept drawings of BoJack Horseman by production designer Lisa Hanawalt.

1: Creating BoJack

Prehistory, Inspiration, Pitching, Producing

BoJack Horseman, Netflix's first animated original series for adults, is a show that boldly asks, "What if humans and talking, humanized animals lived, worked, and loved side by side in a bizarro-world Los Angeles, California?" One answer: "There'd be a lot more animal puns." Ever since its entire first season was released for streaming on August 22, 2014, *BoJack* has amassed a following of viewers who are hungry for its mix of humor, heart, subversive storytelling, and unique visual style. Created by writer Raphael Bob-Waksberg, designed by illustrator Lisa Hanawalt, and produced by Michael Eisner's Tornante Company, the series launches by following alcoholic has-been actor—and literal horse-man—BoJack Horseman (voiced by Will Arnett) as he attempts his big comeback by writing (read: hiring a ghostwriter to write) his tell-all memoir, *One Trick Pony*.

Things have gone decidedly downhill for BoJack since he starred in the beloved nineties television series *Horsin' Around*. Bitter, depressed, and usually drunk, BoJack botches nearly every chance for redemption and alienates everyone he knows, including his human roommate, Todd (Aaron Paul); his cat agent and ex-girlfriend, Princess Carolyn (Amy Sedaris); his human ghostwriter, Diane (Alison Brie); and his yellow Lab arch-frenemy, Mr. Peanutbutter (Paul F. Tompkins). Jumping back and forth between decades, the show stitches together BoJack's evolution from a tiny, cowering foal dressed in a sailor suit, to a sitcom star, to a hungover hot mess.

If that all sounds bleak—well, it is. The show's comedic highs are high, and the depressing lows are low. When *BoJack Horseman* hits us where it hurts, there's no wink-wink moment or sarcastic sidekick deployed to instantly deflate the tension; instead, the writing explores the human condition with believable realism, and it's this sincere interest in what it's like to struggle that connects viewers so deeply to the characters of an otherwise zanily rendered comedy. It's a show that offers its creators endless room to play with its signature motifs—from biting Hollywood parody, to goofy anthropomorphic humor, to funky textile designs. It's the music; it's the animation. It's the amalgamation of efforts from a team working their tails off for months at a time to bring it all to life. It is a funny, sad, and often beautiful experience that audiences binge on as soon as each new season drops

Below: A prescient "About Myself" essay by Lisa from the sixth grade, dated 9/16/94. Lisa writes with either a healthy confidence or a bit of self-aware deprecating humor about her social tormentors before moving on to accurately predict her own future. Note the additional horse drawings bleeding through from the other sides of the paper.

Mustang

This is my favorite of your drawings. I like the sense of movement in the legs

Lisa Hanawalt 9/16/94

About Myself

To start off I'll make it clear that I like horses. I REALLY Like Horses. I Really REALLY Like them! Everybody that knows me says it's more than an obsession. They're probly right. People make fun of me an call me "Horse poop" and "Lady Horse." I Just take it as a compliment, or I figure that they must like Horse Poo a lot, cause I hear them say it whenever I pass!

I get that.

I'm also wild about art. I want to be famous for drawing Horses someday.

What a wonderful goal!

Left, below: Two pages featuring horses from one of Lisa's earliest self-published comics and drawing zines, *It's Sexy When People Know Your Name.*

from the cloud. Viewers are eager to be bruised, tickled, and gut-punched along with the characters they have come to love.

The germ of all of this was, simply, a feeling.

Raphael Bob-Waksberg [series creator]: When I first moved out to LA in 2010, I was staying at this place that was a friend of a friend of a friend of a friend's house. I was paying something like six hundred dollars to live in this little closet, basically, in this gorgeous house—kind of what BoJack's house ended up looking like—up in the hills in Laurel Canyon. I didn't know anybody else who lived there, but this house was amazing: I remember there were rumors from people living in the house that it was the third-highest elevated in all of Hollywood, and that Johnny Depp had lived there once. I remember standing out on the balcony, looking out over the city, and feeling on top of the world—but also never more lonely and isolated. And I thought that kind of irony was an interesting feeling to explore. That was kind of the germ of the idea of the BoJack character: to create this guy who's had every opportunity for success, but still can't find a way to be happy.

A lot more went into germinating the series, too. To explore how Raphael arrived on the Laurel Canyon balcony, first we must jump back further in time, in *BoJack*-ian fashion, to . . . the nineties.

Fruits of Friendship

Two of *BoJack Horseman*'s primary artistic voices, Raphael and production designer Lisa Hanawalt, attended a progressive, academically rigorous high school together in the San Francisco Bay Area, where they eventually connected as friends during their first creative collaboration: a play.

Lisa Hanawalt [production designer]: I knew who Raphael was in middle school because he was acting in a lot of different plays. So I'd seen him, but he didn't know who I was. Then I got into theater when I was in high school. Even though I was really shy, everyone said, "Oh my God, the theater teacher [James Shelby] is really amazing; you've got to take theater." So I took it, and I was a background tech person, building sets. I finally started trying out for the plays, and I was cast in a short one-act play that Raphael was directing called *The Family Continues*, which was sort of an experimental Lanford Wilson play.

Raphael: The play I directed was at the end of that school year, spring of '01, but we'd already been in theater class together all year. We became friends by hanging out in the green room of the studio theater at our school during our prep periods and goofing around.

Left: Lisa's poster design for high school plays which included *The Family Continues*, the play Raphael and Lisa worked on together.

Below, opposite: Lisa with Tony the Pony, the horse that she leased as a teenager. Tony the Pony's markings were the inspiration for BoJack's design.

Below: Future *BoJack* coworkers Raphael (second from left) and Lisa, (front, yellow dress), pose for a pre-prom photo with fellow high schoolers.

Joking around at school, Raphael and Lisa unknowingly foreshadowed their future roles in the studio.

Raphael: We used to come up with dumb ideas for cartoons and do silly voices. I don't think either of us thought any of that nonsense would ever actually go anywhere.

Lisa: Raphael would look through my sketchbook, find a character, and then do the voice for that character, and it immediately made sense to me and I would draw more of that character. And we would make up TV show ideas; we never thought they would actually be on TV, but we'd be like, "Oh, you know that guy we're in math class with? What if he was a pirate and had a chicken on his shoulder?" Just stuff like that. It just felt very kinetic and collaborative. We would sit in the theater classroom and just make up this stuff and annoy everybody.

Thus, *BoJack*'s existence is, in part, owed to the sometimes cruel or beautiful hand that fate deals each of us: the friends we find in high school.

Lisa: I sort of didn't belong to any clique at all. I was friends with a lot of theater kids, but I was also friends with art students and kind of everyone by the time I graduated. I would say it was the kind of high school where nerds and people with really good grades were in the upper echelons of the social hierarchy. We had sports and there were definitely cheerleaders and stuff, but they weren't mean. I was actually friendly with cheerleaders. The arts were really valued there. You know, I was teased because I didn't get a perfect score on my SATs. [*Laughs.*] Raphael teased me. He was like, "Uh, you can go to a good community college, I guess." [*Laughs.*] Oh my God, so mean.

High school provides a delightful opportunity for half-formed humans to bond by railing against mutual enemies. (Parents! Homework! The system!) It is the social gauntlet in which future comics and cartoonists like Raphael and Lisa can first begin to hone their acerbic wit. Classrooms can also double as ideal laboratories for disruptive comic experiments.

Raphael: I feel like a lot of the larger narratives about high school are invented by people looking back. As a teenager, I remember feeling like the cliques and social hierarchy of high school were not as well defined as pop culture had made it seem like they would be. I don't recall railing against the popular kids or mean teachers in any sort of organized way, but I did have ADHD, so I was basically always just railing off in some direction or another. I had very little awareness of what was appropriate, and I would do anything for a laugh. On my less disruptive days, I would draw comics in class when I was bored,

Continued on page 29

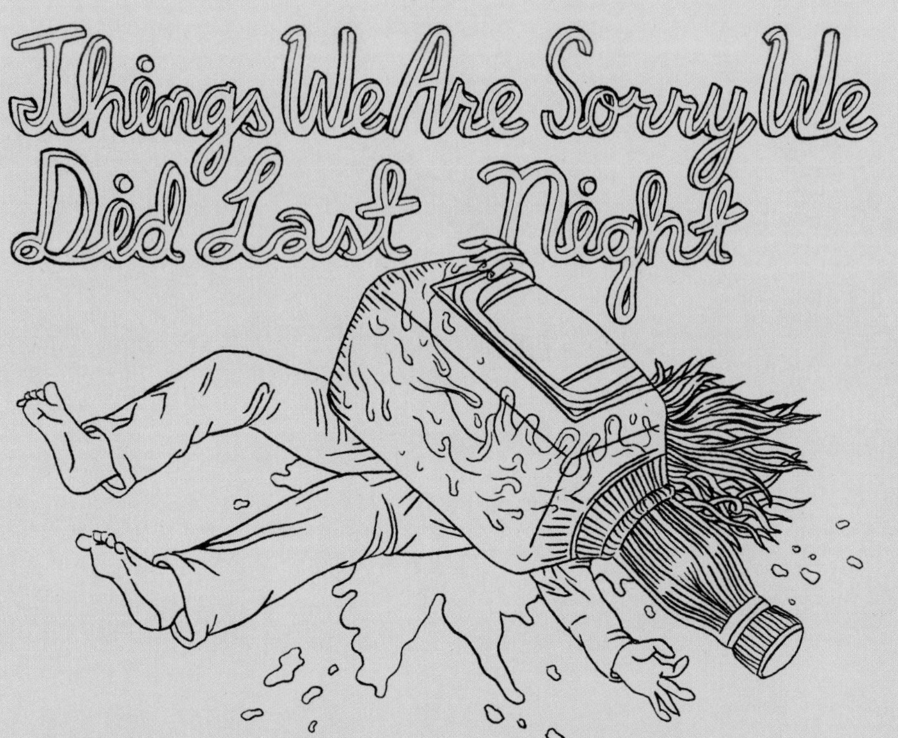
Things We Are Sorry We Did Last Night

① WE SHOULDN'T HAVE GONE HOME WITH THAT GUY

② OUR DECISION TO COOK WAS RECKLESS
MAC N CHEE
SSS!
SSSS!
③ WE DON'T REMEMBER HOW WE GOT ALL OF THESE WELTS
TO THE BEST OF OUR KNOWLEDGE:
① MACARONI BURNS
② VARIOLA-LIKE VIRUS
③ MIXED GRILL
④ PUSSY STAMP
⑤ CAT FACE
⑥ FINGER POKINGS (SELF-INFLICTED?)
⑦ SHARK BITE
⑧ TRILOBITE
⑨ TINY GLASSES

This spread: A comic story from one of Lisa's early self-published zines, *Mistakes We Made*.

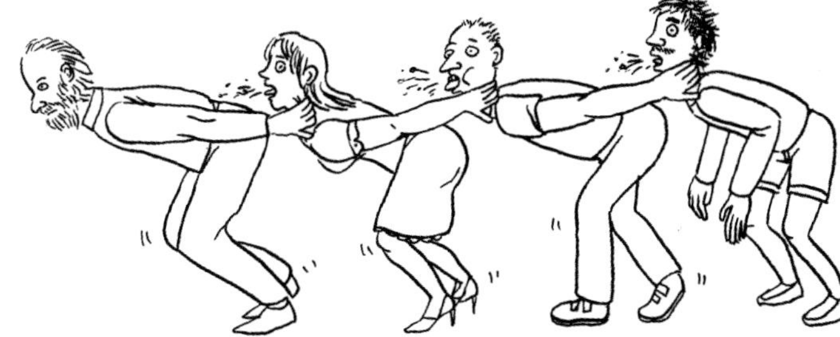

(I DON'T HAVE A NAME FOR THIS DANCE, BUT IT IS HORRIBLE)

"CAT-CALL CONTRA DANCE"
Do-si-do, you sweet pieces of ass! Now allemande left, Honey Haunches!
The "DICK SPIN"
(WE TRIED TO MAKE OUR HARD-ON LOOK INTENTIONAL BY BASING AN ENTIRE DANCE ON IT AND THE RESULTS WERE SHITTY)

The "WORM WHOSE TAIL HAS BEEN CUT OFF AND SO IT IS WAITING PATIENTLY FOR A NEW TAIL TO REGENERATE"

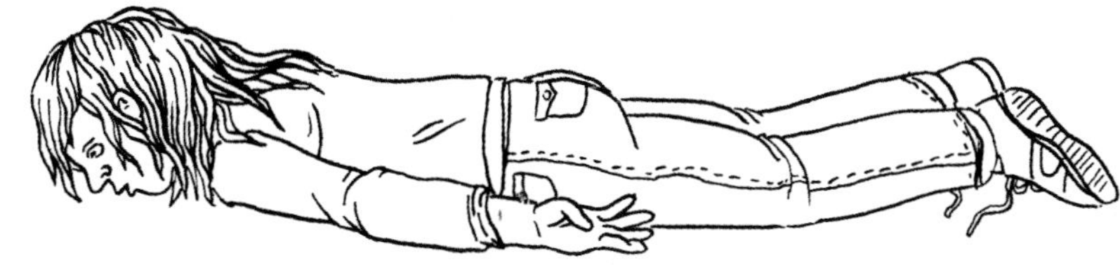

5 WE TRACKED DOWN ALL THE PEOPLE WHO COME UP WHEN WE GOOGLE OURSELVES AND MURDERED THEM

THIS IS MY HAT NOW!

DEATH TO LISA HANAWALT WHO HAS HORSES. I WANT TO HAVE HORSES!

I'M SORRY THAT I MUST DO THIS, LISA HANAWALT WHO TRIED TO ADD ME ON FACEBOOK RIGHT WHEN I STARTED DRAWING THIS COMIC

YOU WERE IN THE WRONG PLACE AT THE WRONG TIME

AND FINALLY, MY NEMESIS, LISA HANAWALT THE REAL ESTATE BROKER!

YOU'RE USING OUR NAME ON LINKED IN, PLAXO, AND NOW TWITTER?!
BUT YOU'RE STILL #1 ON GOOGLE!

This spread: The continued story from *Mistakes We Made*. Lisa's writing and drawing show off an uninhibited, wild, humor—a perfect match for her future work on *BoJack*.

but I also remember dropping my pants in the middle of class or shouting out any funny thing I could think of. I definitely gave off the vibe of a kid who didn't care about anything, but the truth is I just didn't know any other way to be.

Lisa: I was constantly drawing. I was making short comics, sort of in the style of Phoebe Gloeckner—who was my favorite cartoonist at the time along with Renée French—and I was drawing through class every day. My brother had bought me a bunch of comics, so I started reading them and I got really into them. I also was really into zines [self-published pamphlets, usually photocopied and hand-stapled, produced to express any content the author/artist wants, in any form]. So I started making a zine in high school called *Lobster Rags*, and it was just my poetry and product reviews and messed-up musings.

I would make comics about me and how I felt because I was a very emotional teenager. I went through a lot of issues in high school. I was severely depressed and I almost left because I was failing classes because I never went. I almost went to a different school, but then I was like, "No, you know what? I'm going to stick it out." So I kept going and I got really involved in theater. I turned my grades around, and I actually got an award for most improved, because they had thought I was going to drop out—but then I graduated with a really good GPA, so I think theater kind of saved me.

Continued on page 35

 **Stay Away From Other People**

This spread: Lisa's self-published zine *Stay Away from Other People* included several drawings that were used in the initial *BoJack* pitch. The fish-headed woman (left) and dejected goat-man (below) both recall minor characters that eventually made appearances in season four. The fish's jacket includes the distinctive arrow design detail that ended up on Diane's jacket in the series.

Stay Away From Other People

This spread: Intricate clothing detail and patterns have been a hallmark of Lisa's work, on display in these two spreads from her early self-published zine, *Stay Away from Other People*.

WE KNOW THAT WE REPULSE YOU WITH OUR INSIDE-OUTSIDE HUGS, WE'RE THE SEX BUGS SEX BUGS SEX BUUUGGGS!

Opposite: A Sex Bugs concert spread from the early Lisa zine, *Mistakes We Made*. Fun fact: Raphael wrote the Sex Bugs lyrics.

Below: Post-college Lisa and Raphael lived on opposite coasts and maintained their friendship through comics collaboration. A Lisa visit to Raphael in Brooklyn, 2006 (top). A Raphael visit to Lisa in Los Angeles, 2007 (middle). A celebratory dance in DUMBO, in 2009, the day after Lisa moved to Brooklyn. Not long after Lisa settled in NYC, Raphael moved to LA, and the friends' city-swap was complete.

Below: Outside of animal-headed people, a frequently recurring subject in Lisa's earlier work was mangled cars gushing twisted entrails.

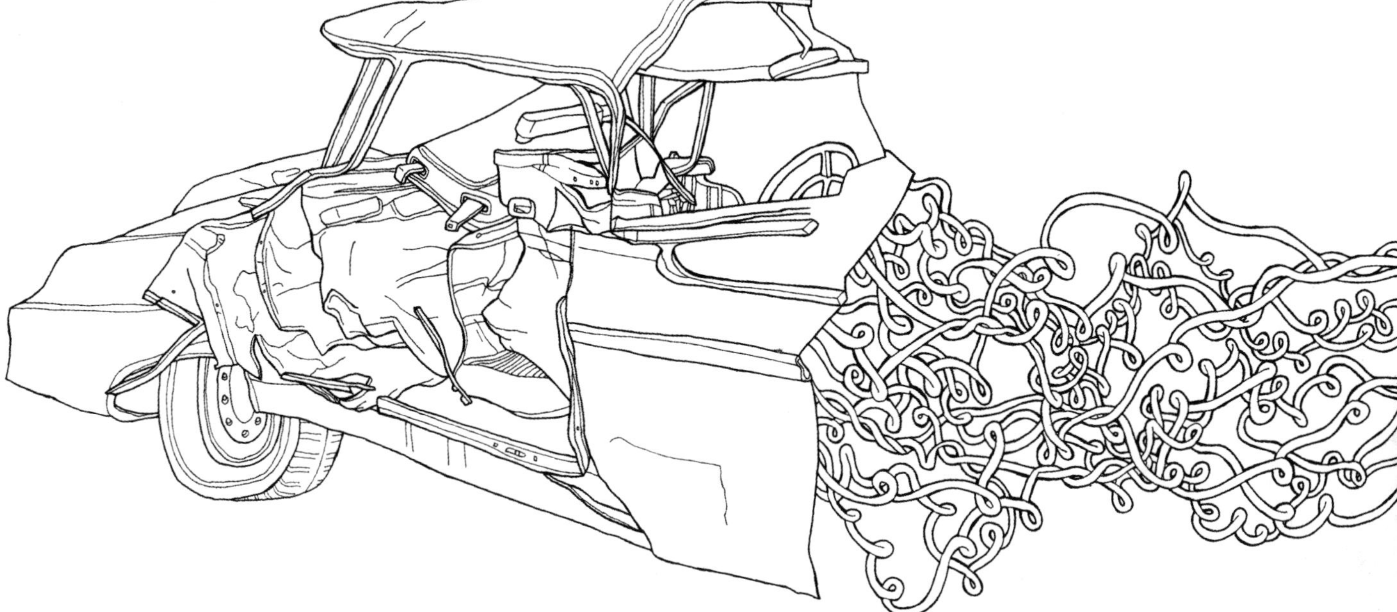

Maintaining good friendships during the turbulent teenage years is impressive, but keeping those friends through adulthood is an advanced achievement. Old friendships have connective tissue based on personal chemistry and a long history of growing together. Contrast this with your average adult-onset acquaintance built on office gossip, sports stats, and/or binge drinking, and you'll find that these old friendships are inevitably deeper and weirder.

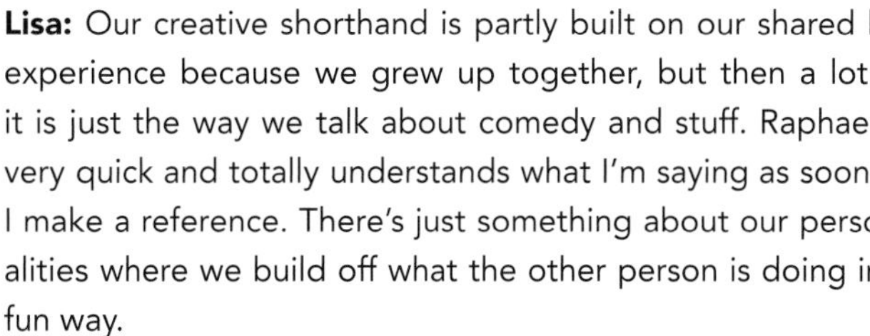

Lisa: Our creative shorthand is partly built on our shared life experience because we grew up together, but then a lot of it is just the way we talk about comedy and stuff. Raphael is very quick and totally understands what I'm saying as soon as I make a reference. There's just something about our personalities where we build off what the other person is doing in a fun way.

Raphael: We just trust and respect each other a lot, which gives us the freedom to disagree without things getting personal, and collaborate in a more giving way. I often can't predict what direction she's going to take something in, and I like that she's still able to surprise me because it makes my life more delightful.

Lisa and Raphael stayed in touch through the mid-2000s while on opposite coasts: Lisa studying at UCLA, Raphael at Bard in New York state. Their largest collaboration yet was a two-year run on the webcomic *Tip Me Over, Pour Me Out*.

Lisa: I was graduating from art school [in 2006] when we started doing *Tip Me Over, Pour Me Out*. It was great because I had just graduated and I didn't really know what I was doing and I wasn't a famous painter like the way art school made it seem like I was going to be. [*Laughs.*] I was like, "Oh, that doesn't happen right away and I need to get a job?" So I was moving furniture for money in my pickup truck and making art on the side. It was the perfect time for me to do a webcomic. So we started working on *Tip Me Over, Pour Me Out*.

TMOPMO, written by Raphael and drawn by Lisa, featured Raphael himself as the lead cartoon hero. Initially conceived as a way to help Raphael "get over a civil and friendly breakup" and as an excuse to work with Lisa again, the strip focused on cartoon Raphael's magnified neuroses and hapless misadventures in relationships and general daily life. For a good third of the strips, you could add a horsey muzzle to Raphael's face and almost have a *BoJack* storyboard in front of you.

This spread: A colored *Tip Me Over, Pour Me Out* comic strip examining the Raphael character's pessimism.

Opposite bottom: A handful of small, sliced cubes of honeydew inflame BoJack's ire in the episode "Hank After Dark" [S2E07], and spun, flavored sugar is rejected from his stomach in "BoJack Horseman: The BoJack Horseman Story, Chapter One" [S1E01].

Raphael: A couple of them feel real *BoJack*. You can see the beginnings of that sensibility. Probably the cotton candy one.

(That's the strip in which Raphael overeats cotton candy to the point of getting sick while exploring why he always anticipates the bad that inevitably will come even when everything is going great—like the fact that his job has free cotton candy. Another *TMOPMO* strip that may seem familiar to *BoJack* fans is the one where cartoon Raphael attends a party, only to spend most of it alone, judging the oblivious revelers from the sidelines. Or the one where his anxious overthinking of relationship steps two, three, and four cripple his ability to get through step one. Or . . .)

Lisa: There's one where you're like, "I feel so fat."

There are ways in which BoJack the character and Raphael the character are different, too. But when BoJack, for example, goes on an unprovoked screed about honeydew pieces in the craft service melon bowl . . .

> Goddammit! Honeydew? Why does cantaloupe think that every time he gets invited to a party he can bring along his dumb friend honeydew? You don't get a plus one, cantaloupe!

. . . the line connecting back to Raphael's comics character is clear.

Raphael: *Tip Me Over, Pour Me Out* taught me how to write economically. When you have only six panels to tell a story or get an idea out, every panel counts. It also taught me how to collaborate and trust my collaborators. When we first started the strip, I would send incredibly detailed instructions to Lisa on how to render every frame. The more I loosened up and gave her the freedom to do her thing, the better the comic got.

Visually, the comic's style could be called proto-*BoJack*. Drawn for the static presentation of a comic strip, it has complex pen work and hatching, with no premium placed on economy of line like there is in television animation. *TMOPMO* features many qualities that Lisa's subsequent comics and illustration work is known for, including careful rendering of detailed clothing patterns and styles (which carries over into *BoJack*) and the semi-realistic, human-proportioned characters presented in comically bizarre scenarios.

Subject-wise, *TMOPMO* also pushed Lisa to explore less-traveled territory for her: drawing people with actual people-heads on their necks. Because she grew up with an affinity for stories about animals—especially horses—her default characters were almost always composed of horse heads, dog heads, bird heads, moose heads, or cat heads affixed to human bodies. Drawing hundreds of Raphael heads and expressions, in addition to the other people in the strips, was a good exercise for expanding Lisa's range.

Continued on page 45

Tip Me Over, Pour Me Out

This spread: In two of the earliest *Tip Me Over, Pour Me Out* comic strips, Raphael's character faces self-defeating anxiety. BoJack can relate.

Tip Me Over, Pour Me Out

Left: One of the most popular (online) *Tip Me Over, Pour Me Out* strips in which Raphael expounds on the seven minute rule for partygoers.

I got invited to a "Back from the Dead" Halloween party. I put together a Back to the Future costume and went as "Guy who Misunderstood the Theme of The Party." Turns out I was dead on.
It's NOT a "back from the dead" party?
No, just a regular Halloween party. Why don't you have a costume?
SEXY GLOBAL WARMING
SEXY ANNE FRANK
SEXY BUNNY WITH SHOPE PAPILLOMA VIRUS
SEXY BAT

We interrupt this comic for a public service announcement. It has come to our attention that SOME of you still don't understand the SEVEN MINUTE RULE.
What are you supposed to be? A guy who fell off a boat?
Basically, if you're a girl with a boyfriend and you meet a guy at a party, you MUST make a reference to your boyfriend within the first seven minutes of conversation.

Girls with boyfriends are shameless abusers of the long-flirt. Since they already have someone to go home to, they don't have to float from guy to guy searching for meat. Because of this, the guys they talk to mistakenly believe the girls are interested in them, ESPECIALLY when they talk for hours without mentioning their boyfriends.
fig.1: GIRL IS FRIENDLY
fig.2: BOY FALLS IN LOVE
fig.3: LEMUR ATTACK
fig 4: EVERYBODY DIES

Here's an example of how you can drop the hint with grace and class...
00:07
ONLY SEVEN SECONDS! EVEN BETTER!
HALLOWEEN PARTY!!!
I used to live in Prospect Heights but now I live in Greenpoint.
That's really interesting. I have a boyfriend who's lived in places.

FREQUENTLY ASKED QUESTIONS
WON'T IT SOUND AWKWARD?
It's okay if it's awkward. He won't mind.
WHAT IF HE'S NOT INTERESTED IN ME? I DON'T WANT TO SOUND PRESUMPTUOUS.
It's still good information. Also, trust me, he's interested.
WHAT IF WE'RE HAVING GOOD CONVERSATION? I DON'T WANT HIM TO GO TALK TO SOMEONE ELSE!
Why don't you go cry about it to your boyfriend?

Besides, if I know this guy, and I think I do, he'll probably keep talking to you anyway, just because he likes the attention.
SEXY WALRUS
SUPERIOR MARTY MCFLY
SEXY GHOST
My boyfriend and I run our own bed-and-breakfast. When he's not touring with his rock band.
Uh-huh.
I think SHE LIKES ME!

In high school, my relationship with the popular kids was a lot like the Taliban's relationship with the U.S.A., pre-9/11. I hated them from afar even though I didn't really know any of them.
DEATH TO THE INFIDELS!
Really? But the infidels are so COOL!
OH...well, do they think that we're cool too?
No, they don't even know about us.
WHAT? DEATH TO THE INFIDELS!

On the plane ride to my high school reunion, I sat next to two frisky teenagers. I felt so old.
PLANE NUTS
The ENTIRE TIME.

I couldn't wait to show everyone at my reunion how much I've changed since high school.
LOL.
2002
2007

I imagined all the popular kids got fat and sad and I would be the coolest person there.
BEAST CLASS OF 02'
WE'RE SAD NOW!
AND FAT!
THAT'LL SHOW US!

Instead it was like the day after high school. All the attractive people were still attractive and I was too scared to talk to them, as if their opinions of me still mattered. I don't even know what we'd talk about.
I'm in publishing now.
OH. THAT'S INTERESTING.
Do you read a lot of books?
IS THE INTERNET A BOOK?

I was angry that all the dumb cliques still existed, but mostly I was angry at myself. In many ways, I haven't changed at all.
Why can't you just feel good about yourself without needing others to validate how cool you are?
PSH. I COULD HAVE DONE THAT AT HOME.

Left: Raphael learns the hard way at his high school class's fifth reunion that people don't change that much. Themes and character traits here are echoed in the writing for *BoJack*.

I've been auditioning for commercials. Fancy stuff!

The actor's life for ME!

I sit in the waiting room, surrounded by real life actors. Everyone's friendly, but the room stinks of desperation. I think, I'm not like THESE guys, am I?

Practices Oscar speech in bathroom mirror

Parents subsidize Manhattan apartment

Not really an actor, just visiting.

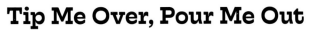

This spread, following page: A six panel *Tip Me Over, Pour Me Out* comic strip written by Raphael and drawn by Lisa chronicling Raphael's pre-Hollywood existence.

I tell myself that if I make enough stupid jokey videos for the internet, maybe eventually Someone will hire me to write Something serious and important.

OH NO! HAROLD PINTER BROKE HIS ANKLE AND SOMEONE ELSE NEEDS TO FINISH THE PLAY!

IMPORTANT PLAY
BY HAROL
PINTERGALACTIC

YOU! CHORUS BOY! HOW'D YOU LIKE TO BE A STAR?

In the meantime, gotta pay the rent...

BLOW GURT

Half the CALORIES, You say?

SPLORCH!

EXPLODING YOGURT!

BLOW GURT

Uh... thanks for coming in. We'll let you know.

HED-SHOT

IRECTOR

There's nothing more degrading than sucking at something you consider beneath you.

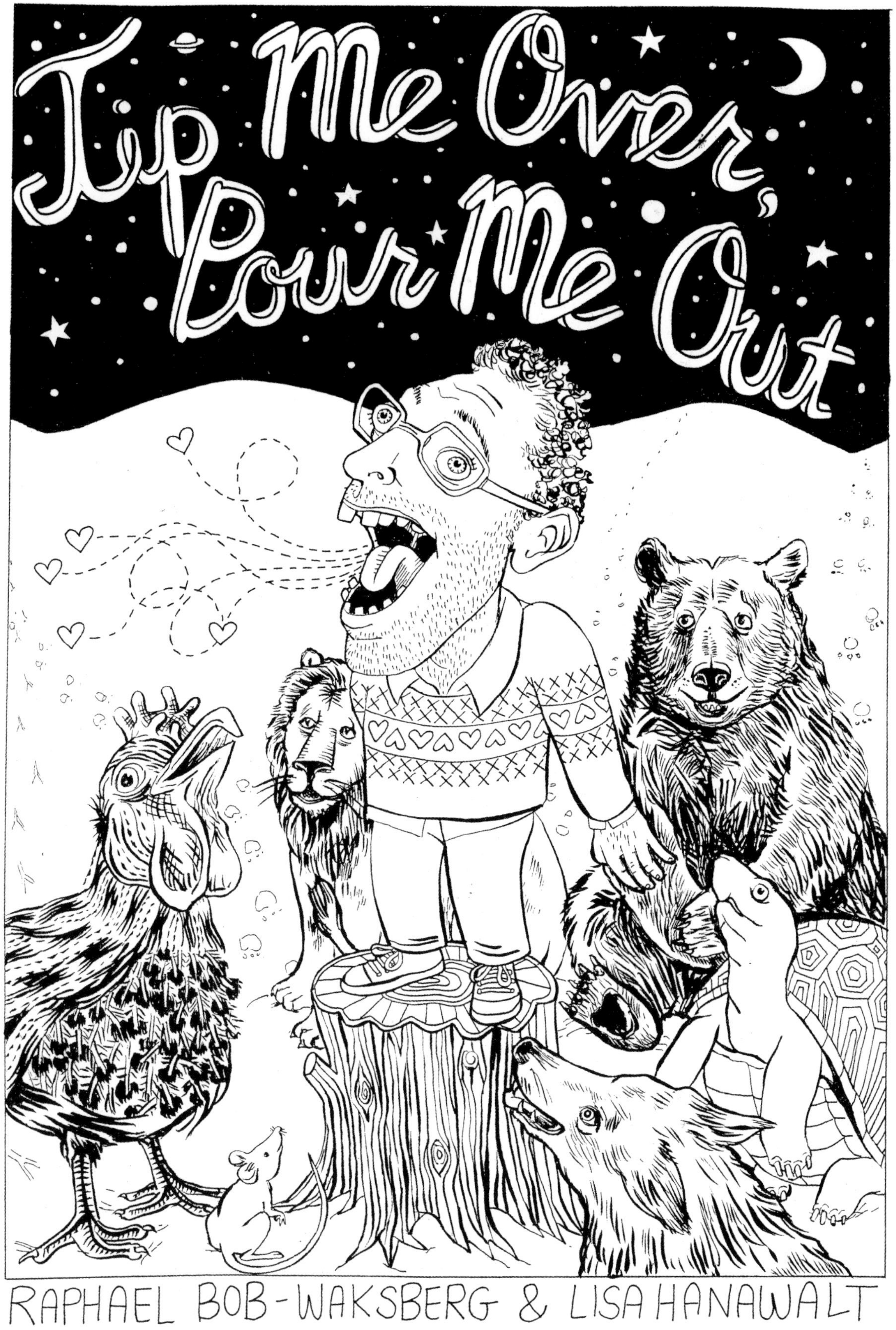

Left: The cover art for the *Tip Me Over, Pour Me Out* self-published comic book collection of the same name.

Below: A panel from another *Tip Me Over, Pour Me Out* strip.

Lisa: I was going to a small comics convention called Super*MARKET that my friend Jessica Gao put together in the back of Meltdown Comics on Sunset, and I was like, "Oh, I have printed copies of *Tip Me Over, Pour Me Out*, but I need to have something else, too—I can't just have one thing." So I made a little zine of my own work, partly work that I'd made in college, and then I met my future publisher Alvin Buenaventura there and he was like, "*Tip Me Over, Pour Me Out* is OK, but I like your work better." [*Laughs.*] So that's when I went solo. Luckily, Raphael was never upset about it or anything; he was like, "Yeah! Do whatever."

Lisa began writing, drawing, and collecting her work for two books that were published by Buenaventura Press (*I Want You* #1 and #2) while she continued to create self-published zines. A confident comic point-of-view runs through all of this work, which features gross-out bodily humor, joke sandwiches, fancy animal hats, impossible dance moves, surreal sex positions, and illustrated dreams. Also prominent throughout these books is a familiar-looking equine-headed figure named He-Horse.

After moving to New York City, Lisa worked as a freelance illustrator, completed several more books—including two published by Drawn & Quarterly called *My Dirty Dumb Eyes* and *Hot Dog Taste Test*—and also cohosted and coproduced a podcast

Continued on page 49

I love She-Moose

HER MUSKY SCENT

HER JAUNTY SKIP

HER MUG, FILLED WITH HOMEMADE HORCHATA

HER CUBICLE, CARPETED WITH BUBBLEWRAP

POP!

POP!

I endorse He-Horse

HIS HUNGRY HEART

HIS CRIMES OF PASSION

HIS SELF-DEPRECATING ANECDOTES

HIS ALLERGIC REACTIONS TO CAT HAIR

This spread: Cover and two of pages from Lisa's book, *I Want You* #1, and cover art from *I Want You* #2, both published by Buenaventura Press.

This page: Interior and cover art from Lisa's collection of comics, *My Dirty Dumb Eyes*, (left, below), and the cover of *Hot Dog Taste Test* (bottom). Both books published by Drawn & Quarterly.

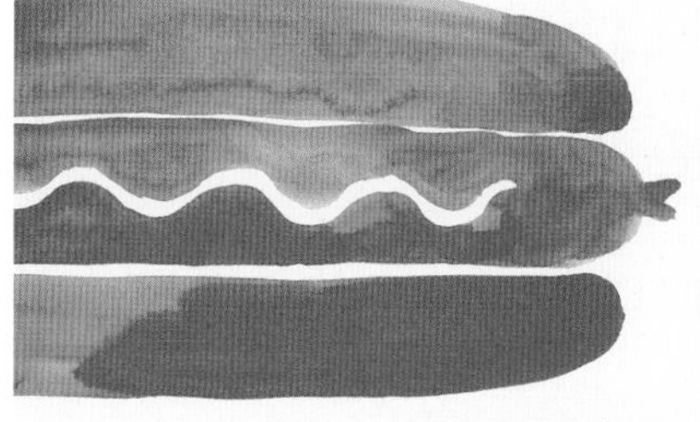

This page: Personal art and an Olde English drawing by Lisa.

with her friend Emily Heller called *Baby Geniuses*. All of this experience served to hone her skills and her comedic voice. Raphael stayed busy, too, writing and performing with Olde English—a New York–based comedy group he joined while in college at Bard. Founded by Ben Popik, other members included future *BoJack* voice actors Adam Conover, Wave Segal, and Caleb Bark, and future *BoJack* music composer Jesse Novak. While active, the group produced more than 150 videos and performed at multiple sketch comedy festivals.

Raphael: Olde English was like a comedy boot camp. We were so rough on each other, and ourselves, to squeeze any kind of joke into every possible crevice. I left that group feeling confident in my joke-writing ability, to the point where now I don't really focus on it. When we're writing *BoJack*, we focus on the stories and the characters without worrying too much about the comedy. I have a room full of comedy writers, not to mention all the hilarious artists and actors and animators—I have faith it's going to be funny.

I also got really into formats while working with Olde English. We were always looking for new ways to deliver comedy, new framing devices for our sketches. That's an interest that has definitely carried over to the storytelling in *BoJack* and how we think about crafting episodes.

After Raphael graduated from Bard in 2006, he moved to Brooklyn for three years, where he continued performing, writing, and making videos.

Raphael: When I was in New York City, I was writing very serious plays on top of the sketch comedy stuff. But by then, I was sick of New York and was looking for a reason to get out.

As a temporary reprieve, Raphael bounced back to his hometown in the Bay Area to teach a high school playwriting workshop for a few months while the bulk of his material possessions remained in Brooklyn.

Raphael: I was teaching playwriting to high school kids and was trying to figure out where to go next. This was fall of '09. Meanwhile, my manager had slipped a pilot I had written to Sony, and they wanted to shoot a presentation of it and try to shop it to networks, so I flew down to LA for a few days to do that. It was the first time I had ever been on a professional set, and it blew my mind. I remember asking if I should help move a table for a shot and being told, "No, there are people here to do that." The presentation ended up going nowhere, but the fact that Sony thought I was good enough for them to spend that kind of money on made me think I was ready to come to LA to try to make a go of this TV thing. That's when I decided I would move to LA, but first I went back to New York to put up a play I had written, pick up all my stuff, and make my for-real good-byes.

Of course, once I got to LA, I didn't know what to do next, and there was a lot of just hanging out on the deck of this house I was staying at, writing things I was sure nobody would ever read, and going to meetings I was sure would never lead anywhere. I was taking on odd writing jobs wherever I could. I spent a few days working freelance for a small production studio, writing up pitches for reality shows. A couple guys hired me to write a movie for one of them to star in, but the project fell apart because I had much weirder ideas than they wanted for what kind of movie it would be. I remember one time my friend Matt Wing commissioned me to write him a poem, just because he knew I needed money fast for rent.

Left: "Hot Dog Show" personal art created by Lisa during her freelance illustration period in NYC.

Raphael had no way to foresee which idea might rise to the top during this chaotic time, but the *BoJack* feeling was surfacing there, on that deck, in 2010.

Pitch of a Lifetime

The email from Raphael to Lisa on March 22, 2010, was to the point:

> Hey, do you have a picture of one of your horse guys, by himself? I came up with this idea for a show I'd like to pitch. Tell me what you think:
>
> *BoJack the Depressed Talking Horse.*

Lisa: I was like, "That sounds too depressing. Can you make something more fun and whimsical?" And he's like, "What about *The Spruce Moose and the Juice Caboose*?" And I said, "Oh great, they can have cocktail waitresses called the Spicy Mice." I think we should still make that show. For kids.

Raphael's Sony pilot marked the beginning of his professional television-writing career. When his manager sent some written samples to Tornante—an entertainment company founded and run by former Disney honcho Michael Eisner—Raphael's work passed the sniff test, and attempts at scheduling a general meeting with two of the company's producers, Noel Bright and Steven A. Cohen, began. The meeting was prefaced with an unintentionally long buildup of anticipation.

Raphael: I had gone back up to Palo Alto to teach another high school playwriting workshop in the fall of 2010, and when I got back down, Steve was very eager to meet me. Apparently while he was waiting for me to be available again in LA, he kept asking my manager, Joel Zadak, to send him more stuff, so Joel eventually sent him everything he had: a couple TV pilots, a short story, a spec feature script—all the stuff I did with Olde English. He might have even sent him a link to my blog. The first meeting was a "getting to know you" meeting.

Noel Bright [executive producer]: I was on a phone call, and so Raphael came in and started talking to Steve first. Steve's office is next to mine, and if a meeting was worthwhile or there was something urgent but he couldn't disrupt that meeting, he'd pound loudly on the wall. It's like our own fire drill: Wall-pound means, "Get in here." So I got off my call and played it like I just casually walked in. Steve said, "This is Raphael." That meant that I should sit and talk, and clearly this was a meeting that was going to go well.

What was it about Raphael that was evident right away to the executive producers (EPs)—that indicated good things to come? What could Steve have seen?

Steven A. Cohen [executive producer]: Why was it "bang-worthy"? A term I already regret! [*Laughs.*] I don't know if it was specifically *BoJack* related, but it was probably Raphael related. It's so fun when you read stuff by people and every page you're thinking, "This is fantastic," and then you spend five minutes with them and you're like, "This is really interesting." Every day in this town you're trying to meet someone who has something new to say or a new way of saying it, and you can feel it right away when they do. It's exciting.

Noel: There are very few creators that are able to channel what's going on in their brain into an exciting and intelligent and cohesive story at any step of the way, and Raphael's just a master at doing that. He's well-spoken and he likes to pry at certain things in an interesting way.

Raphael: After that general first meeting, my manager called and said, "They really liked you. They want to meet you again because they have something they want to throw at you." So I went back and they pitched me this property they had for

Continued on page 54

Below: A drawing from *I Want You* #1.

Right: An email exchange between Raphael and Lisa in which the initial idea for *BoJack* is discussed and Raphael gets notes, opinions, and an art-usage-blessing from Lisa.

Raphael Bob-Waksberg Mon, Mar 22, 2010 at 4:22 PM
To: Lisa Hanawalt

Hey, do you have a picture of one of your horse guys, by himself?

I came up with this idea for a show I'd like to pitch. Tell me what you think:

BoJack the Depressed Talking Horse.

BoJack is a horse-dude in a world full of humans, and other animal people. He used to be the star of the 90s sitcom, Horsin' Around!, about a wise-cracking horse who raises three precocious human pre-teens. Now he's a washed-up misanthrope who lives in a gorgeous bachelor pad in the Hollywood Hills, complains about everything, and wears colorful patterned sweaters. Insufferably self-deprecating, neurotic, abrasive and stubborn (Larry David meets Bender from Futurama meets a horse), he has burned all but a few of his bridges:

TOPHER (human) is BoJack's childhood best friend and freeloading permanent houseguest. Cheerful and excitable, he always tries to get BoJack to go on adventures, meet girls, and have parties, or at least stop sitting on the couch, eating sugar cubes and watching old episodes of Horsin' Around! on DVD.

MR. PEANUTBUTTER (dog-person) is BoJack's agent. Easy-going and smooth-talking (think: Shaft), Mr. Peanutbutter is constantly convincing BoJack to take on embarrassing projects that he considers beneath him and that usually don't even go anywhere.

HONEYBUCKET (horse-person) was another star from the mid-90s TV-shows-about-talking-horses trend (his show was called Horse Patrol! and it was about exactly what you think it was about). Stupid and shallow, but friendly and well-adjusted, he's the opposite of BoJack. He's good at shmoozing and he's the life of the party, and BoJack secretly hates him, but keeps hanging out with him for vague masochistic reasons and to give him something to hate besides himself.

DIANE (human) is Honeybucket's girlfriend. Cynical and clever, she's a development exec who likes BoJack and wants to help him make his comeback. BoJack is in love with her, but he's too proud/stubborn/lazy to put the effort into trying to win her over, because not trying is better than trying and failing.

CHELSEA (human) is BoJack's ex-girlfriend. After throwing away the majority of her twenties on the immature man-child-horse-pony, Chelsea finally broke up with him when it became clear he was never going to give her the baby that she wants. High strung and high maintenance, she makes a terrible match for BoJack, but they keep sleeping together anyway, because in the great grand scheme of things, why does anything we do matter at all, right?

The tone of the show is darkly funny with a melancholy Great Gatsby-ish center. Most of the show is NOT about show business, rather about a guy who gets annoyed by everything and constantly makes big deals out of nothing (obsessing over getting the exact right wording of an email, "I think that guy in the parking lot looked at me funny," etc.). Stories come out of BoJack reluctantly getting roped into schemes by Topher (to try to get girls) or Mr. Peanutbutter (to try to jump-start his career), or from BoJack going to great lengths just to prove someone wrong ("You think I'd make a terrible father? I'll show you...") or trying to improve himself to impress Diane.

Let me know what you think about all this! Or if you have other ideas that you think would help flesh out this world! And send me whatever sketches you have that would fit for this pitch. Also, if you feel weird about repurposing your animal characters for something like this, let me know and I will come up with something else!

-R

Lisa Hanawalt Mon, Mar 22, 2010 at 4:53 PM
To: Raphael Bob-Waksberg

Hey!

Haha, I like it, BoJack the Sad Hack! And featuring Topher Grace.

My only caveat is that earnest characters are always more appealing and interesting to me than cynical ones...like, my current favorite cartoon character is Flapjack, the most positive of protagonists! Or even the main guy in SuperJail, who could easily be an abrasive type but is usually pretty upbeat. Maybe there's a way for BoJack to not be too much of a bummer?

What if BoJack was incredibly neurotic and phobic but also optimistic about his abilities to break back into showbiz to the point of delusion? And he doesn't realize or won't admit to himself that the projects his agent books are embarrassing? Just a thought, I'm not an Eeyore fan..

Here's some drawings that could fit!

This spread (artwork): Personal art by Lisa featuring her signature animal-people whose designs hail from a unique Lisa Hanawalt universe. Based on the complexity of details and the relative realism of the creature's head designs, Lisa's charcters relate more to designs found in illustrated picture books of fairy tales and fables—and modern classics, such as the work of Beatrix Potter or Maurice Sendak—than they do to most mainstream animated cartoon *funny animal* types like Mickey Mouse or Bugs Bunny. Content-wise, Lisa's adult humor and stories have a strong connection to the underground and independent comics world where anything goes and personal expression is paramount.

Raphael Bob-Waksberg — Tue, Mar 23, 2010 at 3:04 PM
To: Lisa Hanawalt

Hm, I was thinking Topher was more like Flapjack, and BoJack was more like Captain Kanuckles. Or Archer, if you've seen that show (if you haven't you should; the first seven episodes are on Hulu). Maybe depressed isn't the right word--more cranky, or detached. What I'm interested in is getting to the vulnerable center of the too-cool-for-school. Like on Daria, whenever Jane's cute brother would flirt with her, and she would blush, I always thought that was really neat, and that's what I want to explore. This is definitely not supposed to be a show about Eeyore; maybe I can clear that up somehow. Good notes!

I will try to come up with another pitch that's a little more cheerful; but cheerful is not my forte. I of course also love Flapjack, and David Wain's character on SuperJail, but it's hard to get into that mindset when you're in a new town and you don't know anybody and you don't have any money. I've been in more of a TMOPMO-y mood recently, so I was hoping I could exploit that for comedy, TMOPMO-style.

Okay, what about this:

Spruce Moose in the Juice Caboose.

Spruce Moose is a dapper fellow with his finger on the pulse (and he's also a moose). He works as a bartender in the bar car of a swingin' locomotive (The Juice Caboose) where meets all sorts of people and solves their problems. Dig that crazy rhythm, baby, juice, baby, POW.

It's Cheers! On a train! With a moose!

[Quoted text hidden]

Lisa Hanawalt — Tue, Mar 23, 2010 at 7:54 PM
To: Raphael Bob-Waksberg

I hope you aren't kidding about Spruce Moose. Because I'm not kidding when I say he should work with twin cocktail waitresses called the Spicy Mice!

Oh ok, I like that Daria reference. That was such a good part of Daria, man. Maybe the only good part. Ok, I'm interested in where this BoJack character goes! And what crazy cosby sweaters he will wear!

I wish I could offer some soothing words about that whole new town/no friends/no money thing, but it's been almost a year and I'm just barely adjusting. Good thing I'm too busy for friends!

Well, we'll move back out there eventually...after BoJack gets picked up and I have to come out and art-direct it. Riiiight?

[Quoted text hidden]

Raphael Bob-Waksberg — Thu, Jan 20, 2011 at 4:49 PM
To: Lisa Hanawalt

BoJack update!

Thought you might like to read the full treatment I wrote up for BoJack Horseman, attached. If not, NO WORRIES.

I hope it's okay I used your illustrations to help set the tone (last page, I credited you)-- don't worry; you and your characters are not attached to this project if you don't want to be, but I thought some pictures of animal-people would help sell the idea and Richard Scarry and I are on the outs. Also, I think you are great and I wanted to share your work with a bunch of Hollywood big shots (Michael Eisner is reading the treatment as we speak).

Lisa Hanawalt — Thu, Jan 20, 2011 at 8:24 PM
To: Raphael Bob-Waksberg

Niiiiiiice, this is WEIRD AND HILARIOUS. BoJack is like Greenberg (note: I never actually saw that movie. But he's sad and wears sweaters, right?)! And, what, Michael Eisner is reading it right now?!!? Thanks for slipping Ol' Eiznee my drawings, heh heh.

This is so exciting. Eisner knows you're the next Charlie Kaufman, right?!

And yes, feel free to use any of my drawings, of course!

Opposite (emails): Raphael and Lisa's initial *BoJack* email discussion continues, edited only slightly for content: extraneous banter and personal details removed. Notably, Lisa predicts her future in writing a second time.

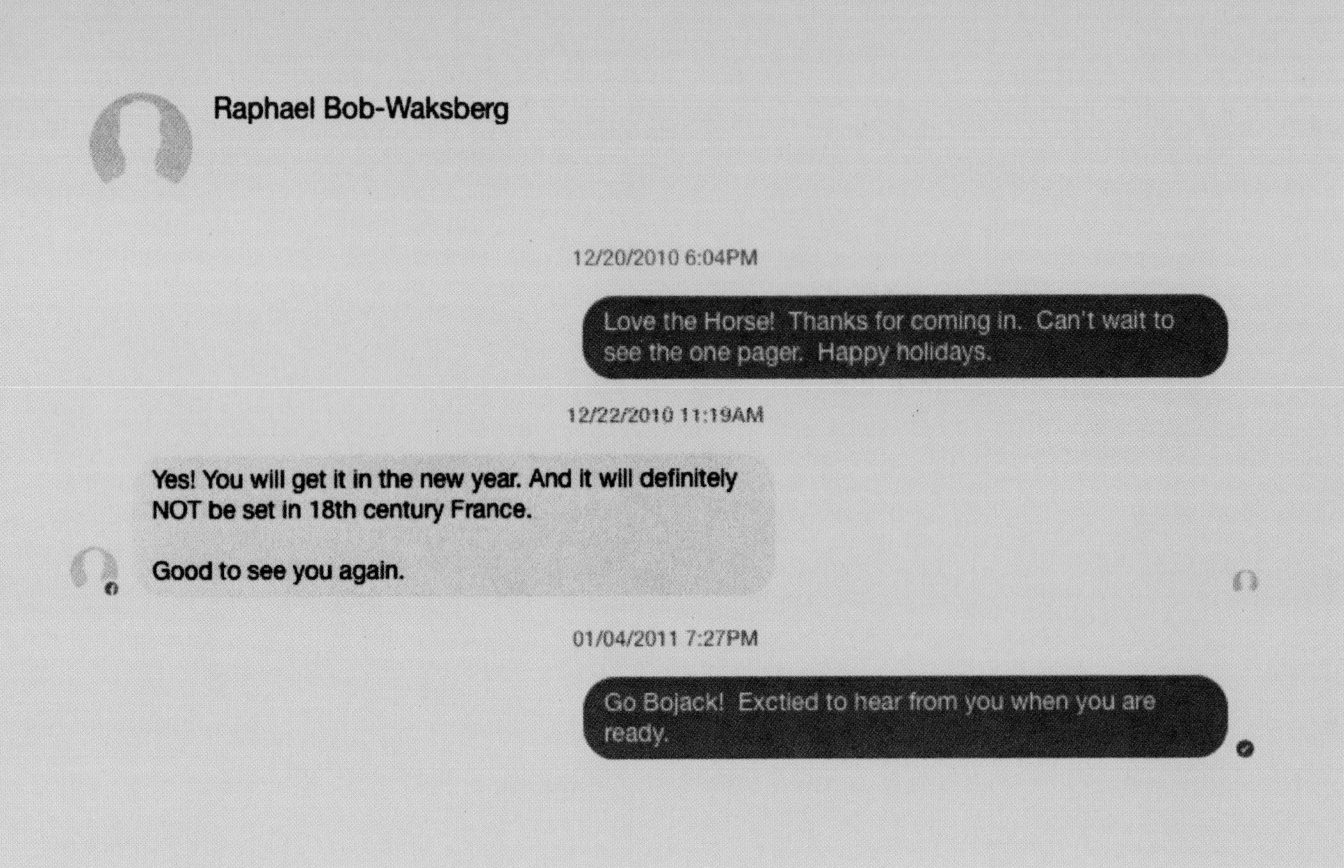

Raphael Bob-Waksberg
12/20/2010 6:04PM
Love the Horse! Thanks for coming in. Can't wait to see the one pager. Happy holidays.
12/22/2010 11:19AM
Yes! You will get it in the new year. And it will definitely NOT be set in 18th century France.
Good to see you again.
01/04/2011 7:27PM
Go Bojack! Exctied to hear from you when you are ready.

Left: Executive producer Steve Cohen follows up with Raphael after the first meeting in which *BoJack* is verbally pitched (one of Raphael's other pitches was set in eighteenth-century France). A month later, Steve would find Raphael on Facebook and check in on that one-pager's progress, finally setting Raphael into high-gear on writing pitch materials.

me to develop, and I was like, "I don't know, I'll think about it." And then my manager called and I was like, "I don't know. I don't think it's for me." And he was like, "All right, well, Steve called again, and he wants to see what *you* have. And I was like, "Awww, now I got to come up with my own ideas? I should have just said yes to their thing!" [*Laughs.*] When you live in this town you do a lot of meetings, and most of them don't turn into anything. And sometimes you really have to do a lot of prep work.

So then I came up with five ideas—all different animated projects—one of which was *BoJack*. I go in again and pitch them out, and Steve asks which one of these is most interesting to me. I said, "I think the horse one is the one I really like." Then he asks if there is anything written up, like a treatment they can look at and show around, and so I was like, "OK . . . I'll get that to you." And I was thinking, "Now I gotta do *more* work!" [*Laughs.*] And then I just forgot about it.

A month later, Steve found me on Facebook and was like, "Hey! How's *BoJack* coming?" [*Laughs.*] And I was like, "Almost done!" And then I was like, "I gotta do it! I gotta do it!" So I wrote this thing and sent it to them. Originally there was an agent character, who was a man, and an ex-girlfriend character. In the process of preparing for the formal pitch, I combined them and made the ex-girlfriend the agent. I think some of the characters had different names and other things like that. Diane was a network executive who was going to help BoJack with his comeback before she became the ghost-writer of his book. But that was really early. That's even before we pitched it to Tornante. I kind of settled all that down.

Then we met with Michael Eisner, and I was like, "OK, this is for real now." [*Laughs.*]

Michael Eisner [owner, The Tornante Company]: Told that there was a meeting in Steven Cohen's office with a well-respected young writer, I happened to be in the hall as the meeting ended. In a one-minute hallway conversation, I was told three ideas. One of which being: "This one is about an animated show about a living 'person' who has a body of a man and a head of a horse." Thinking that sounded interesting, original, and theatrical in this century—yet harking back to my youth of *Mister Ed*, the talking horse from the early sixties—I simply said, "Yes, let's do that one."

Clearly the horse idea was the winner. A more formal meeting for a detailed pitch was arranged soon after.

Noel: Meetings don't get to that level [with Michael Eisner] until we want to get a yes. That was the meeting to say, "This is a project we want to do. We want to go write a script and, ideally, go make a presentation—make a pilot or some test footage on our own and go sell it to a network or distributor. We believe in the idea, we think it's great, and you should hear it—and you should hear it directly from Raphael." The only times those meetings happen are when we're prepared to fight for it.

The Tornante plan for *BoJack* followed the model that independent production companies use if they have the will and capital to go through the initial development phases of a series themselves. Noel and Steve needed this meeting with Michael Eisner to achieve an internal green light, which would allow them to spend the necessary chunk of Tornante's money on writing and developing a *BoJack* presentation pilot as a proof of concept to pitch to networks—the risk being that even if an impressive presentation was produced, it did not guarantee that a willing broadcast partner would be found.

In Raphael's formal meeting with Michael, an idea was floated about altering one of the central concepts of the *BoJack* story.

Raphael: The question was: "Could it be sports? Instead of a former sitcom actor, could he be a former racehorse? And what would that look like?" I had some pitches for that, and how the story would change, but I said, "I really like the show-business angle and here's why . . ."

Continued on page 63

Below: To commemorate production on *BoJack* season two, character supervisor Lotan Kritchman illustrated this group shot of some of the supervisory and executive team, including executive producers Steven A. Cohen and Noel Bright, who shepherded the series development from its infancy.

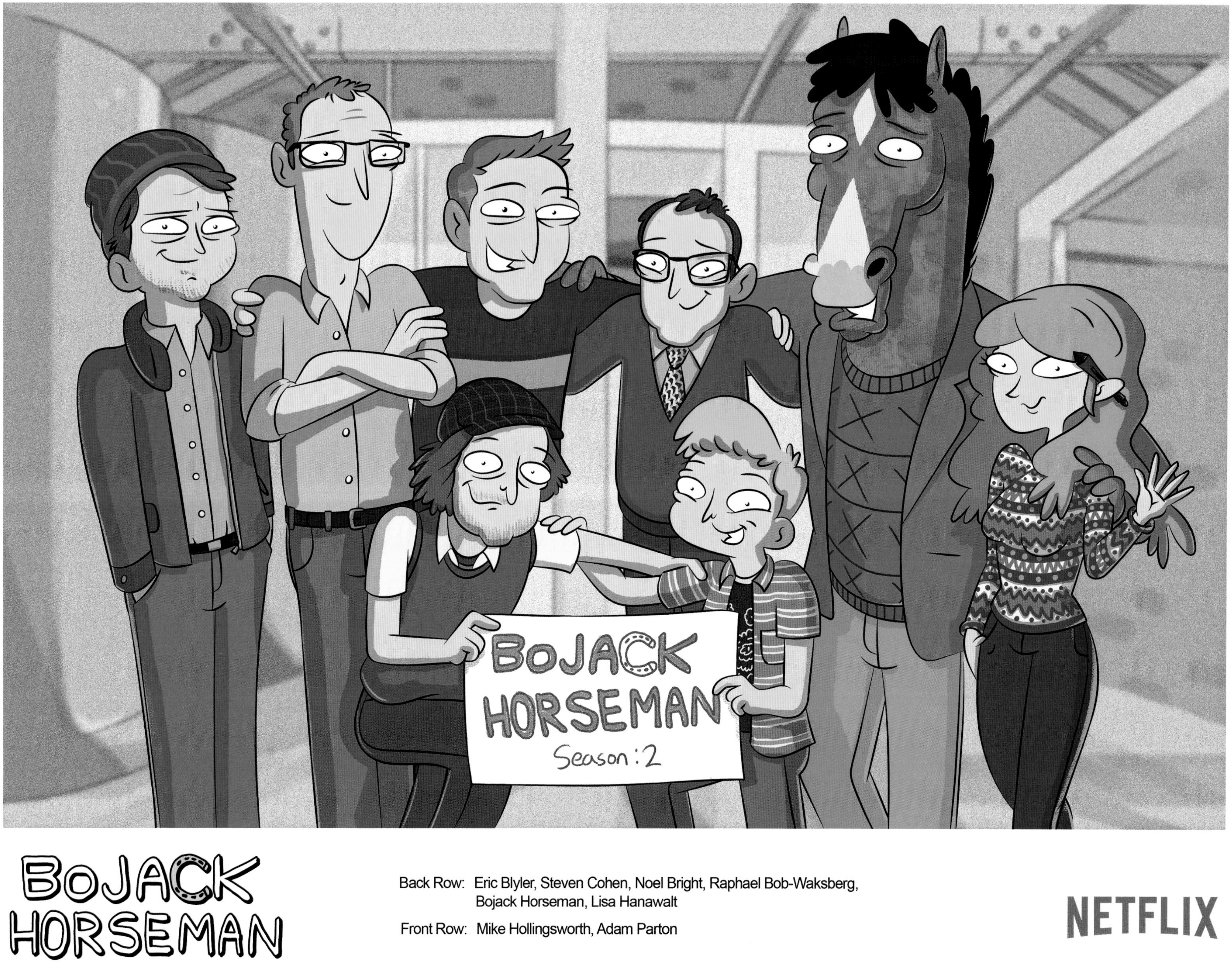

Back Row: Eric Blyler, Steven Cohen, Noel Bright, Raphael Bob-Waksberg, Bojack Horseman, Lisa Hanawalt

Front Row: Mike Hollingsworth, Adam Parton

This page: Raphael's original treatment for *BoJack*.

BoJack Horseman

By Raphael Bob-Waksberg

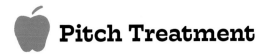

Set in a Los Angeles in which humans and anthropomorphic animal-people coexist, BoJack Horseman is an animated show about one man (who is also a horse) who peaked early and is trying to figure out what to do with his life now.

An outrageous and dark comedy with a melancholy center, the show asks the question, What happens when you have the world at your fingertips and you still can't figure out how to be happy?

Characters

BoJack Horseman (horse) – star of the 90s sitcom Horsin' Around, a show about a wisecracking horse who raises three precocious human children. Now he's a washed up misanthrope who lives in a gorgeous bachelor pad in the Hollywood Hills, complains about everything, and wears colorful sweaters.

Insufferably cynical, BoJack engages the world with a nihilistic prickliness that's a clear front for a well of neuroses. Acerbic, self-righteous, self-destructive, and as alienated as he is alienating, he's Larry David mixed with Jay Gatsby mixed with a Noah Baumbach character mixed with a horse, someone with high impenetrable walls around a lonely and scared center.

Deemed untreatable by just about every psychiatrist in L.A., BoJack vacillates wildly between extreme narcissism and extreme self-loathing, seeming to simultaneously believe that he is both better than and not as good as everyone he talks to.

He spends his days lounging by his pool, watching reruns of his old show, venturing out into the world as little as possible, and idly jabbing at half-finished projects including his long-delayed memoir "One Trick Pony" and a script for a romantic comedy he calls "Love Is An Illusion And Happiness Is Fleeting And There's No Such Thing As God And The Beatles Beat Their Wives" which he describes as "basically three hours of people crying."

Since the show follows BoJack's day-to-day life, the supporting cast is used when needed, but there's no guarantee that everyone will appear in every episode. Some episodes will utilize all of them, while some might feature none of them.

Other characters include:

Todd Chavez (human) – BoJack's best friend and permanent houseguest. A happy-go-lucky twenty-something who sleeps on BoJack's couch and spends his days working on various internet start-ups, Todd is the cheerful yin to BoJack's depressed yang.

Todd throws parties at the house and goads BoJack into going out and meeting people. BoJack is often annoyed by Todd's energy and enthusiasm, but it's clear that if it weren't for Todd, BoJack would rarely interact with the outside world.

Princess Carolyn (cat) – BoJack's agent and on-again off-again girlfriend/employee-with-benefits. Princess Carolyn (not actually a princess) is constantly breaking up with BoJack because of his toxic attitude and inability to commit. However, she continues to work for him, because she takes pride in her ability to separate her personal life from her professional life.

As his girlfriend, she complains that he's a miserable washed up hack whose best work is behind him, while as his agent she promises that new exciting work is just around the corner. BoJack recognizes this is probably an unhealthy professional relationship, but is too lazy/self-destructive to end it.

Pinky Penguin (penguin) – BoJack's contact at Penguin Publishing. Like everyone in the publishing industry, Pinky is just barely hanging on. Desperation wrapped in a used suit (a suit he got cheap because a guy died in it), Pinky is constantly getting suckered in by pyramid schemes and other get rich quick scams. He is eager for BoJack to finish writing his memoir, as he believes it's the book that will keep his company afloat.

Diane Nguyen (human) – a ghostwriter Pinky hires to help BoJack finish his book. BoJack is initially reluctant to work with her but is won over by her charm and wit. Upbeat, but not cloyingly so, with a dry sense of humor, Diane is the first person who BoJack feels really gets him, and he is crushed to learn that she's dating his friend/enemy Mr. Peanutbutter.

Mr. Peanutbutter (dog) – a dashing golden retriever and former star of "Mr. Peanutbutter's House," a mid-90s sitcom in which he played a wisecracking dog raising three precocious human children, a premise BoJack dismisses as ludicrous and hackneyed.

BoJack hates Mr. Peanutbutter for being essentially a less miserable/more deluded version of BoJack, relentlessly positive and free of neuroses and shame. Comfortable being a C-list sitcom actor and an A-list schmoozer fifteen years past his prime, Mr. Peanutbitter is currently filming a pilot for an E! reality series (or a Vh1 reality series, or a Bravo reality series—he's filming a new identically premised pilot every time we see him) and is followed around by a camera crew everywhere he goes.

This page: A variety of extra character designs by Lisa from the earliest development phase of *BoJack*.

This page: Raphael's original treatment for *BoJack* continues.

Episodes:

Every episode is made up of stand-alone segments that range in length from five minutes to the full half hour. Possible segments include:

BoJack throws a party!

After Princess Carolyn breaks up with BoJack, Todd tries to cheer him up by convincing him to throw a party at the house, even though BoJack hates parties; at his last party, he just sat in the corner the whole time eating cotton candy until he threw up.

Meanwhile, Pinky tries to get BoJack to take on a co-writer for his memoir to help him speed up the process. He gives him a book to peruse by a young writer named Diane, emphasizing that the book is a loan, because he can't afford to be giving books away. Pinky tells BoJack to invite Diane to his party so he can get to know her.

As Todd and BoJack prepare for the party, BoJack alternates between being insulted by the implication that he needs a ghostwriter and frightened to meet a real writer because he's sure she'll see what a phony he is.

After spending several hours standing by himself in the corner eating cotton candy, BoJack finally works up the nerve to talk to Diane, who quickly wins him over with her charm and genuine interest in his life. After they agree to work together, BoJack learns Diane is dating Mr. Peanutbutter, which makes him throw up.

Lights, Camera, BoJacktion!

Carolyn gets BoJack a cameo in a movie about Hitler's horse (as it's explained to him, it was going to be an Eva Braun biopic, but it got retooled), playing Hitler's horse's Jewish friend.

As the shooting of his scene is repeatedly delayed, BoJack spends the whole day in his trailer, pigging out on sugar cubes, making small talk with the bizarre P.A.s, and rehearsing his one line, which is about how important it is to live every day to the fullest.

At the end of the day, the director asks BoJack to come back tomorrow, but instead BoJack quits, complaining that he's already wasted a whole day, a day he complains he'll never get back. He goes home and watches a Match Game marathon on the Game Show Network with Todd.

BoJack supports the troops!

At the supermarket, BoJack gets in an argument with a greyhound over the last box of muffins. The greyhound claims that he had dibs on them, but BoJack claims that his dibs are nullified because he left the muffins unattended. The greyhound argues that since he left the muffins in a place where muffins don't belong, it should have been obvious that he was planning on returning for him. BoJack dismisses this argument as completely without merit and leaves with the muffins.

The next day, the greyhound appears on Fox News. It turns out he's a soldier on leave for two weeks. He tells a story about how all he wanted when he got home was his favorite brand of muffins, but BoJack Horseman, a fine example of the Hollywood Elite, hates the troops.

BoJack calls in the show and argues that a) the fact that he's a soldier has nothing to do with it, b) if people would just look at what really actually happened they would see that BoJack was right about the dibs being nullified, and c) he can't return the muffins because he already ate the muffins. When pressed on whether or not he ate all the muffins, BoJack admits that yes, he ate all the muffins in one sitting, because he's a big fatass with no self-control, is that what you wanted to hear?

Diane tells BoJack she could never be the center of attention like he is and that sometimes she climbs onto Mr. Peanutbutter's roof just to escape the cameras.

Mr. Peanutbutter has a great idea. He'll host a reconciliation of the two. Since he's currently filming a reality show about the remodeling of his kitchen and another reality show about his second career as a conflict resolution mediator, if he invites BoJack and the greyhound back to his kitchen to talk things out, it could be a great crossover event for his two reality shows.

BoJack reluctantly shows up to Mr. Peanutbutter's house with a new box of muffins. The greyhound has parlayed his recent fame into a reality show deal of his own and has brought his camera crew along too. Additionally, the director of the greyhound's reality show also has a camera crew following him for a new reality show about reality show directors.

BoJack tries to give the greyhound the muffins, but the different camera crews continually get in each other's way, causing a production pile-up. While everyone's distracted, BoJack climbs onto the roof where he meets Diane, and they share the box of muffins.

BoJack makes a public appearance!

BoJack's car breaks down in Beverly Hills on the way to a promotional event. When the OnStar operator recognizes his voice, she demands he sing the Horsin' Around theme song, which he reluctantly does, to her delight. Then she asks him to do it

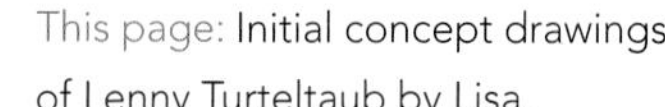

This page: Initial concept drawings of Lenny Turteltaub by Lisa.

This page: Raphael's original treatment for *BoJack* continues. The final page (not pictured) included Lisa's artwork of the pre-BoJack horse-man and other animals from her zine *Stay Away from Other People*.

again, for her friend, which he does. Then her friend asks him to sing the Growing Pains theme and he hangs up.

BoJack tries calling AAA, but his phone dies—Todd drained the battery while talking on the phone all night with his internet girlfriend (he couldn't use his own phone, because he wanted to play snake on it while he talked)—so BoJack is forced to knock on strangers' doors asking to use their phones, and he gets in various misadventures around the neighborhood.

BoJack does lunch!

Pinky, Diane, and BoJack visit a café in Echo Park to discuss a potentially lucrative product placement deal for BoJack's memoir with the café's owners.

The meeting goes well until BoJack notices something strange about his meal; there seems to be the same amount of soup in the cup of soup as there is in the bowl of soup, even though the bowl is twice as expensive. The café's owners apologize that BoJack "feels that way" but this offends BoJack even more, as the issue isn't about how he feels, it's about very real measurable evidence.

Diane and Pinky try to get the conversation back on track, but BoJack refuses to move on until the owners admit that their soup deal rips customers off, a subject they repeatedly avoid commenting on directly.

BoJack says no to drugs!

In support of National Hugs Not Drugs Week, BoJack is invited to speak at a local high school, an invitation he accepts while expressing a supreme ambivalence about advocating hugging, as he is someone who doesn't like to be touched.

At the school assembly, BoJack barely hides his disdain for the other washed up celebrities present, the panel of "Hugs Not Drugs Heroes," and goes off on long tangents about his depressing life. At one point, he lets it slip that he uses horse tranquilizers to help him fall asleep each night. The students are confused - aren't those drugs? - and BoJack explains that some drugs are good drugs. The next day, the news is all over the internet: BoJack loves drugs and hates hugs.

BoJack is asked to apologize and retract his statements, but he refuses, arguing that labeling all drugs as equally dangerous is an irresponsible message to send to children. However, when Pinky tells him that this P.R. snafu could shutter his book deal, thus depriving him an excuse to see Diane every day, BoJack agrees to make amends.

Carolyn arranges for a high profile mea culpa: he is to deliver a public apology during the halftime show of the Super Bowl, after which he is to hug the president of the Hugs Not Drugs Council.

Flanked by a clearly high halftime show rock star and a clearly on-steroids pro football player, BoJack makes his half-assed apology: an admission that both drugs and hugs should be used in moderation. The football player grabs the microphone and offers a simpler way to live: Say yes to hugs and no to drugs.

This sets BoJack off on a tirade about the dangers of hugging. From child molestation to perfectly innocent relationships that end in heartbreak and bitterness, BoJack argues that more lives are ruined by physical intimacy than by drug abuse, and if children really want to live happy adult lives, they should say yes to drugs and no to hugs. BoJack leaves the stadium to a chorus of boos.

Plaaaaaaay BoJack!

When BoJack complains about how little he contributes to the world, Diane convinces him to do some charitable work and BoJack volunteers to coach an underprivileged inner city little league team.

BoJack enjoys working with the kids and teaching them things like, "The point of baseball isn't to win; it's to try your hardest and then lose anyway so you learn that no matter how badly you want something, there's always someone better than you that deserves it more." But when Mr. Peanutbutter starts coaching another team in the league, BoJack's competitive side comes out.

Mr. Peanutbutter claims that his team is a ragtag crew of underdogs, but BoJack is convinced that his team is ragtaggier and underdoggier. The two compete over who can make their team more pitiful, buying worse and worse equipment, and replacing their best players with kids from the cancer ward.

This page: Additional art collected in Lisa's zine *Stay Away from Other People*, (see pages 30–33 for more), included some tough lady cats, a preview of the resilient Princess Carolyn. Notably some of these characters have tails—a rare appendage in Lisa's designs for animal-people.

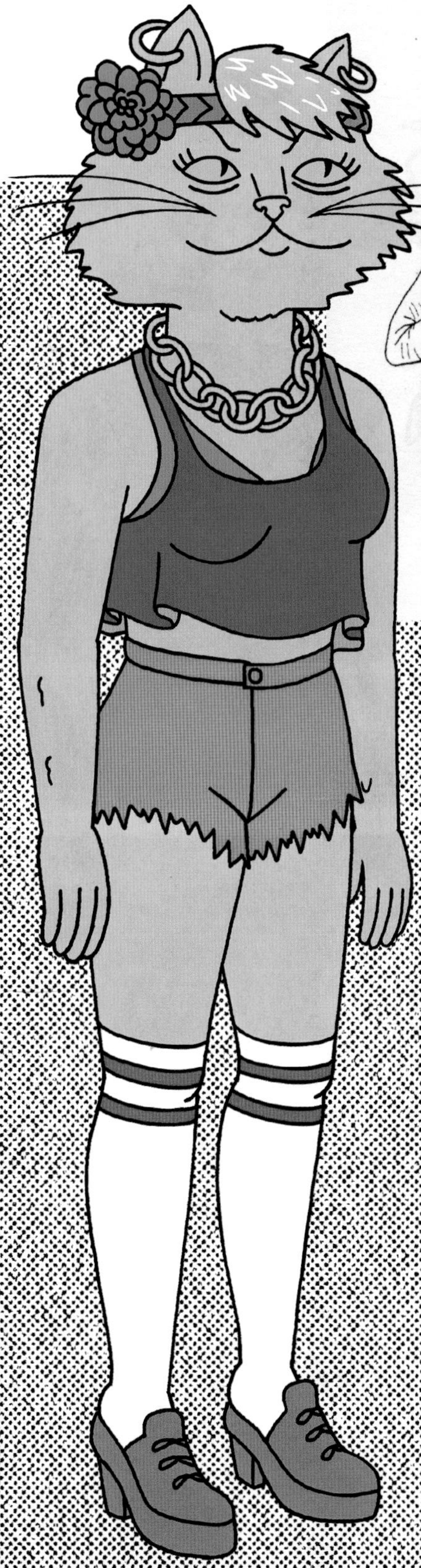

"Judith & Holofernes" by Caravaggio

Opposite: Development drawing of Princess Carolyn by Lisa.

Below: Raphael introduces Lisa to Steve in an email.

From: Raphael Bob-Waksberg
Sent: Wednesday, May 11, 2011 3:57 PM
To: Lisa Hanawalt; Steven Cohen
Subject: Introduction!

Steve, this is Lisa Hanawalt, the fantastic artist whose work I included in my treatment. She knows a little bit about BoJack (I think I sent her the treatment), but she has not read the script.

Lisa, this is Steve Cohen, Head of Development at Tornante. He is a cool dude, and wanted to discuss your possible involvement in this project.

You should get to know each other! Lisa will be visiting LA for three-six weeks this summer, so we should at least all have a party when that happens. I'll bring cups!

Steve: I think one of the great things about Michael is that he'll come in and try to push something to a certain place—or maybe try just to push Raphael for the first time, to see how much he really believes in this idea. I think he was impressed by Raphael's conviction, and he was won over.

Raphael: Less on the idea and more on the "Oh, this is a thoughtful guy who knows what he's doing. He can make smart choices; he can do the show right." Which is good, because now that we're here, if it was the sports version, I don't know how we'd do it! [*Laughs.*] I don't know anything about sports or racing!

Mike Hollingsworth [supervising director]: If you're a former actor, you can still act. But if you're a former athlete . . . it's like, "OK, I'm going back into the NFL at age sixty."

Raphael: The whole tagline for *Secretariat*—"He's tired of running in circles"—came out of that meeting with Michael about *BoJack*, where we talked about how BoJack is tired of running in circles and he wants to do something else. So it was helpful! [*Laughs.*]

The green light from Michael Eisner to proceed was secured. Meanwhile, back in New York . . .

Lisa: I hadn't heard from Raphael in six months, since the initial *BoJack* email, and then he emailed me again and was like, "I just showed your drawings to Michael Eisner!" I was like, "Michael Eisner, former head of Disney?! What?!" Then Steve and Noel brought me in for a meeting in the summer of 2011 to propose working on designs for the presentation. I was still living in NYC, and I was visiting LA. But I wasn't sure how much work it would be, and I was kind of commitment-phobic, so I said no.

Noel: Lisa gave us kind of the opposite reaction that you could want: "So we have this show, and we'd love for you to be a part of it!" And Lisa's like, "I'm not sure . . . I'm kind of busy." [*Laughs.*]

Lisa: When I first said no, Steve emailed in response, "Best of luck." And I was like, "Oooooohhhhhh." [*Laughs.*]

Steve: Is it possible that I just meant "best of luck"?

Lisa: I have no idea, but to me it was like, "Oh, this is a Hollywood fuck you."

Noel: This is why I never email people.

Lisa: It had a period instead of an exclamation point.

Raphael: I think an exclamation point is insincere: "Best of luuUUCKk!"

Lisa: It could have meant anything.

Mike: The worst would have been a question mark: "Best of luck?"

Lisa: Part of it was that I'd just finished illustrating a children's book and it was kind of a bad experience. It took six months of work and felt endless, and I didn't want to commit to another big project. I made the mistake of not jumping aboard a good thing.

Noel: But that wasn't actually a mistake because if you weren't ready at the time, you wouldn't have been happy to do it. When you eventually agreed, you were ready.

Lisa: I got lucky that you guys came back six months later. 'Cause you could have gone with someone else.

Raphael: [*Laughs.*] We did . . .

Lisa: Nobody could get the horse right. Is that what it was?

Noel: We couldn't get the tone right.

Continued on page 66

BoJack Concepts

This spread: Rough sketches and refined color concept drawings of BoJack by Lisa.

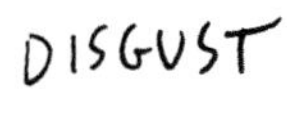

Subject: Re: Bojack
Date: Thursday, March 22, 2012 at 12:27:20 PM Pacific Daylight Time
From: Lisa Hanawalt
To: Steven Cohen
CC: Raphael Bob-Waksberg, Noel Bright, Laura Hilker

Hey everyone!

Yaay, I'm so excited to join the Bojack team! I'll look over the script this weekend.

Thanks!! Lisa

On Thu, Mar 22, 2012 at 2:53 PM, Steven Cohen wrote:

> Hey Lisa,
>
> Great catching up. We are thrilled that everything has worked out and we have our dream team in place.
>
> As promised here is the last version of Raphael's script. We will coordinate a time for us all to get on the phone at the beginning of the week and move things forward.
>
> In the meantime, welcome aboard.
>
> Steve

In fact, development had proceeded after Lisa's initial rebuffing of the proposal, with several seasoned Hollywood animation pros taking a whack at formalizing the character designs for the main cast of *BoJack*. The qualities that made Lisa's work unique, especially in animation, were still part of the original horse-man drawing that was seared into everyone's imagination from the early emails and proposals. Nothing else seemed to be doing the job as well as Lisa's indie comics linework and curious characters, which could only hail from a Lisa Hanawalt universe.

All along, Raphael had been working on writing—glad to be working, but mentally preparing for, and expecting, the worst.

Raphael: I'm thinking, "At least I'm getting paid for these scripts, but this is going nowhere. No one's going to buy this. No one wants this."

Lisa: I feel that way about everything before it becomes a thing.

Raphael: It felt like, "OK, this is my career now, writing stuff that never gets made, wasting my time in development for the rest of my life."

Lisa: So when Noel and Steve called me six months after I said no and were like, "So . . . sorry to bother you, but could we ask again?" I had just joined a shared studio space in Greenpoint and was doing illustration work for the *New York Times*, and I was bored, and so I said yes.

Raphael: Part of your hesitation was that you were really nervous about what the job would be like and what the time commitment was, and no one could give you a solid answer. The thing we said at the time was "Let's just work on this presentation together, and if there's a show, we'll figure out what your commitment is." We even said that if you want to walk away after the presentation, you can do that.

Lisa: And then my agent outlined super-specific things, like "There will only be two revisions per character"—which later we threw out, of course. I did, like, ten revisions on Todd; it didn't matter. . . . A lot of things were set up to protect me in case I hated it.

Noel: I remember those conversations with your agent: "She will do one set of revisions." "Well, what if we want to change the color of the nose—is that a revision?" We wanted to make you feel comfortable.

Lisa: I'd never done anything like this, so I was just worried about being exploited.

Noel: Our goal was to make a presentation. If you make it and cast it and show it, that gives you your best chance. The script process, once we hired Raphael to write the script (and he was "wasting his time" getting paid for it) [*laughs*], was also the beginning of knowing how it would be to work with him. We're an independent studio, so it was immediately a very collaborative process and we wanted the presentation to be in his voice and not screw it up.

To start, Raphael was tasked with writing an outline for the first episode.

Raphael: I had to write an outline for Tornante, and I literally did not know what an outline for an episode of television looked like. So I handed them, like, this two-page document. Now, a typical outline is ten to fifteen pages. And they looked at it and they were like, "Uh . . . OK. Um . . . [*laughs*]. Yeah, I don't know . . . This doesn't really look like an outline that we're familiar with." But I had no experience. [*Laughs.*] It was like an outline for an outline. But what's even funnier is, because I didn't know how to write an outline, unbeknownst to them, I actually wrote a full script and then tried to make an outline out of it. [*Laughs.*] I wrote the full episode, I sent it to my manager, and I said, "Should I just send this to them?" He said, "No . . . you get paid on different levels. So send the outline first; you get paid for the outline." I looked at the scenes in the script and I was like, "OK, what's happening? I guess this

Continued on page 72

This spread: Lisa's initial concept drawings of BoJack immediately captured the character.

Diane Concepts

This spread: Diane (and Todd) proved to be relatively harder to capture in the design phase than the animal characters, necessitating much more exploration. Drawing hundreds of variations is entirely typical during the design phase for a main character.

Diane Concepts

This spread, following spread: Diane's character was relatively challenging for Lisa to design, but the process did allow her to utilize her enthusiasm for creating clothing and textile concepts.

happens, then this happens, then this happens." In my outline, there's a little paragraph for everything that happens.

BoJack development spanned all of 2011 and 2012.

Raphael: In those two years, I developed a show for NBC—a workplace comedy about the United Nations starring Kal Penn—and I learned what an outline looks like. Obviously, that show never happened, but soon after I got staffed on a Comedy Central show starring Matt Braunger that also didn't happen, and then I got staffed on *Save Me*. I was in the *Save Me* writers' room for the fall of 2012, and into 2013. That show was canceled before it even aired. I learned a lot more about what I want a TV show to be, and also how to make a TV show. Because I was ludicrously green when I first started working on the *BoJack* pitch. [*Laughs.*]

Noel: We ended up with two scripts and a presentation script. The next step in the process was to interview animation production studios.

Because Tornante doesn't have its own animation production facilities, a production studio would need to be hired for the job of animating the *BoJack* presentation, as well as the potential series. Noel and Steve turned to a studio they'd worked with in the past, ShadowMachine (known for producing *Robot Chicken*).

Alex Bulkley [ShadowMachine]: When Noel and Steve sent over the *BoJack* script we had an immediate and visceral reaction to the material. It took a whole five seconds to call Noel back and say, "We're in!"

Corey Campodonico [ShadowMachine]: Very few projects make such a strong first impression. We knew we needed to bring in a strong director that would build on the visual language that Lisa and Raphael had honed together over the years.

Alex: We interviewed a bunch of directors to take on the pilot with us, but none of them could mimic a slide-whistle like Hollingsworth.

Mike Hollingsworth was hired to be the *BoJack* supervising director. Lisa, working from New York, logged many hours on the phone with Mike, who talked her through the specifics of designing for animation.

Lisa: I remember when we were working on the presentation, I hadn't yet met Mike, and we were just on the phone all the time talking about these character designs and backgrounds. Mike taught me how to draw through the backgrounds so that when you pick up a piece of furniture, there's still background behind it. I would just flatten everything, because I was thinking like an illustrator, not an animator . . .

Mike: Yeah, if somebody had to walk behind a couch . . .

Raphael: I remember the first draft of BoJack's house—

Lisa: It was drawn just, like, a small apartment.

Raphael: Yeah, and we'd be like, "BoJack's very rich, and this just looks like *your* house. [*Laughs.*] Let's imagine . . . Look, here's some pictures of rich people's houses."

Noel: After Mike came on board, we arrived at a place where we felt like the show had a unique perspective, was incredibly well written, had the right art, the look, the feel—it all felt right. So it was like, "OK, now we actually have to make it." So casting was the next thing.

The *BoJack* casting approach was to aim high to secure the kind of big-name talent that could achieve dual goals: to deliver funny and dynamic performances, and to help sell the show in the first place.

Linda Lamontagne [casting director]: We just went for really strong actors—comedic and dramatic actors. A lot of people will pigeonhole actors: If you do comedy, you're strictly comedy; if you do drama you're strictly dramatic. Casting directors get pigeonholed that way, too. What's unique about *BoJack* is that it's not just comedy—there's real dramatic moments in there—and you get the best performances out of people. I loved Lisa's designs. I loved that it was anthropomorphic, I loved that it was different than anything else. And the script was really smart. I knew when I read it that it was going to be a fun thing to cast. It was not that difficult to get people, because of the caliber of the project and the people involved. Michael Eisner's name really goes far. I got great responses from agents and managers and talent.

The EPs and crew delighted in securing their dream cast one by one, thanks to each actor's enthusiastic response.

Will Arnett [voice of BoJack Horseman]: I knew Raph was funny the moment I read the first pilot presentation. It wasn't until we were a few episodes in that I realized just how deep he was prepared to dive.

Aaron Paul [voice of Todd Chavez]: From what I remember, I was presented with a seven- or nine-page written spec treatment. I didn't see any animation for it; I just heard sort of the broad strokes of what the show was about. And I read it, and I loved it, instantly, of course. The world, the setting, you know? In Hollywood, in the industry, where animals and humans coexist, and there's nothing weird about it. It's just how it is. And I read it and I thought it was just so smart. Raphael explained to me that he wanted to not only do a cartoon that was funny, but also a cartoon that was incredibly tragic at times. I thought that was such a brave, cool idea.

Noel: I love how Raphael tells the story about how the casting went: "Can we get this person?" "Sure!" "Wait—we really can get that person?" And then, all of a sudden, "Yeah, that person just said yes."

Steve: Well, one casting story we always point to is the line Raphael had written in the script was that there was "a Keith Olbermann type" for Tom Jumbo-Grumbo.

Raphael: "Keith Olbermann whale," which is what I think the script described it as. It was just trying to describe the character!

Steve: Right. We didn't think he was going to be Keith Olbermann.

Raphael: Linda said, "Let's get Keith Olbermann! We can do it!" And then we recorded him and we did all the lines, and afterward we just said, "OK, now can we just get some whale noises from you?" And this is in New York; he's over the phone, and he says, "Mmmmmmwrrrrwrwrwwrwr!" [whale noise] and it's like, "That's Keith Olbermann! Making whale noises for our dumb little cartoon!"

Mike: We were like, "Can you make a noise like you're spraying water out of the back of your head?"

The final presentation cast featured three of the main actors that continued on into the series: Will Arnett as BoJack Horseman, Aaron Paul as Todd Chavez, and Amy Sedaris as Princess Carolyn. When the series went into production, Alison Brie was cast as Diane Nguyen and Paul F. Tompkins as Mr. Peanutbutter, completing the impressive ensemble.

Continued on page 79

Mr. Peanutbutter Concepts

This spread: Mr. Peanutbutter comes to life in these initial concept drawings by Lisa.

Princess Carolyn Concepts

This spread: Princess Carolyn sprung almost fully formed from Lisa's pencil and was refined through the sketching process.

AGENT PHONE CALL
IRRITATED

This spread: Princess Carolyn's hair color was still up for debate well into the presentation pilot phase as the design options below illustrate.

Noel: For each actor, really we were just offering, "Come in and do this for us," because we didn't know where we were selling the show. Netflix wasn't even a buyer at that point. But in the middle of making the presentation, they announced *House of Cards*. Once we came through the presentation phase, I remember Steve and I wondering, "Is it going to be hard to convince Raphael that we think we should be taking this to Netflix?" Going into our pitch, we knew that we would only be their seventh original series; so much was unknown about their model of serialized content that, at that time, it seemed like an unnatural place to go.

However, as the time approached to pitch the presentation, in October 2013, everything seemed to be falling into place for *BoJack Horseman*.

Raphael: By the time we were ready to pitch *BoJack*, *House of Cards* season one, *Orange Is the New Black*, and *Arrested Development* season four had all come out, and so Netflix felt like a real company doing good stuff. But it was interesting: The different places that we went to affected the pitch. With Netflix, I pitched it as a Netflix show. I talked about how serialized it was going to be and how it was gradually going to change over the course of the first season, which is not something I was vocal about on pitches to other networks. Different places got different versions of the pitch. I ultimately think that the Netflix version was the best possible version it could have been.

Mike: I remember when you pitched it to Animal Planet you really played up the animal aspects. [*Laughs.*]

Noel: So we had the show, we had the presentation, we had all the elements so that you feel like you've gotten it—everybody felt we were ready. The hard part was selling it. Part of it was that we had to wait a while because Raphael was working in New York again. We had to wait and find that window when he was done.

Raphael, continuing to keep many projects up in the air simultaneously, had once again been staffed on a series, this time being written in New York City in the spring of 2013. The kind of contract that Raphael signed made it difficult for him to leave to head up his own show.

Raphael: I got hired on a show in New York called *Us & Them*. So I moved back to New York. The show got canceled before it even aired. As soon as I heard the news, I booked a flight back to LA and pitched *BoJack* to Netflix. This was October 2013.

Noel: We had a few things going for us at Netflix at the time, which was just an insane coincidence. Number one, we had cast Will Arnett and Aaron Paul. Both of them were the leads in two of Netflix's most high-profile shows [*Arrested Development* and *Breaking Bad*].

Raphael: Well, one Netflix show, and one AMC show that Netflix helped popularize. [*Laughs.*]

Noel: Yeah, that's right—they were open about it. That was their most watched show at the time. So we had Aaron and Will, who were the first people aboard the project and who also were so passionate about it that, at the outset, we talked about them becoming producers, to help in the sales process. They were great.

Initially, we could not get Netflix to look at the show because they weren't buying animation. The feeling was once they said yes to an animated pitch, then they'd have to hear a pitch from every other animation producer in town—and they weren't set up for that; they were still really so new that it wasn't their focus. We were very lucky that a personal connection led us to a new executive at Netflix named Blair Fetter. Every project needs a champion, and Blair very quickly became ours. Even though Netflix was just ramping up their efforts in original

Continued on page 84

Todd Concepts

This spread: Todd's design proved difficult to settle on and required many sketches by Lisa.

WELL THAT WENT SLIGHTLY BETTER THAN THE WORST IT COULD HAVE POSSIBLY GONE. SO, HOORAY?
STRUDEL

Right: Aaron Paul's reaction to seeing the completed presentation animation for the first time.

From: Aaron Paul
Date: Wednesday, October 23, 2013 at 6:43 AM
To: Noel Bright
Cc: Linda Lamontagne
Subject: Re: "BoJack Horseman"

Noel,

So, I'm laying here in Spain with a giant fake beard on my face waiting to get called back onto set and I just watched BoJack. The entire time I had to hold my fake beard in place because of my laughter. The beard kept coming loose and this thing took almost three hours to put on. I knew Bojack was going to be a lot of fun but this my friend completely went way above and beyond all of my expectations. It so good!! I love this show. I would absolutely have this on my dvr and I am thrilled to be a part of it. Thanks for the kind words about BB. We had such an amazing time doing it and I loved being jesse so much. I miss the kid.

BoJack looks like it is going to have awesome potential. I can't wait to hear what people think about it. Where are you shopping it around??

Ap

On Oct 21, 2013, at 7:32 PM, Noel Bright wrote:

> Aaron,
>
> Wanted to say thanks again for being part of the "BoJack" team and send you the finished product. We are just starting to take the show out with Raphael and feel like we have something incredibly smart, funny and unique. It's already getting exciting feedback... With Will Arnett as Bojack and you as Todd there's a really great dynamic at the heart of the show.
>
> The link to the presentation is below. Hope you like it and that I'll be following up shortly with some news... By the way it would be insane for me to not tell you how much of a BB fan I have been from the start. I loved every season and especially the way it ended. Congrats on all your success as JP. I'm thinking we can get at least five seasons out of "BoJack" too!
>
> Noel

Todd Concepts

This spread: Todd could have been a drum-circle guy or surfer dude if these directions were pursued.

This page: The *BoJack* crew created these extra characters based off some of the executives who have helped to produce the series, including the Netflix execs who were at the pitch meeting.

series and not really interested in pursuing animation, Blair still agreed to watch the pilot presentation.

Blair Fetter [Netflix]: The proof of concept presentation Raphael created with Tornante was undeniably funny. It felt like I had that video playing on a loop in my office for weeks after. I was dying to meet the guy that created it. Even his name [Bob-Waksberg] made me laugh.

Noel: A few days later he called to tell us that their creative team—which at the time was Cindy Holland, Peter Friedlander, and Kris Henigman—thought it was really great and asked if we had a full-season pitch to present them. Blair had just met with the creative team from *Bloodline* and was blown away by their level of detail in presenting episode ideas and character arcs for multiple seasons. We passed this intel on to Raphael, who had always envisioned *BoJack* as a serialized show with long character arcs.

Raphael: Noel and Steve had heard that they pitched all three seasons of *Bloodline* in that first meeting—the full arcs of the first three seasons! So it was like, "Do kind of something like that." [*Laughs.*] I was like, "Guys, I know I have the first season—should I have a second and third season ready to start, too?

Steve: Raphael sat at a table with no notes and walked the executives at Netflix through all twelve episodes, for over an hour, in incredible detail. One episode at a time. Not just the thumbnails, but the A, B, and C stories, when there were any.

Cindy Holland [Netflix]: Raphael is a masterful storyteller and his passion for, and command of, the story he wanted to tell was infectious. This was *not* going to be a typical animated series—this was an at once silly and serious exploration of what makes us human (and horse, etc). About halfway through the pitch we were hooked, and we knew we could find an audience who would love this story.

Raphael: Every episode had a B and C story at this pitch! [*Laughs.*] I said, "Here's episode one, here's episode two," and all the way through, I was kind of showing what the scope of the season would be and how it was going to change. The pitch was that we were going to start with a wacky goofy cartoon show and it was going to start getting darker and darker so it becomes like a *Girls* or a *Louie* or even a *Mad Men*—those are the examples I pulled in the meeting to show what I wanted to do with it.

Noel: Raphael skipped over the fact that you only get one shot to be in that room and to have that chance. And he's underselling it—there were four Netflix executives in that room (Cindy, Peter, Blair, and Kris) who all had to be sure that our team could deliver a great series. Talk about pressure . . .

Aaron: I am dear friends with Peter Friedlander. After the pitch, I called him up and just expressed my love and passion for this project. And you know, they didn't buy it in the room, or even that night when I was speaking to him on the phone. But we all knew it was just such a love fest, the moment that pitch was done.

Raphael's in-depth pitch was thorough and convincing, and with the strength of the all-star cast's passion for the project, and the presentation pilot, the package was enough to sell Netflix. With one condition.

Raphael: In a follow-up meeting they said, "Can you have the series ready this summer?" We said, "Well, I dunno, *this* summer?" . . . And they said, "This summer or we don't want it." Basically. [*Laughs.*] So we said [singsongy], "We sure caaAAaan!" We got back and were like, "Hey guys . . ." and Mike was like, "YOU PROMISED THEM WHAT?!"

Alex: I'll never forget the moment, standing outside the studio on the sidewalk with Noel, contemplating a thirty-five-week schedule to produce twelve half-hours.

Cindy: When I think about *BoJack*, I think summer—doesn't everyone? We wanted to give the series its own time to shine and thought keeping it out of the crowded fall network schedule would be best. We knew it was ambitious, but we believed in the team and they rose to the occasion.

You Promised Them What?!

Corey: The season one production margin for error was razor thin and is a testament to how organized and decisive the entire team was in getting the show up on its feet.

In order to have the first season proceed with maximum efficiency right from the beginning, Lisa made the move to Los Angeles.

Lisa: I had to come out to LA for a funeral, really sadly, for family, and I got the news that *BoJack* sold while I was at the

This page: Todd becomes puppy-like in these color drawings with a floppier body and larger head.

funeral, and then I had to go straight to work here before going back to New York to collect my things. I worked here for a couple of weeks, stayed at Airbnbs. It was a really crazy time. I had never done anything like this before. I had been working by myself, completely solo freelance, and then suddenly I had to work in an office with meetings, and I had to stand in front of the character designers and be like [dopey voice], "So this is, uh, my aesthetic, and uh, this is the kind of stuff I like, and let's make the clouds purple, and uh . . ."

Mike: We put one of Lisa's books, *My Dirty Dumb Eyes*, on the server, and it was mandatory reading.

Lisa: I don't think anyone looked at it. They didn't have time. We didn't even have time to hire people. We just basically rolled people off of another show at ShadowMachine onto ours.

Noel: We had to be lining up the show even though we hadn't quite gotten the official green light yet on paper. Raphael had to start writing.

Raphael: We had the first two episodes written, and I started writing the third episode without a staff, thinking, "Well, all right, let's get ready." Then we started building a writing staff. We had a table read that first week; we didn't have any of the prep time that you normally have.

Noel: We had a week of prep. We had the writers come in, and we told every writer we wanted to hire that they might work every day of the week, weekends, late nights, and that they wouldn't get the holidays off, because we started right after Thanksgiving. It was a schedule built around working through the holidays because the start day was effectively the first week of December, and we had to deliver the show in July 2014. All twelve episodes, in nine different languages. [*Laughs.*]

Raphael: It had to happen. We signed the thing! I mean, it was always clear to me that the work was going to get done, but it was like, "How miserable are we going to be?"

Lisa: And was it going to be good?

Mike: We wanted it to be the best possible quality, so it was like, "What is going to be the end result of this crunch?"

Noel: We set up a process. It was crazy, and way too fast, and not an ideal situation, but the one silver lining in it was—a lot of times, when you're doing a pilot, you just have to make decisions, and usually maybe you get them right half the time. Every decision we made had to be made quickly and it was instinctual—there was no time to second-guess it.

Raphael: It's so funny that we spent two and a half years to make fifteen minutes, and then seven months to make the additional eleven and a half episodes.

Lisa: I'm so glad we made the presentation episode because we solved a lot of problems in it.

Raphael: We would have been screwed if we hadn't done that.

Noel: Initially, when we started series production, I kept saying, "Well, we have twelve minutes, at least, done. So we can reuse that."

Lisa: Yeah, you didn't know we had to redo it.

Noel: A couple weeks in they were like, "Oh yeah, we need to redo all of that."

This spread: Todd's design in the pilot presentation (left) was still only half-baked, and was one of the main reasons why the pilot footage had to be redone when season one was ordered from Netflix. Todd's final, fully-baked design still retained a lot of the attitude and details from all of these concept drawings (this spread), but with a simpler, more child-like face with less jaw, nose and brow definition.

Lisa: We had to change Todd.

Noel: I haven't watched the presentation in probably two years, but even back then it was really weird to see the old Todd.

Lisa: He's ugly. [*Laughs.*]

Pilot-presentation Todd was one of the elements that Raphael and the crew weren't too happy with, so Todd's design was one of the main things that changed between the presentation and the first episode.

With little to no stopping, the bustling studio worked for seven months to crank out the premiere season in time to release all twelve episodes simultaneously for streaming. The culmination of more than three years of talking, writing, drawing, and animating saw Raphael's "Depressed Talking Horse" become *BoJack Horseman* at the stroke of midnight on August 22, 2014, when the series went live.

Among the factors that have been disrupted by the recent ubiquity of streaming video is the old way of understanding whether a series is successful or not. Television viewership ratings are available for the public to see and are usually the justification for a show's renewal or cancellation. Netflix keeps its viewing stats secret, thus its executive decisions can seem magical. One of the few remaining public metrics of success, the critical review, initially provided a mixed opinion of *BoJack*.

Aaron: When we first premiered, people didn't understand what they were getting. And so I think a lot of critics maybe didn't even finish the season, because they were like, "What is this?" I thought the first season was brilliant, and I'm a tough critic on myself: If I don't like something, and I'm a part of it, I will say that it's terrible. I thought that the first season was really special. But it just didn't perform all that well in the critics' eyes.

In fact, a handful of the first reviews were written based on the preview episodes that had been provided to the critics in advance. Watching only three episodes of season one could give anyone a skewed sense of what the show might be before it completely unfurls its complex bouquet of relatable sadness. The critical tides turned once critics and fans who had actually watched the entire season began to write reviews.

Paul F. Tompkins [voice of Mr. Peanutbutter]: It found an even bigger audience in the second season and then the critics started understanding that, oh, this is not what we thought it was. I think it's a really wonderful lesson not only for the people who create stuff but also for the people who consume stuff: There might be more to something than you thought there was. Raphael could have made that show just a funny cartoon for grown-ups, and it probably would have been fine. But I just think the fact that he challenged people's perceptions and did it the way that he did it was very courageous. Because he must have known, "People might check out of this. If I save this turn until the third episode, people might not get there." But the fact that you are rewarded for hanging in there and giving the show the benefit of the doubt—because when that turn happens it's so sharp—I think is a terrific thing.

Aaron: Ever since that first season, it's kind of been a critical darling, in a way. But it's all the same show. I think a lot of people just didn't understand, or went, "Well, this isn't funny. It's *kind* of funny. . . . And then why am I feeling bad about myself right now? What's happening?" [*Laughs.*] You know?

Alison Brie [voice of Diane Nguyen]: I was struck by how smart, funny and moving the show was. It was the most honest portrayal of loneliness in Hollywood that I'd ever seen.

Continued on page 90

This page: Lisa's meeting notes regarding her character-design assignments for the pilot development (white) and the notes she received back (yellow) included the essential question "What is a character design?" and a note to make Todd "less dreamy."

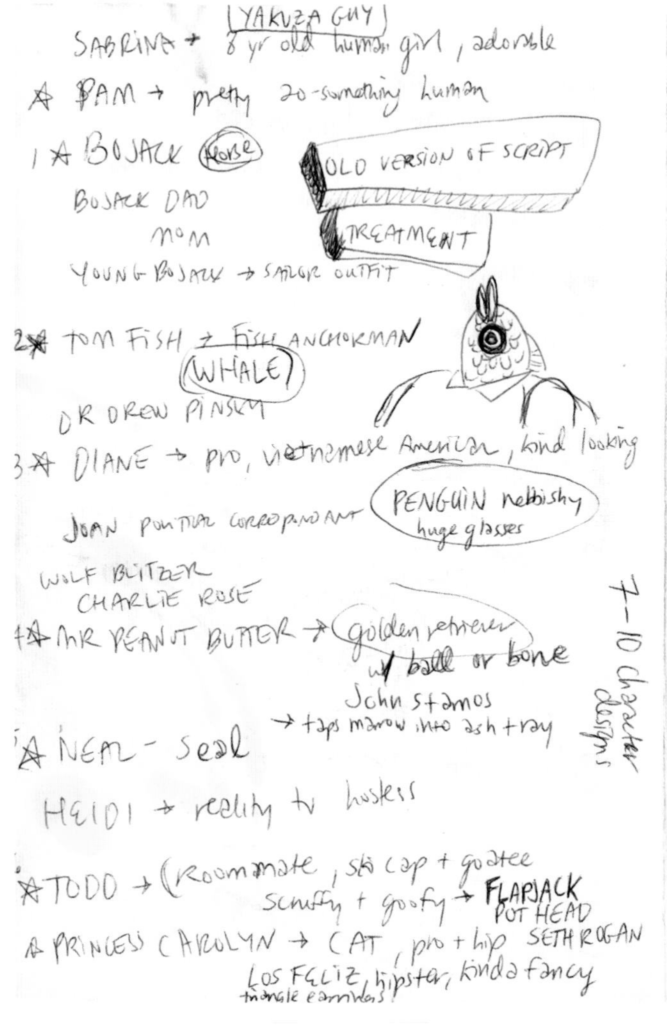

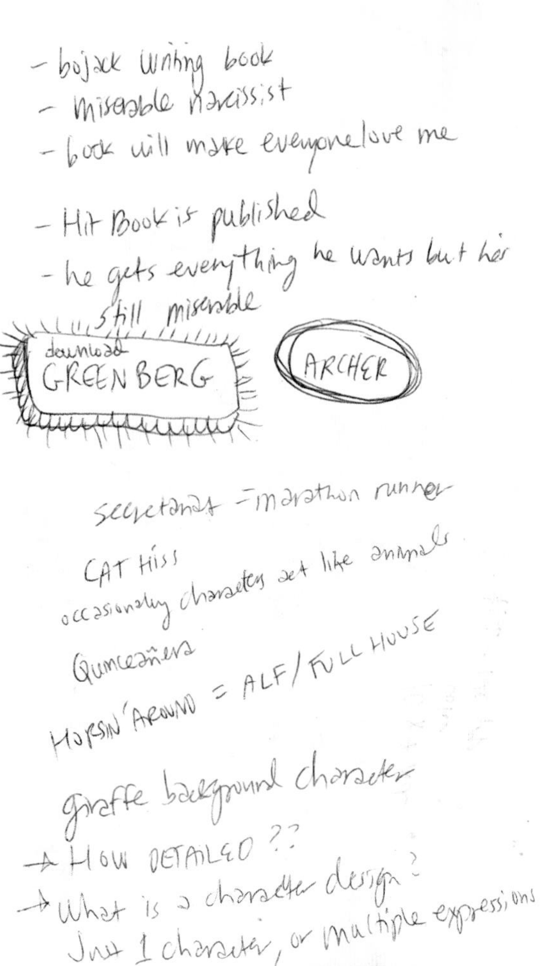

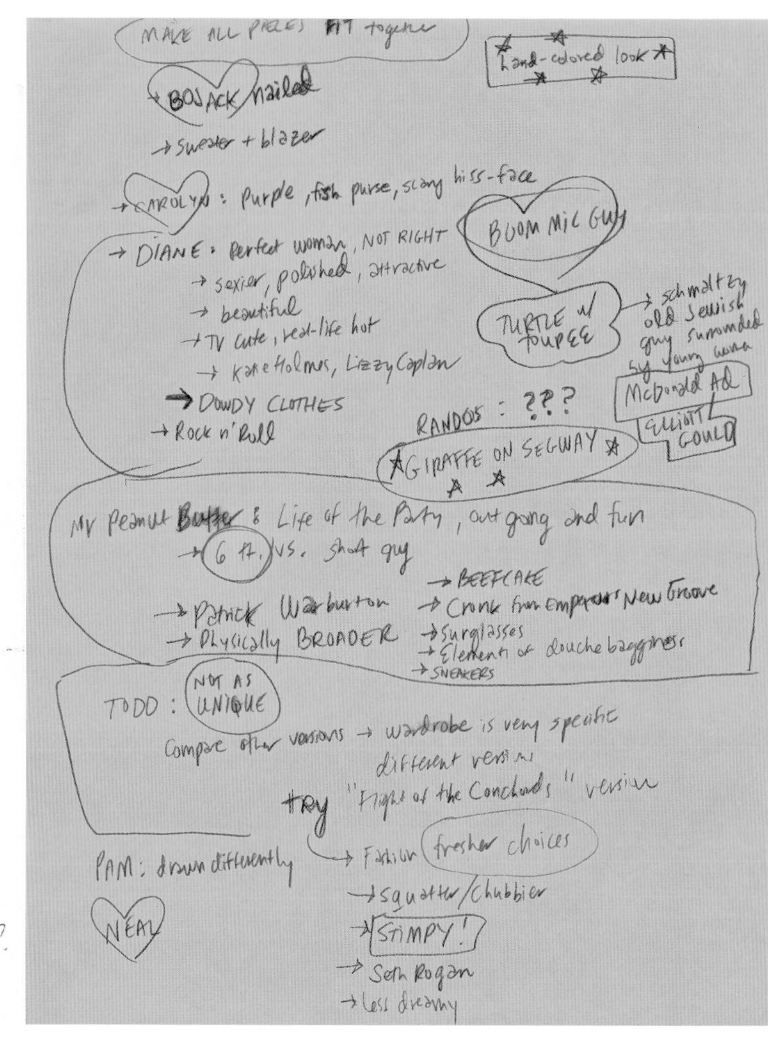

BoJack Horseman

BoJack Horseman

BoJack HORSEMAN

BoJACK HORSEMAN

BoJACK HORSEMAN

BoJACK HORSEMAN

BoJACK HORSEMAN

BoJack

BoJack Horseman

BoJACK HORSEMAN

This page: Presentation pilot development of BoJack's living room including perpetual houseguest, Todd.

Aaron: When we first aired, I got an email from Rian Johnson [director, *Star Wars: The Last Jedi*, *Breaking Bad*, *Looper*, *Brick*] saying, "I just finished *BoJack Horseman* season one for the second time, and I had no idea that I would cry so much watching a cartoon on television." And then we actually ended up getting him a role on the show [Bryan, an improv troupe member from season two]. He just had to be a part of it. People's reactions are just so great. People are really getting personally affected by this cartoon.

Indeed, it turned out that the many gut decisions along the way turned out a cartoon that keeps jabbing audiences in the guts—in the best way possible.

Michael: Who knew Raphael Bob-Waksberg would deliver a brilliant, clever, funny, and emotional script, with the brilliant series to follow? That kind of talent shows up about once a decade.

This spread: Additional concept art created by Lisa for the presentation pilot.

This page: Voiced by real-life news anchor and commentator Keith Olbermann, Tom Jumbo-Grumbo spouts off about the latest news. Concept drawing by Lisa.

2: The Horse's Voice

Writing and Acting BoJack

BoJack craves people's approval and attention, but he sabotages his relationships. BoJack wants love, but his emotions have long been scarred over. BoJack's oldest friends are gone, and those who remain mostly work for him, or are dependent on him. BoJack fantasizes bitterly about the roads he didn't take. In his darkest periods, BoJack wallows in drug-fueled benders. BoJack's mood rarely rises above sad dissatisfaction, even when getting the opportunity to portray his personal hero, Secretariat, in a movie. Instead of lulling its viewers into a dark pit of despair along with its hero, however, *BoJack* entertains—the show and the character are funny. There is a structure and science at work behind the scenes, in the writers' room, to keep the dark balanced with light.

Root for Him; Don't Aspire to Be Him

Raphael Bob-Waksberg [series creator]: We were trying to find that balance of, "How do we show this character, and sell this character and what he is, but not have that be the point of view of the whole show, and not feel like we're endorsing his behavior?" I think the challenge for a lot of shows like this, where you have your asshole protagonist, is that you glamorize it, or just by the nature of showing it, you kind of soften it, or make it feel, like, "cool."

Lisa Hanawalt [production designer]: Yeah, you're supposed to relate to it.

Will Arnett [voice of BoJack Horseman]: And I don't know if I'd say that BoJack's condition is that he's an asshole. That's too simplistic. Certainly being an asshole is sometimes a symptom of his overall condition. Maybe he can learn to act less like an asshole if he could somehow deal with his multiple, deeper issues.

Raphael: Something very early on that we wanted to make clear with BoJack was that we want you to empathize with him; we want you to feel his wound and feel his pain, and we want you to want him to get better. We never want him to be an aspirational figure. He's not a cool guy. With some of these other shows, it feels like, the writers are in love with this badass who tells it like it is, and is a fucking dick to everyone. As the first

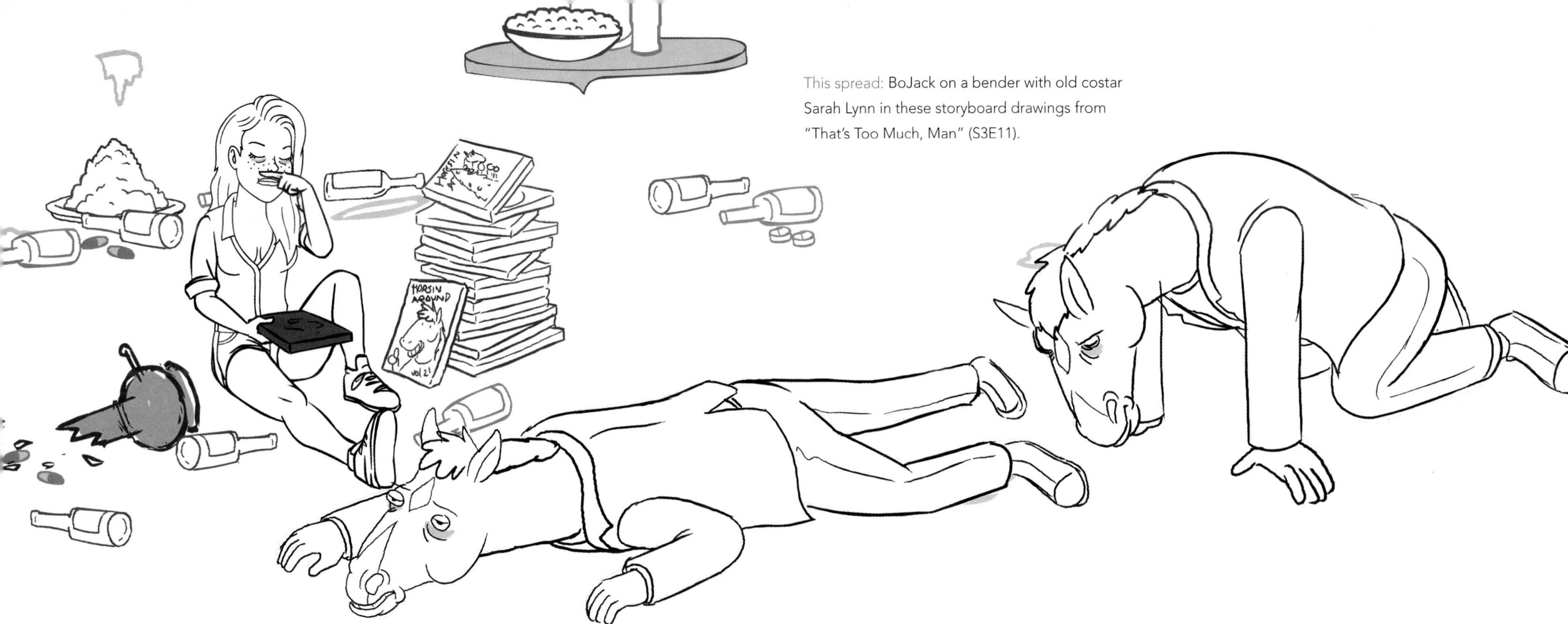

This spread: BoJack on a bender with old costar Sarah Lynn in these storyboard drawings from "That's Too Much, Man" (S3E11).

season of *BoJack* progresses, it gets increasingly clear that there are consequences to BoJack's actions, and that he's *not* a cool guy, and he's not happy, and he's not good—that he's not better off for the way that he is.

Like many other recent critically acclaimed series, *BoJack* features a deeply flawed protagonist. But comparing BoJack to other antiheroes, like *Mad Men*'s Don Draper or *The Sopranos*' Tony Soprano, is a mixed bag.

Raphael: I like those comparisons to a point.

Lisa: Those are such great characters.

Raphael: I want BoJack to be his own thing, though. I don't want it to feel like, "Oh, they're just doing Don Draper as a horse, or Tony Soprano as a horse." I think there are some ways in which those comparisons are helpful. I'd rather BoJack be compared to Don Draper and Tony Soprano than, like, [*Family Guy*'s] Peter Griffin. [*Laughs.*] It's kind of nice that it takes the show out of the animation conversation for a little bit: "Oh, *BoJack* also has something in common with these other different kinds of shows, and different kinds of textures." But the show in general is a mix of many influences and many original things.

Relatable, Not "Likeable"

Raphael: "Likeability" is a very loaded term in television development, and a lot of writers kind of push back against that. I don't think it's a bad instinct. You want your characters to be likeable, but the *way* you make them likeable is wider and more open than what some people may think. There's this narrower kind of philosophy that you have to make a character likeable by making him or her good, or generous, or kind, or admirable in some way. The wider approach is, for example, that if they're good at their job, the audience will like them.

Lisa: It's more important for them to be relatable.

Raphael: That's what it is. And I think you like your characters if you understand them, if you understand what they want, if you understand where they're from, if they feel vulnerable in some way. Vulnerability makes a character "likeable."

Lisa: A lot of people are like, "I relate to BoJack. He's a lot like me. How can I change that?" [*Laughs.*]

Raphael: "How can I not be that?" [*Laughs.*] Yeah . . .

BoJack plays out a scene that reflects this approach in "Downer Ending" (S1E11) with Diane, who is in Penguin Publishing's office arguing for her version of the BoJack book she wrote:

DIANE
See, people respond to the flawed portrait I painted of you. They see themselves in it. Why do you love Secretariat?

BOJACK
Uh, because he was awesome.

DIANE
No, because he was flawed. BoJack, when people find out that someone like you, who is larger than life, is actually just as wounded and vulnerable as they are, it makes them feel less lonely.

BOJACK
Ugh, no! Maybe that's what flawed, sad fatties want from other celebrities, but from BoJack Horseman they want a heroic horse stud who is awesome and who can save them from their flawed, sad, fatty lives.

Clearly not taking Diane's words of wisdom to heart, BoJack then claims he will rewrite an entire autobiography himself in less than five days that will "kick your dick off."

Real-World Issues

Beyond sculpting a dynamic, damaged protagonist, the crew must craft scenarios and stories to throw him into to see

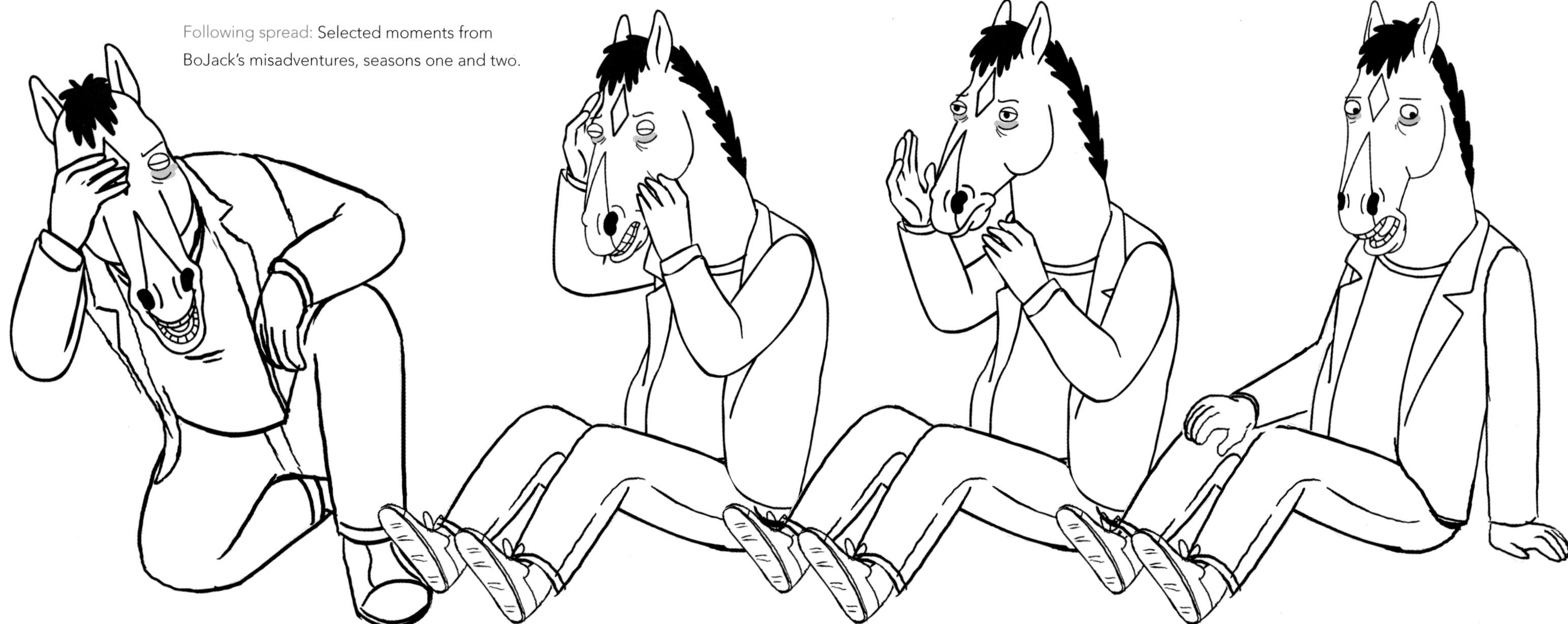

Following spread: Selected moments from BoJack's misadventures, seasons one and two.

what he does. The writing of the series is ambitious. *BoJack's* storylines dare to go to serious, potentially controversial places that are not often explored in adult comedy cartoons, where the amount of raunchy humor tends to be the main measure of their "adultness."

Kelly Galuska [writer]: We get to examine real-world issues under the guise of making this comedy cartoon. We've written episodes about guns, and about how men behave in Hollywood, and things like that. We're able to explore some really deep topics, but with this comedy layer of these animals going through these things. That kind of allows us to slight the blow of how heavy things get sometimes.

Kate Purdy [writer]: One thing I really like about working on the show is that we have interesting, flawed female characters, and through them we explore ideas of feminism.

Nick Adams [writer]: In season four, we have an arc where Princess Carolyn deals with her miscarriages. There was a lot of talk last year about miscarriages; like, we needed her to have more than one to convey the scale of trauma that we were going for, but we had to ask, "How many is too many miscarriages, and how much are we going to discuss it? Are we going to see her going to the doctor's office?" At some point we decided: "Let's just talk about this; we don't want to get into the doctor's visit or what the procedure is like or anything like that." I feel like just talking about it was impactful, but it's also still a comedy. . . . We don't want it to be—too impactful? I mean, there's also so much other strong, emotional stuff. It still feels like Princess Carolyn is comic relief—BoJack is the character who's allowed to wallow in pure sorrow, and the things that everyone else does have to have a more comedic element at all times.

Joanna Calo [writer]: We take it all really seriously; we talk it all the way through. Like Nick was saying, we talk about "how many is too many," and we talk about what's real for a woman and what has the biggest emotional impact. Then we find ways to make it funny, or we subvert it in some way. But we take it all really seriously.

Elijah Aron [writer]: If we're dealing with topics like abortion, for instance, we are very conscious of what we're trying to say, and Raphael really feels like we have a voice. Not a lot of people do, so we try to make sure we are using our platform to say something meaningful and useful to society. It's also meaningful to us, but we're all conscious of what message we're sending each time we bring up something controversial.

Everyone Fart-Jokes

At the same time, acknowledging the seriousness of *BoJack* doesn't suggest at all that the crew members are above indulging base humor, too—within limitations. On Netflix, almost any content goes, which shifts the onus of defining taste parameters over to the showrunner.

Raphael: With Netflix, there are no language restrictions, no nudity restrictions, no thematic restrictions. I mean, we get some pushback on story points sometimes, or some jokes . . .

Lisa: I've had maybe one design note, and it was like, "Make sure this horse character doesn't look too much like BoJack." And I was like, "Huh, good note."

Raphael: It never feels like "the man" is clamping down on us. Well, sometimes it feels that way, but it never actually *is* that way. [*Laughs.*] Sometimes we tortured artists like to decide, like, "How dare they?! They're going to kill this Scott Baio joke? This is the crux of the whole episode! Those PHILISTINES!"

Mike Hollingsworth [supervising director]: Probably the biggest limitation we have—the thing we all have to deal with a lot of notes on that's a little soul-crushing—is Raphael's aversion

Continued on page 98

ABSINTHE
MENU

HORSEMAN
3

to bodily fluids. That is blood, that is piss, that is sweat, and that is pus. And boogers! And vomit.

Raphael: Is that really the biggest challenge?

Noel Bright [executive producer]: The seven months to produce season one is nothing, but this—

Mike: This is the biggest challenge.

Raphael: Early on in season one, I had a realization in the writers' room: Fart jokes are like farts; everyone thinks their own don't stink. People would keep trying, and I would be like, "C'mon, c'mon—you're better than that!" Then at one point I throw a fart joke in there and everyone's like, "WHAT!" And I'm like, "Yeah, but it's not, it's not—it's—*this* one, it's *classy*!" [*Laughs.*]

Lisa: Have we ever had a fart joke on the show?

Raphael: A couple. Well, one that comes to mind is not really a fart joke. It's when Turteltaub tells BoJack, "I've laid farts that have lasted longer than your entire career," which is not really a fart joke—it's a mention of farts.

Lisa: Do farts exist on this show?

Mike: I have a fart in the show this season. There's that ketchup thing; it goes [imitating the score of *Psycho*], "*REEE REEE REEE thbpbpbp!*"

Raphael: Yeah, that's not a fart.

Mike: No, but we got a real fart noise. We looked up fart noises.

Raphael: Eh, you snuck it in. But yeah, I think just any kind of body humor is kind of grossness.

Lisa: It's one place where we are different.

Raphael: I can't pin it on any sort of high-society taste—it's just that I'm squeamish, and it's a personal problem. Early on, though, there was pressure on us to prove ourselves as not being like those other shows. We didn't want to just do, you know, boner and poop jokes. We wanted to kind of indicate that we've got a higher range, that we're going higher here. Now that we've kind of established the tone, we can sort of—

Mike: Our boner jokes aim higher.

Raphael: Exactly. I remember I was in the third episode, where Sarah Lynn takes a dump on a floor model in a store, and there are storyboards of her, like, dropping her pants and squatting and I'm like, "GUYS! C'mon! What are we doing here? Let's class this up!" And they're like, "You wrote the script! What did you think we were going to be seeing?" And I was like, "No, they just talk about it!"

Lisa: It can happen offscreen.

Raphael: It can happen offscreen, exactly. And so that's what we did.

BoJack, Lover or Lothario?

Mike: Raphael has been the protector of this world, but there will be moments in editorial reviews when we're talking about what would happen here—what could these characters be doing—and I'll be like, "Well, BoJack could be in this bar and a beautiful woman could walk by and he ogles her." And Raphael will be like, "What? That's gross." Meanwhile, BoJack is having one-night stands all the time and he's drunk—he's always drunk! Raphael's like, "No, no, I can't have BoJack objectifying this woman," and we're like, "He just had a one-night stand in the previous scene!"

Lisa: BoJack written by anyone else would be more like a Charlie Sheen–ish type of character.

This spread: Todd studies humor writing; BoJack gets frisky with Heather Manatee in "Start Spreading the News" (S3E01).

Following spread: Selected moments from BoJack's misadventures, seasons three and four.

Raphael: I'm probably trying to project a little bit, but I'm like, "Can we give him a little bit of dignity?" One thing I remember, from before *BoJack*—when I was staffing [preparing to apply for a writing job on one of many shows gearing up for a season of production]—was, I'd read all these scripts of pilots for other shows. My agent sent me, like, the whole packet, saying, "Here are all the shows that are going. Tell us which ones you spark to, and we'll try to set up meetings so you can meet on those shows." One thing I discovered that I was very annoyed by, with all these scripts, is the tendency for there to be a central male character, and then every female character in the script is defined by whether or not male characters want to have sex with them. That's, like, the primary characteristic of the female characters. So I had a rule for myself: If a script doesn't have a female character that isn't solely defined by the romantic or sexual possibilities of her, then I would throw it away. So when it was time to sit down, and I'm like, "All right, I get to make my show; I get to make *BoJack*," and I looked at my female characters, I go, "Oh. One is his ex-girlfriend, and the other is his love interest. Um—a problem." [*Laughs.*] So we very quickly tried to find ways to define those female characters outside of their relationship with BoJack, to give them more dimensionality. That's part of the challenge on any show, because all of your characters are defined by their relationship with the protagonist, male or female. But especially with the female ones, we really tried to—we struggled that first season to, you know, make sure we weren't just falling into that trope, and just defining them by whether or not our protagonist wants to sleep with them.

Lisa: It's hard, because BoJack just wants to sleep with everyone.

Raphael: Exactly. [*Laughs.*] Yes . . .

Lisa: But he's classy. He's classy. . . .

Bad Behavior

Discussion in the writers' room has often centered around how far they can push BoJack's behavior without making him irredeemable. In just one episode, "Horse Majeure" (S1E09), BoJack gets Todd to commit several crimes, including breaking into Mr. Peanutbutter's house. He then encourages Todd to eat a cyanide pill via walkie-talkie when the plot goes sideways; couldn't care less when he thinks Todd ate it; is vaguely interested later when he sees that Todd is not, in fact, dead; and hires character actress Margo Martindale to stage an armed robbery—all to sabotage the wedding of his friends Mr. Peanutbutter and Diane, out of jealousy.

As in most comedies, the consequences BoJack faces for his misdeeds aren't always realistic. Such over-the-top antics are a familiar part of broad cartoons and cartoonish live-action comedies. Every cartoon cat that has blasted a giant hole in its head or stooge that has puffed on an exploding cigar knows that the damage inflicted was never going to be permanent. Typically, though, neither the cat nor the stooge would spend the following scene on a rooftop under the stars having an introspective dialogue about intractable depression with a sympathetic friend. What makes BoJack unique among comedic protagonists is his capacity to be both a cartoonish heel and a flawed, dramatic antihero who has to cope with the havoc he wreaks upon his own life.

In "That's Too Much, Man" (S3E11), BoJack and his old costar Sarah Lynn's epic, often hilarious, weeks-long bender ends with her fatal overdose in a planetarium, having silently died while sitting in the darkness next to BoJack, composed in silhouette against the projected starry sky. When considering the serious consequences BoJack has had to face for his actions, it's hard to top the permanence of death.

Kate: One thing we talk about when we're writing him is making him remorseful and regretful. He really wants to be a good person—but seems to struggle with what it means to be good.

Joanna: Also, he's a real person to us. We all can be bad people, but we know why we do it and we know that sometimes

Continued on page 102

PUPAE SITTING
BOJACK KILLS
BOJACK HORSEMAN
"SECRETARIAT"
YOU ARE
SECRETARIAT
CABRACADABRA TEAM

PIGARONI PIZZA
PIGARONI
EVIL WRINKLED WHORE!
Mercy, dear, save me from this DEMON RAISIN!
Tilda Madison
TO DO:
LAUNDROMAT
CALL BIV
PICK UP BULBS!
FINISH FANFIC
DESTROY TILDA
96
NO LOUD TALKING
WAIT UNTIL CALLED BY CLERK

This page: BoJack betrays his old friend Charlotte's trust and hospitality. The writers craft scenarios that test the audience's empathy for the lead sad horse.

we make mistakes. For BoJack, we think about the emotion that's beneath the really bad behavior and just try to keep it really grounded.

Kelly: We'll always talk about the consequences of his actions—as Joanna was saying—as though he's a real person. We'll get into arguments with each other about whether the things that he does are forgivable or not. We think of him as another human being, and that's also part of what keeps him grounded.

One particularly precarious moment for BoJack's redeemability came in the episode "Escape from L.A." (S2E11): After initially rebuffing his old friend Charlotte's teenage daughter, Penny, Charlotte catches BoJack and Penny in bed, moments away from an intimate act. The writers wrangled with this scenario extensively.

Joe Lawson [writer]: That was days and days of conversation. I mean, not just the detail of how old she is, but mainly the conversation was: "Can we make BoJack irredeemable?" And the answer is no. But we wanted to get right up to that line: "Are we going to be able to come back from this?" And so, as a room, we discussed that for a long time. We were very concerned about how to protect the characters but also be realistic; how to not be off-putting but still be extremely human.

LA Stories

The showbiz subject matter of the series continues to spark the imaginations of the writers, especially Raphael. Before the green light, however, it was a concern, as Raphael had become aware of a stigma that focusing a show around Hollywood, or Hollywoo as it is called in the show, could be a turnoff to some network execs who might consider it too insider-y, or overexposed.

Raphael: As a kid, I always liked the show-business stories. Then again, maybe I was predisposed—clearly now I work in this business. [*Laughs.*] I'm the kind of person it appeals to. But that was never a stumbling block. I loved *The Muppet Show*. *The Larry Sanders Show* I loved. *The Critic*. *30 Rock*. It's never been a turnoff point for me; I don't understand it.

By virtue of continuing to make the show, Raphael has gained access to even more of Hollywood's true weirdness.

Raphael: The longer I live here, and especially given the success of *BoJack*, the more I kind of see kind of the, uh—the upper echelons of Hollywood, kind of, living, kind of—

Lisa: [*Laughs.*] He's in high society now.

Raphael: I'm more tangentially, you know, adjacent to it.

Lisa: Yeah, you're in it.

Raphael: I observe all sorts of new ridiculousnesses that I would have thought were too cartoony, maybe, when starting the show. But now that I've been able to go to some of these houses and meet some of these people up close, um . . .

Lisa: It's good fodder.

Raphael: It is. . . . [*Laughs.*]

Lisa: I mean, really . . . Some of it you can't use for the show. [*Laughs.*]

Raphael: Right. But even the experience of having a successful TV show, all of a sudden I can relate to BoJack in ways that I couldn't when I first started writing the show.

Joe: We all live here in California, and I think we all are sort of interested in an anthropological view of celebrity culture and Hollywood. Personally, I find the stories interesting when we are able to sort of step back and [examine Hollywood] in a way that a lot of shows don't—really call it out for what it is and how many sort of different layers are involved. We're working in this business and trying to remain normal and grounded, like BoJack isn't.

This page: In a world where humanoid animals, insects, and invertibrates are people too, the doctor's office waiting room is ripe for visual gags.

Talking Animals

The most obvious surface-level curiosity about *BoJack* is its cast of coexisting humans and anthropomorphic animals—not a first, as far as fictional worlds go, yet *BoJack* offers a unique take on such a society.

Raphael: I think the thing I was kind of thinking about was the world of *Roger Rabbit*, where you have this world of real people and 'toons. It's kind of like that. You have people, and you have animal-people. What helps is that you kind of start with an idea: "Oh, this horse was on this TV show. Oh, I get it. It's like *Mister Ed*, and he's the horse." And then you expand that out into the world and show that there can be both animal-people and people-people.

Lisa: I'm always surprised when people think *that's* the weird thing about the show, because to me, growing up, all the books I read and all the shows I watched were about animals treated equally as people.

Raphael: I mean, we live in a post–*Family Guy* world. Where you have the dog who is the dog, but who also walks around and drinks cocktails.

Mike: On paper, there's not much of a difference from Bugs Bunny.

Raphael: But you normally see either animal worlds, where it's like Mickey Mouse and Goofy, or *Zootopia*, or you see talking animals in a person world, like a Bugs Bunny or a *Family Guy*. It's rare to see animals as people mixed in with other people.

Steven A. Cohen [executive producer]: Concerns about whether people would understand the premise came up a good number of times. For me, one of the early watershed moments was something that Mike put in the presentation: this gag where BoJack yells at a chicken and an egg pops out.

Lisa: She's wearing a skirt and the egg falls out when she's startled—it's ridiculous. [*Laughs.*]

Steve: That really became a signature of the show. Gags like that are a reminder that you can live with one of these characters, like a chicken and human, and for ninety percent of the scene, it's just a girl on a girls' night out with her girlfriends . . . and then, all of a sudden, you're reminded that we're playing by a different set of rules.

Raphael: That's really the Mike Hollingsworth influence on the show. When I first started thinking about it, even in early conversations, my whole thing was that I wanted this to be really real—I wanted people to feel like this was really happening. Mike put a joke in the presentation that the grocery store was "J'Vons," which is a combination of "Jons" and "Vons"—which are two different grocery stores, and I was like, "No! It should be Jons or Vons; it should be a *real* grocery store! And all the restaurants should be *real* restaurants! I want it to be in the real Los Angeles as it actually is!" I didn't want to make jokes; I wanted it to feel like the real world, with animals as people. Loosening up on that edict really improved the show [*laughs*], and I'm thankful for Mike's influence. Going to those goofier places—more cartoony, animals doing animal stuff—a lot of that comes from Mike.

A logline [a short description of a project's premise] that I kind of landed on for describing the show was "Real, grounded characters in a crazy cartoon universe." But also the characters are pretty crazy and cartoony, too. It was going to go to these wacky places but have this real, grounded heart to it. A melancholy to it that we would keep coming back to.

Mike: In the end, the flights of fancy kind of ground it.

Raphael: Yeah, so it actually works. They ended up complementing each other really well. We kind of found this alchemy in that the sadder you go, the goofier you can go, and the goofier you go, the sadder you can go.

This page: Though Mr. Peanutbutter's Seaborn Seahorse Milk commercial from the episode "Fish Out of Water" (S3E04) references some familiar tropes of funny Japanese commercials (big-eyed cartoon mascot, nonsensical scenario, seemingly random American celebrity spokesperson), the balance of the underwater world was designed not to read strictly as a Tokyo-esque equivalent.

Opposite: J'Von's was an early background joke that foretold the torrent of silliness to come.

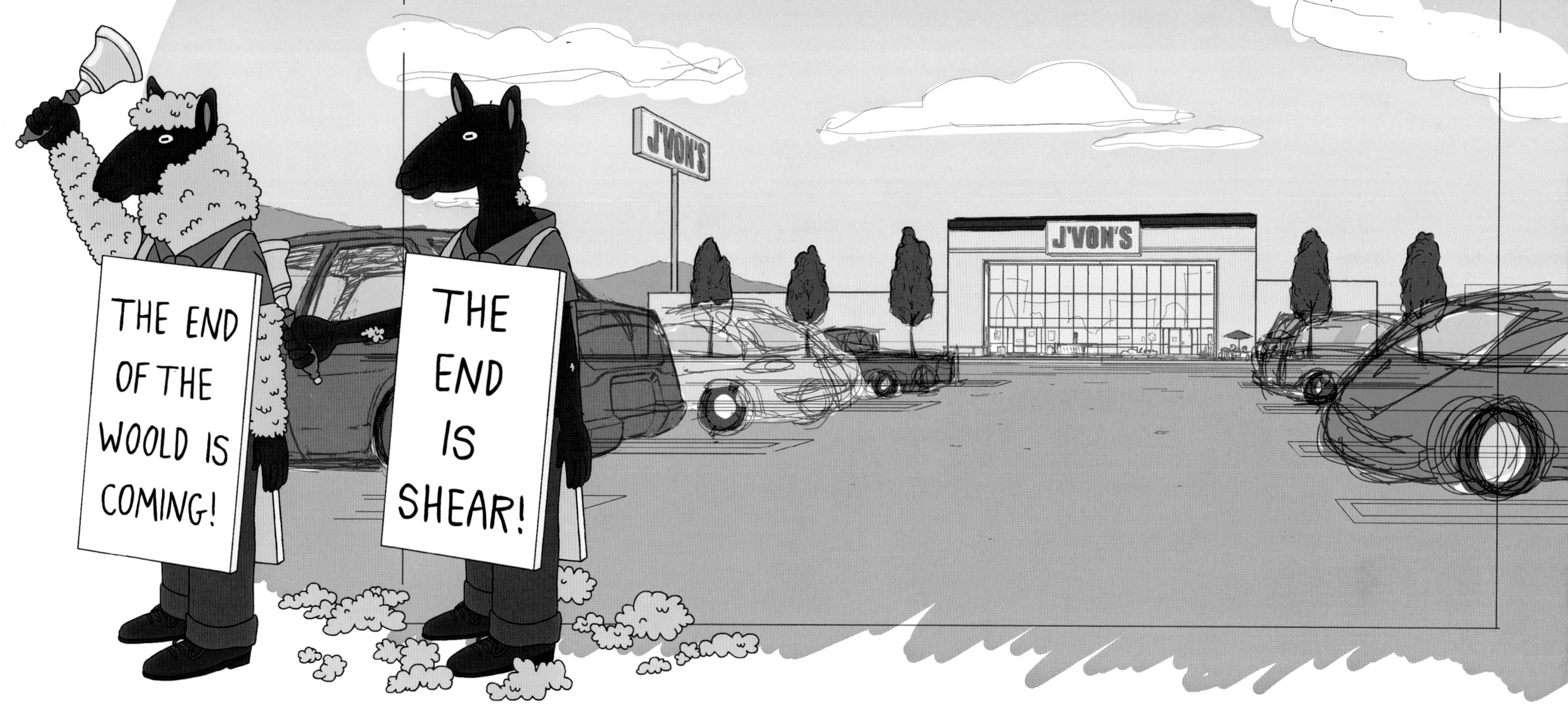

Mike: Without seeming like we're—

Raphael: Self-indulgent—

Mike: Punishing the audience—

Raphael: We really get this salted caramel kind of flavor.

Does a Bear Pray in the Woods?

Despite being conscious creators and populating the *BoJack* world with a diverse variety of human people in an attempt to reflect the real world, the crew has to be careful not to carry human-specific signifiers of ethnicity or religion over to animal characters, for fear of audiences trying to spot ostensibly intentional correlations (and inevitably taking offense).

Lisa: We don't want to associate certain species of animals with certain races, for example.

Mike: Yeah. We were very careful in that underwater episode ["Fish Out of Water" (S3E04)]. Because there's also a tone that we were in a Tokyo-type place. And so we didn't want the fish to read as Japanese.

Raphael: Right. It draws on *Lost in Translation* a little bit, and certainly . . . our commercial is very much a Japanese commercial. But we didn't want it to feel like we were saying, "This is Japan."

Mike: Yeah.

Raphael: Early on, in the first season, we had a bunch of writers who—just coincidentally—had all worked on the *Cavemen* show on ABC, including the creator, Joe Lawson. He said that one of the things they got dinged on immediately by audiences was when they had a joke that seemed to be trying to say that the cavemen were black people. And then it's like, "Well, *are* you saying black people are cavemen?" And once you try to get into the specifics of the analogy, things kind of break down a little bit, and you have to go back and go, "Oh, no, no, we weren't saying that; we were just saying it's kind of like this . . ." Even *Zootopia*, which I thought was a fantastic movie, got criticized for [making some animal jokes that relate to real-world scenarios involving race], and when you try to track those analogies, you go, "Oh, well, this is that, and that means this is this, and this is that . . ." They muddied things up enough that it's not a clear one-to-one analogy. I think some people were even kind of angry because they wanted it to be *more* specific, but it wasn't. That kind of specificity is something that we've really stepped aside from. We'll have a joke every once in a while, in which an animal gets offended by, like, an animal joke that feels racist in that way. But we really try not to go too deeply into that.

Mike: Ultimately, what's great is that throughout the history of animation, and the history of storytelling, animals can serve as placeholders for people, but in a way that allows us to shed all of the different societal hang-ups. You have all these animals in these stories, and they're not from a place. They are just from the earth; they're just animals.

Lisa: That's why it's easier to design the animal characters than the human characters, because the humans are so specific and are tied to a background of what that kind of person looks like.

Raphael: I think that is a key to the show's success in some ways. That even though BoJack is in many ways coded as an affluent white man, he's not a white man. He's a horse. And you are able to latch on to him. You could be any kind of person and see yourself in BoJack, or Princess Carolyn, or Mr. Peanutbutter. And I think there is a power to that—because

in a sense he's more iconic, because he has this animal face. You're not thinking, like, "Oh, he looks like me," or "He doesn't look like me." You can kind of project yourself onto him.

Mike: We make sure to put in people from all different cultures.

Raphael: Part of what's hard is that, because we have these animals, we have fewer humans to play with than a normal show does. But even still, we really want to be inclusive in all our humans and show the wide spectrum of what humanity can be.

Mike: Raphael is writing these characters who are so human, who are so relatable—what they're going through is really, you know, human. But then, in the very next scene, Mr. Peanutbutter is thinking about lifting his leg on a fire hydrant.

A Horse Is a Horse, of Course

Outside of his prominent facial features, BoJack doesn't often exhibit horse-specific attributes or behaviors. But what is a horse like? Do horses have a variety of personalities? In an urban environment, it is common to grow into adulthood with no firsthand horse experience. Fortunately for the production, Lisa Hanawalt grew up horse-obsessed.

Lisa: Horses all have a lot of similarities. There are, maybe, ten different horse personalities. [*Laughs.*] They're fearful. It takes a while for them to trust things, you know, because they're prey. So they're always looking out. They're always vigilant. They're herd animals, too, so they warn each other.

Mike: My mother-in-law told me that the reason you have to try so hard to get a horse to accept you riding on it is because that is what scares them: something on its back.

Lisa: Yeah, it's like a mountain lion pouncing on their back.

Mike: Yeah, that's how they get attacked.

Lisa: So it's weird for them to have an omnivore, a predator, you know—an animal that eats meat—on their back, riding them. There's this place where I go out riding in Joshua Tree, where people rent out their horses. And one of them told me, "You know, they can smell on you that you eat meat." And so you have to be aware of that when you're on them, and you're strapping, like, dead cowhide to them and then riding them. [*Laughs.*] And I was like, "Riding is brutal . . . Why do we do this?" So pretty much every time I ride now, I try to be very respectful of that dynamic.

Mike: As scripted in the first episode, BoJack throws up a tremendous amount of cotton candy—

Lisa: And horses can't throw up.

Mike: And Lisa's like, "Well, um . . . I should say, as a point of record, that, uh, horses actually cannot throw up. This is not accurate."

Lisa: So, BoJack's digestive system is human. [*Laughs.*] It's in the human part of his body. There were a couple horse people who were like, "It's weird that he throws up," and I was like, "I know, I know."

Raphael: It's also weird that he has arms and legs, and wears clothes, and drives a car . . .

Lisa: There's not a ton of horse-specific behavior that comes into the show, except when he mentions, like, getting spooked by a bag in a parking lot, which I thought was the funniest joke ever. [*Laughs.*] Animals—not just horses, but animals in general—if they see something, like a different silhouette than usual, they freak out. Like, if you put a hat on, a dog will be like, "Who are you?" Your shape has altered. So, yeah, that's very funny to me.

Like, we kind of forget that they're animals on this show, and then we'll bring in just slight references or jokes—

Raphael: Yeah, a minor involvement, like in the middle of a big fight between Diane and Mr. Peanutbutter, she'll say, "You're a good dog. Yes you are. Yes you are. You have a cute, furry face."

Lisa: Yeah. I love the dog jokes especially.

Raphael: It kind of just comes in and leaves again just as quickly.

Diane: The Flawed Idealist

Diane's outlook on the world is defined by her terrible high school experience and strained family relationships. Married to Mr. Peanutbutter by the end of season one, she begins to feel stifled and directionless. She and BoJack share certain critical and pessimistic attitudes about people and life in general, which is part of what bonded them as friends—until she rebuffs BoJack's inappropriate romantic advances in "The Telescope" (S1E08) and BoJack struggles to cope with his intense jealousy of her relationship with Mr. Peanutbutter.

Raphael: I think Diane was a difficult character to crack in the writing because we kind of knew from the beginning that out of five characters, she's our fifth funniest. Like, she's never going to be that "hard laugh" punch-line driver the way some of the other characters are. But we didn't want her to just be a straight woman, or a wet blanket. I think having Alison Brie really helped a lot in finding her voice, and finding the kinds of jokes that she can tell, and the comedy you can get out of her.

Lisa: Yeah. She really brought a warmth to the character. Diane could have come across as so cold.

Raphael: Yeah. And so I think we found a lot of different ways that Diane can be funny. You know, a lot of it is her being, comically, the straight woman sometimes, kind of being that stick in the mud and nobody is listening to her. Also when she goes off on a rant. In episode three ["Prickly-Muffin" (S1E03)], I think we have that long speech she gives about Sarah Lynn and third-wave feminism, and that really felt like we were finding her voice in a cool way. Like BoJack, I think once you find Diane's wounds, and what her vulnerability is, that's when maybe she pops and becomes more interesting. And so when she has these kind of weird tensions left over from feeling left out in high school, and that anger and that aggression come out in weird ways . . . or when you see that she wants to be making a difference in the world, and how hopeless that is, and how she struggles and fails to do that—that can be very funny as well. When we found more of what her character is, and not just in relation to BoJack, that's when she really blossomed to life.

Lisa: I like that she's this character who really wants to be better, and wants to save the world, but in many ways, she's just as much of a selfish asshole as, like, anyone else.

Raphael: Yeah. And she knows it, too.

Lisa: She knows it. She's kind of shitty. She's kind of a shitty friend.

Raphael: I think that is very relatable, to a lot of people. That feeling of, "I know what's right and good, and I have trouble holding myself to that standard, or even knowing how to hit that standard." You know, "I know I am a bad, gross, dumb human, but I want to be better. But I don't really see the opportunities. . . ."

Mike: "But I also want a coffee."

Raphael: Yeah. [*Laughs.*] Exactly.

Left: Diane and BoJack in the Blow Hole room at Whale World investigating the mystery of a dead whale floating in Cuddlywhiskers's pool in "BoJack Kills" (S3E03).

Opposite: A sampling of Princess Carolyn moments.

Lisa: And she's talented, but she's not, like, living her full potential, maybe. It's like she's still not doing exactly what she wants to be doing.

Alison Brie [voice of Diane Nyugen]: One thing I love about Diane is how she'll change her mind about something and then go all in on it. Hard. Like her view on guns, or how to represent abortion in the media. Even in her relationships she can be a surprising character.

Diane and Mr Peanutbutter are definitely wrong for each other, and that is what makes them one of the more realistic relationships on TV. There are aspects of both of their personalities that draw them towards each other, at times even bringing out the best in each other, but they will never fully understand each another. Perhaps they both represent the type of person they think they should be with rather than their actual perfect match. That is something I think a lot of people struggle with when looking for love.

Princess Carolyn: Textured but Ruthless

The world of talent agencies, managers, publicists, and casting directors is often portrayed as full of scrappy, cutthroat players who would stop at nothing to score big-name clients and land big-dollar deals. In spite of Princess Carolyn's occasionally less-than-ethical business practices, viewers still feel a lot of empathy for her. The writers try to make a point of exploring that tension between Princess Carolyn as a hardworking heroine, a sometimes morally bankrupt Hollywoo power player, and a cat just trying to achieve some work-life balance.

Amy Sedaris [voice of Princess Carolyn]: She shows you her flaws from the get-go, and I think people can really relate to her. How she tries to be a hard-ass at work. . . . her love-life. I like how sentimental she can be. And every cat-person in the world . . . I'm like their leader now.

Raphael: In the first three seasons, I think we like her because we know her, and she's our gal. But if you look at the episode with Gekko and Rabitowitz ["Old Aquaintance" (S3E08)], you kind of see the story from their perspective: She's just as ruthless as they are. There's no reason, necessarily, that they are worse or better than she is. You know, I think Rutabaga has been a real heel in many moments in the show. But Princess Carolyn has double-crossed and outsmarted, and outwitted, and she's been just as ruthless.

Lisa: Yeah. She lied to her previous assistant.

Raphael: Yeah, to Laura. She kind of throws her under the bus, because she wants to keep her as an assistant; she doesn't want to promote her out of it.

Lisa: Yeah. She's not an ideal feminist hero or whatever.

Raphael: Right. I think that's interesting. That there's texture to her. And I think she is, on some level, a good, decent person who cares about other people and wants what's best for her clients and puts them ahead of herself sometimes.

Mike: Certainly BoJack.

Raphael: Yeah. But I think also she has her baser qualities as well, her ruthless qualities. I think that's what makes her interesting, that she's not just this perfect character who does the right thing all the time and believes in a code. I think she's as flawed as anybody else.

But, you know, one thing that we want to be careful with, is making sure that she doesn't fall too much into the cliché of the woman who has a great work life, but her personal life is in shambles. We kind of skirted that line a little bit. In episode seven of season one, which is her first big spotlight episode ["Say Anything"], she's kind of won all the professional battles

PHILBERT

Cat on a Hot Tin Roof
Snappy...
ELIZABETH TAYLOR PAUL NEWMAN BURL IVES
When Tabby met Snappy...
JUNIOR

This spread: Princess Carolyn's very bad day in "Ruthie" (S4E09) included a dramatic break up with her boyfriend, Ralph, after she'd revealed to him that she'd suffered a miscarriage; seen here as frames from the final storyboard.

but her personal life is a mess, and she feels sad and lonely because of that. At the end of season two, I wanted to tell the opposite story, even though it's kind of the same: Her career is going great but her personal life is a mess, and yet she can feel good about that—she doesn't have to feel sad that her personal life's a mess. In other episodes, we've shown that her personal life is going better, and she's happy in a relationship, but her work life suffers. Or sometimes both things are going well at the same time, and sometimes both things fall apart at the same time. To use the spinning-plate metaphor, she has different plates going, and she has to kind of tend them all, but sometimes some do fall down, and others get stronger.

Mike: We might want to do something in the book where we maybe have a picture of what spinning plates are? [*Laughs.*] Because that seems to be a favorite metaphor of Raphael's. I don't know how many of these kids who are going to buy this book have seen *The Ed Sullivan Show*.

Raphael: Well, *we* have . . .

Lisa: Could it be, like, "multiple fidget spinners"?

Raphael: So Princess Carolyn has multiple fidget spinners that she's spinning. [*Laughs.*] Yeah, yeah. But we shouldn't dive too deeply into it, because even in the explanation it's like, you know, with all plate-spinners now, some plates fall down, but other plates get stronger. Like, that's not . . . how it works . . .

Lisa: The one plate you're spinning just grows larger and larger—

Raphael: *Raahhh!*

Mike: When I was talking with a young lady in Costa Rica, and I mentioned spinning plates, she said, "What's that?" So I explained to her what it was: "You know, and then you're spinning them all on a series of dowels." She said, "Dowels?" I'm like, "Never mind . . ." [*Laughs.*]

Raphael: But I do think one defining characteristic of Princess Carolyn is that she often puts the needs of others in front of her own. Which is admirable, but also dangerous. And sometimes she does that to a fault. She does not, maybe, practice self-care as much as she should.

Mike: Yeah. It's a real easy way to put your own problems on the back burner.

Amy: The writing is so heart-felt, and it's so dark. You can get away with more in animation. I like that the writers go there with all the characters. And the show biz stuff—playing a manager—is fun. She's got her home life and the workplace, and she always tries to keep them separate, but they always merge. And I like that she has bags under her eyes. That always applies for me!

Mr. Peanutbutter: Sunny Optimist

At first glance, Mr. Peanutbutter the yellow Lab is an energetic, sunny, surface-deep Hollywoo schmoozer. But the audience learns much more about him with time.

Raphael: One of the first things we talked about in the writers' room—and also to Paul F. Tompkins, when I was explaining the character to him—that I wanted to be very clear on was that Mr. Peanutbutter seems very shallow and superficial, but he isn't. When he says, "BoJack, I want to talk to you!" and then goes, "Erica!" Like, that's not him being a douchebag—although it *kind* of is—but it's him genuinely being interested in BoJack for that moment, and then getting distracted and being genuinely interested in Erica.

Lisa: [*Laughs.*] He has a short attention span.

Raphael: He has a short attention span, a low IQ, but he's very genuine.

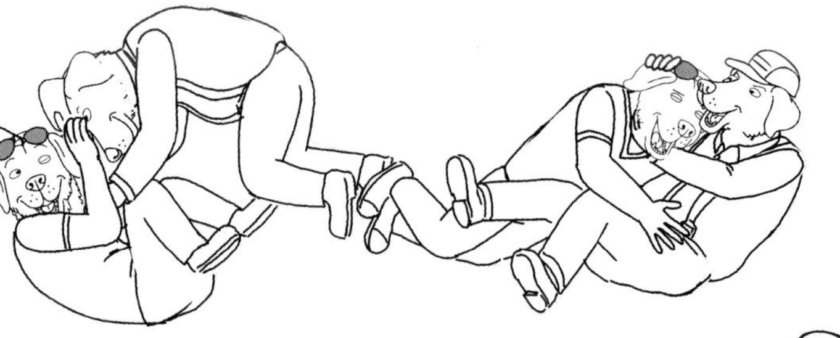

This page: Mr. Peanutbutter is greeted with some light airport roughhousing by his brother Captain Peanutbutter in the Labrador Peninsula; storyboard images from "Old Acquaintance" (S3E08).

Opposite: A sampling of Mr. Peanutbutter moments.

Lisa: He has a low IQ?

Raphael: He's not the brightest bulb in the box.

Lisa: Yeah, that makes sense. Sometimes he's weirdly intuitive.

Raphael: I think he also has an emotional intelligence.

Lisa: Yeah, he does.

Raphael: Um . . . but not always. [*Laughs.*]

Lisa: [*Laughs.*] Yeah, he's mostly a dummy.

Raphael: He's often a dummy. But I also think he enjoys *playing* the dummy sometimes. You know, I think you see it in moments like in the first episode, when BoJack and Princess Carolyn are breaking up, and Mr. Peanutbutter goes, "Oh, would it be awkward if I joined you right now?" Or at the end of season two ["Out to Sea" (S2E12)], when he's talking to Diane at a restaurant, and he says, "You know, there's a woman here who looks exactly like you." And it's kind of unclear in that moment whether he knows that's Diane.

Mike: The storyboarders kept asking, "So, does he see her?" And I was like, "I don't think so . . . ? Talk to Raphael." Raphael says, "He doesn't *think* he sees her . . . ?"

Lisa: I think he does.

Raphael: I think he does, too. But I enjoy the ambiguity of that moment. I think it's a sweeter moment if he knows and he's letting her off the hook.

Lisa: Well, then later it seems like he thought a little bit more about what had happened, and it's like they're trying to repair that.

Raphael: There's something funny about not quite being certain if he knows, and that the audience can kind of draw their own conclusions. There are other moments of that as well. Like, "Is he playing dumb, or is he actually dumb?" In the first season, I enjoyed starting with BoJack as our point-of-view character, because you think you have a handle on Mr. Peanutbutter, and then you gradually realize, "Wait, no, actually, I love this guy." [*Laughs.*] He's really sweet and fun and, like, not a douchebag at all.

Lisa: Yeah. He's my favorite.

Paul F. Tompkins [voice of Mr. Peanutbutter]: It takes a little bit longer to see the emotional turns that Mr. Peanutbutter has. They don't happen right away, since so much is focused on BoJack and Diane. During the show it's been so exciting because it keeps surprising me and I keep getting to do different things—in this cartoon! It's way more of a nuanced character than I've ever gotten to play before. To have the ups and downs and the complexities of this character has been really a gift.

Mike: Also, at least in season one, one of the most important functions of Mr. Peanutbutter is that he and BoJack have basically the exact same backstory.

Lisa: They respond to it in opposite ways.

Mike: Two sides of the same coin. BoJack is very pessimistic about where he is, and Mr. Peanutbutter is very optimistic. I mean, Mr. Peanutbutter also doesn't have a lot going on.

Raphael: Right. He's like, "Oh, you want me to do a commercial? You want me to do a cheesy reality show? Sounds great! What a joy to be alive!"

MSNBSea
Dutch
FETCH
SIT
STAY

Left: A nineties-styled Mr. Peanutbutter starring in *Mr. Peanutbutter's House*, the contemporary rip-off of BoJack's sitcom, *Horsin' Around*.

Opposite: A nightmare vision of Mr. Peanutbutter appears during BoJack's extended hallucination in "Downer Ending" (S1E11).

Lisa: Maybe his parents were more supportive.

Raphael: Yes, certainly. [*Laughs.*]

Lisa: I started understanding who Mr. Peanutbutter was by seeing how he responds to Diane, and the way he's emotionally intelligent. He's kind of a goofball, and he's kind of got a sunny personality. He's just like a golden retriever. He's always happy to see you. He sees the best in people.

Raphael: Well, Mr. Peanutbutter is not a golden retriever.

Lisa: Oh, is he a . . . He's a yellow Lab.

Raphael: He's a yellow Lab.

Lisa: Yeah, I always confuse them.

Raphael: You, of anybody, should know that.

Lisa: I know. They're very similar kinds of dogs.

Raphael: Yeah, I don't know the difference.

Lisa: Basically one just has slightly longer hair. But I think, personality-wise, they're pretty similar.

Raphael: Oh, OK.

Lisa: Same kinds of genetic disorders, too. Yeah, he's just a ray of sunshine. He's a break from all these characters that are cynical, a balance to them.

Raphael: And one thing that's been really interesting for me to explore in the Mr. Peanutbutter/Diane relationship is never quite being on solid ground, or knowing—because I think we're very used to seeing stories where we know, like, "Oh, this is the bad relationship, and they should break up." Or "This is a good relationship, and they'll be happy for the rest of their lives." And it's like most relationships in the real world—you never quite know. You can be, like, ninety-eight percent sure . . . Or you can be fifty-two percent sure. But there's never that moment where it clicks and you go, "Oh, this is definitely right." Or there's a moment where you could feel that click, but then a week later you could be like, "No, I was wrong. I don't know." And to kind of play that shaky equilibrium with them felt really interesting. When we realized that, I think toward the end of season one and into season two, it became clear that we're not saying we need to break this couple up. But we're also not saying they're in love and everything's going to be perfect from now on. We're saying it's going to be a struggle, and both of them are going to be second-guessing it, and you're never going to quite know how you're supposed to feel—if you're supposed to be rooting for this relationship or not.

Mr. Peanutbutter also reveals depth to his character when the audience starts getting glimpses of other moods and turmoil under his sunny exterior. In "Horse Majeure" (S1E09), he's pulled over by the cops and gets his license suspended for chasing his enemy, the mailman, in his car. In "Brand New Couch" (S2E01), he attacks his own reflection in the mirror after drinking too much and cuts his arm, which then requires him to wear a cone to prevent him from chewing his stitches. Later, when he enthusiastically brings his Mighty Mighty Bosstones mix CD-Rs to BoJack's movie trailer in anticipation of them attending the group's concert together, but BoJack rudely rejects him, he walks away deriding himself under his breath for being so stupid.

Lisa: He looks up to BoJack.

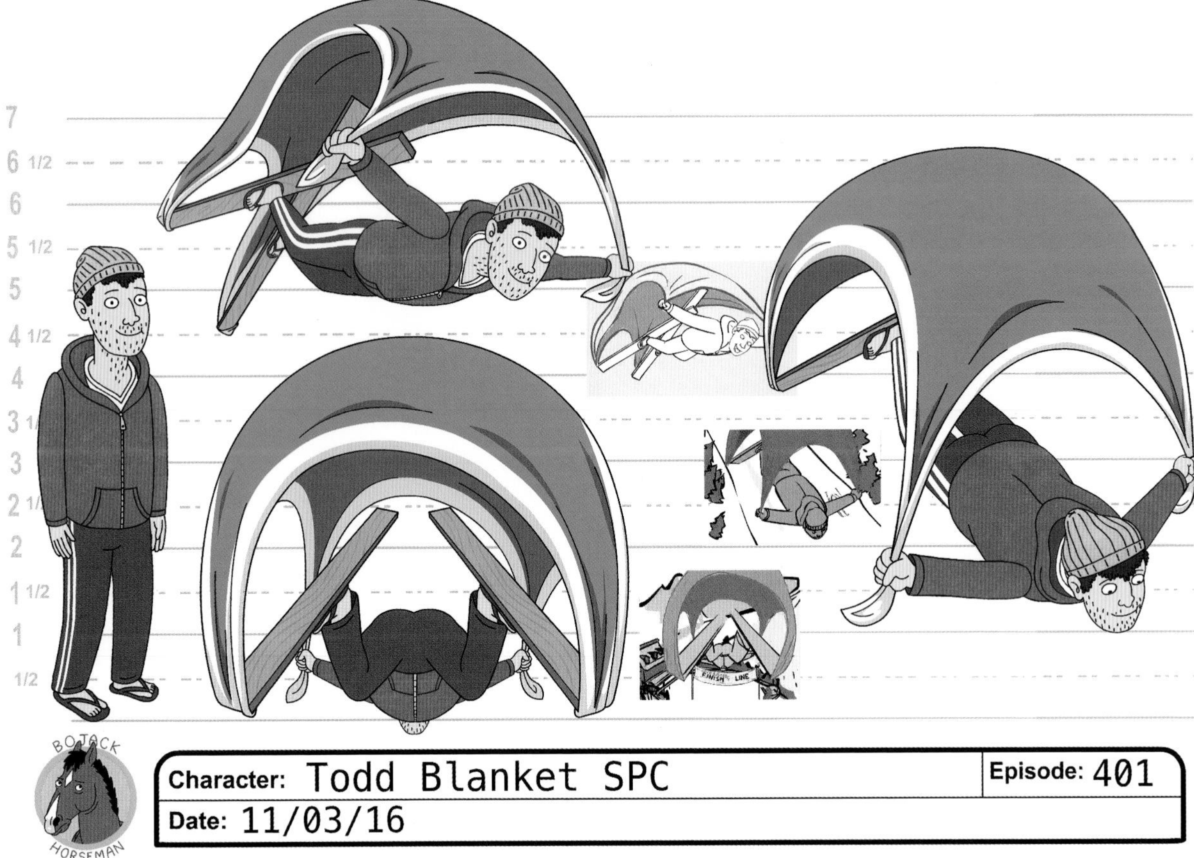

Left: Special pose models of Todd with skis and blanket parachute from "See Mr. Peanutbutter Run" (S4E01).

Opposite: A variety of Todd moments.

Raphael: In season two, in the game show episode ["Let's Find Out" (S2E08)], he confronts BoJack and says, "Why do you make fun of me all the time?" And up until then, you kind of assumed that he doesn't get it; that he's an idiot and it all goes over his head, when actually he does hear all that, but he smiles and puts on a good face anyway.

Lisa: Yeah. He's pretty sharp that whole episode.

Sweet, Stoned Todd

Todd is potentially a confusing character to comprehend if you've never encountered a carefree couch-surfing dude. But Todds do exist.

Mike: Lots of people in LA are like Todd—they just seem to be floating and have nothing going on but . . . are so happy.

Aaron Paul [voice of Todd Chavez]: I absolutely know a couple of people like that.

Raphael: Early on, at least, he was somewhat based on my friend Kevin, who would kind of jump from scheme to scheme, in a very lovable way.

Lisa: He's always got a scheme. [*Laughs.*]

Raphael: He's always got something going on. For a while, Kevin was living with this rich lady in Pasadena and kind of, like, being her Guy Friday in many ways. He has a story in which she asked if he would drive her daughter to school. He said yes. And then it was revealed to him that school was college on the other side of the country, and so he had to go on this weeklong road trip with this woman's daughter, and this guy was like, "All right. Guess I'm doing this now!" And that was—that's kind of his attitude, he kind of always—

Lisa: He's very open to new experiences.

Raphael: Yeah. He's, like, open to the adventures of the world, and Todd was kind of based on that a little bit. He kind of falls into stuff, and he's like, "All right, this is what I'm doing now," and doesn't let it faze him.

Lisa: Not a planner.

Raphael: And Kevin always has the best attitude. He is always, like, delighted to be around, and is like, "All right, let's see where this goes." And so that was kind of the early idea for Todd, like when I was describing it to the writers, I said I don't want to make him too stupid. Because it's not quite that. Although he definitely has gotten stupider as the seasons have progressed. [*Laughs.*]

Mike: And it's also, like, there's being stupid, and then there's just not caring. Kind of, like, letting it roll off your back. He's stoned a lot, too.

Raphael: He's definitely stoned a lot. [*Laughs.*]

Mike: That helps with the not caring.

Lisa: He's the perfect balance to BoJack, who cares so much what people think about him and is so worried about everything.

Raphael: We thought he would be a good foil, especially early on. BoJack could hurl abuse at him, and he would just kind of take it with a smile and be like, "Ah, you. You're zazzin' me, and I'm loving it." And BoJack's like, "No, I'm not zazzing you. I'm asking you to clean up your shit." Early on, Joe Lawson, one of our writers, pitched a line for him that I felt like, "OK, Joe's getting him." It was when BoJack is complaining in the

PB Livin'
A DIVISION OF
PB
ENTERPRISES
CC

first episode, saying, "Why did I say I could write this book?" And Todd says, "Because you have an amazing story to tell."

Lisa: Yeah . . . [*laughs*].

Raphael: That sweetness really gets to the heart of who Todd is, and his outlook on the world. We also thought he'd be a great way to tell these more cartoony, off-the-wall stories.

Aaron: He's just got a kind of childlike wonder. I love that Todd is sort of an under-the-radar genius, you know? I get that when I'm reading the scripts; I'm just amazed at what Todd Chavez is coming up with right now. Because most of his ideas are just so idiotic, but so fun and innocent, and then all of a sudden he'll have this epiphany where you're like, "Wow, you're so profound, Todd Chavez." I love that about him—he's just so endearing. I have so much fun with him. He's just so over-the-top.

Raphael: Sometimes you get a hint of a C story with Todd, but you don't quite know how he got into that mess or how he's getting out of it. You're just getting a little insert in there of, like, "Oh, there's a whole other thing happening with Todd right now," but we don't even get to see all of it.

Todd's generosity also gives BoJack monumental leeway to be unabashedly self-centered. But even their friendship gets strained beyond the breaking point.

Aaron: I was about to describe it as a love/hate relationship, but I don't think there's hate at all within that relationship. I do believe that it does stem from love. But with BoJack in particular, he was raised in such an abusive, unhealthy household, you know? So it's so hard, because it's almost not even his fault. It's just all he knows. With Todd, you realize that he has lived so many different lives, and it's just so fascinating that he has so many new secrets revealed. He comes at it in such an honest, innocent, kind of pure way, and he loves BoJack just endlessly at the beginning of the show. But he also becomes BoJack's punching bag. And Todd is just letting it happen. But then he can't take it anymore. And he ventures off on his own.

Mike: It's also fun with Todd, from the animation and storyboarding point of view. Even though he is a human, and we generally view the animals as our sillier, "they can do stupid stuff" kind of characters, Todd actually acts kind of the most like a cartoon.

Raphael: Like, he's a real puppy dog.

Mike: Yeah, like—when we're brainstorming, he has his own rules for what he can get away with. He can do cartoonier things, which is a lot of fun.

Raphael: Right. Early in season two ["Still Broken" (S2E03)] there's the story where he has to take ten dollars to a vending machine. And then the wind blows the bill away, and he chases the bill a little bit, then it gets stolen by a mouse, and then the mouse gets picked up by a hawk, and the hawk has the mouse in its legs and it flies in the air and it gets hit by an airplane. And that is, like, so cartoony, and so silly—

Mike: And if that were to happen to BoJack—

Raphael: Yeah, you'd be like, "This doesn't feel right." But with Todd it's, like, perfect. [*Laughs.*] Oh! BoJack also, once, picked up a toddler from a stroller, climbed in the stroller, and rode the stroller all the way to the studio. [*Laughs.*] All of our characters have that cartoonier side, if they choose to. But I think Todd lives in that world a little more.

Lisa: Maybe Diane the least.

Raphael: Right, yeah. When the hawk got hit by that airplane, I think Todd's line was "Why does this always happen to me?"

Opposite: BoJack and Princess Carolyn loom large over the writers' room conference table (left), which is situated in the cubical just beyond the character designer island (right) at ShadowMachine in Los Angeles.

Right: BoJack's mother, Beatrice, admonishes all who pass by the white board in the writers' room.

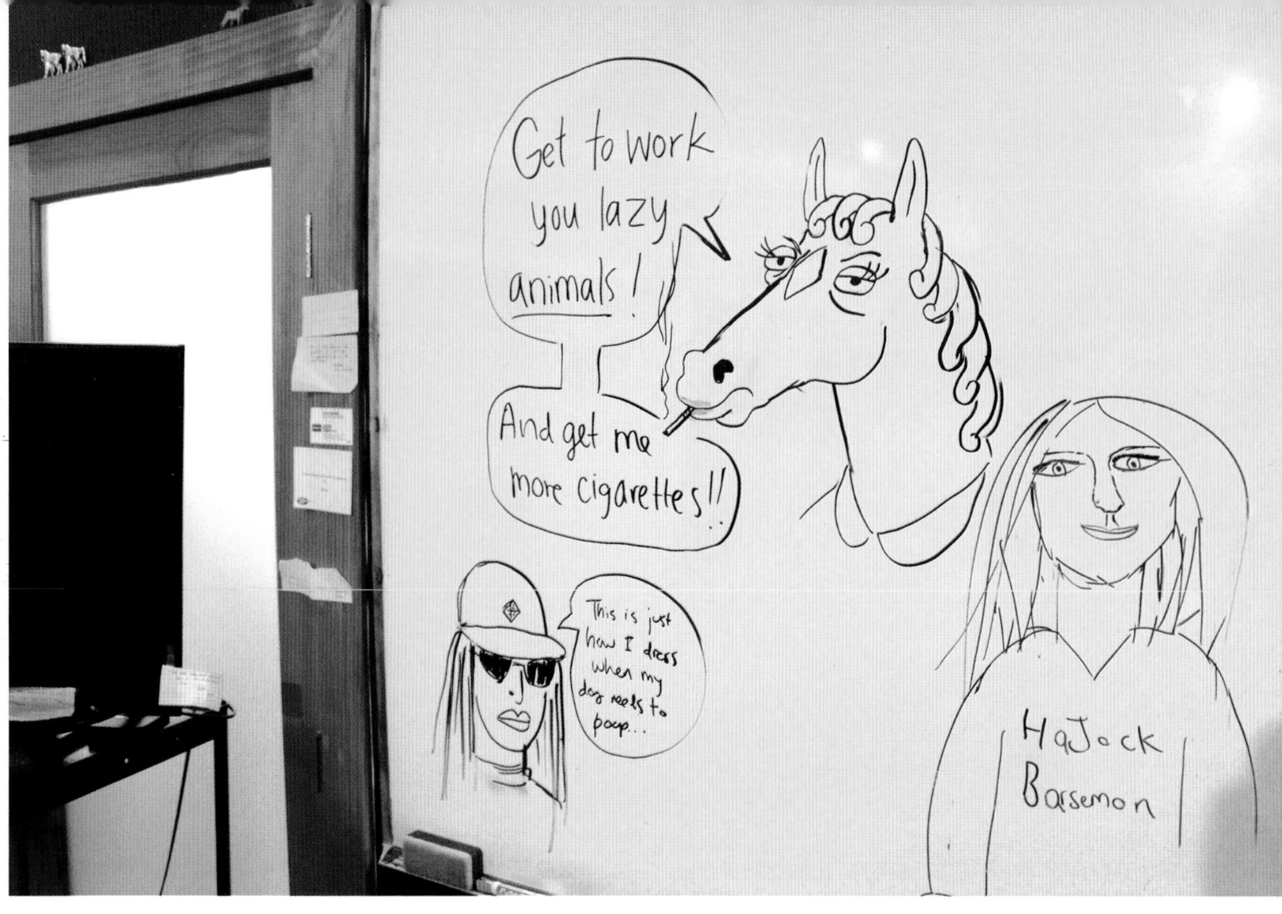

In the Writers' Room

In addition to Raphael, the *BoJack* writers' room includes both well-seasoned, award-winning comedy writers and writers who are brand new to "staffing" on a show. Many television writing rooms function with staffers hierarchically arranged by experience. *BoJack* has found a sort of hybrid structure in which Raphael is the leader, but the process is still highly collaborative.

Raphael: Every show kind of discovers itself. I feel like this show's process figured itself out in that first season. It turned out to be not too different than most other shows.

Kate: Yeah, I think that structurally it works the same, but the tempo and rhythm and beat of the show is very particular in a way that I especially love. I think that it's actually top-down: It comes from Raphael, and it feels like it's just a very egalitarian environment. It's diverse, it's gender neutral—

Raphael: We don't have a lot of hierarchy in the room like other shows do, for good or for ill.

Kate: For good, in my experience! [*Laughs.*]

Raphael: It works for us. I guess the hierarchy is I'm in charge, and other than that . . . [*Laughs.*]

Kate: Yeah, but I think you give us a lot of room to be creative on our own, and then you come in and make it yours. I mean, make it the voice of the show.

Raphael: I've really enjoyed the collaboration of it. I've worked on shows in the past where I've felt like, "Oh, this boss just wants us to be clones of him, and if he could just do everything himself, he would; he's annoyed that other people are contributing, but that's how you make a good show." I know what I bring to the show; I'm not looking necessarily for other people to have my own sensibilities. I like that other people bring their own flavor, and it was a real joy that first season to see how everyone made the show better at each step of the process. It just keeps getting better and better and better and better! What a treat to get to work with so many talented people.

The actual process of writing a script-based animated show (as opposed to a storyboards-based animated show, which is largely written visually during the storyboarding process) is functionally the same as writing most kinds of live-action scripted shows. A writers' room wrestles an episode through many revisions until it is ready for the actors to perform it.

Raphael: The first thing we do every season is talk for a week about the whole season, and we kind of plot out the big stories. We've gotten increasingly laissez-faire with that. The first few seasons it was very much like, "Episode one, episode two, episode three, episode four," all the way through twelve. I think for season four it was kind of like, "All right, this is the broad arc of this story, and this is the broad arc of that story." We want to at least have the big ideas of what we're doing in a season, and then I'll pitch that to Netflix, just to, you know, put on their radar, "Here's what we want to do." If they have any concerns, they can come back to us and say, "Well, maybe not in this direction . . ." Then we say, "We want to!" And they say, "All right, fine . . ." But usually they say, "Sounds great! We can't wait to see it." So then once we do that, we start breaking one episode at a time.

Peter Knight [writer]: In breaking a story, you start with the general idea—you know, "This is the episode where BoJack is going to play Danny Zuko in a *Grease* revival" (that's not happening; I'm just making that up)—but then you go back and identify the beats of the plot and organize them on a whiteboard, and you try to see what fits well with other things. The process is a little bit like building a snowman, where you try to build it up and support it and make sure everything fits into a cohesive structure, and that you're satisfied that it has twists and is interesting. There's no one way; it depends on the particular story.

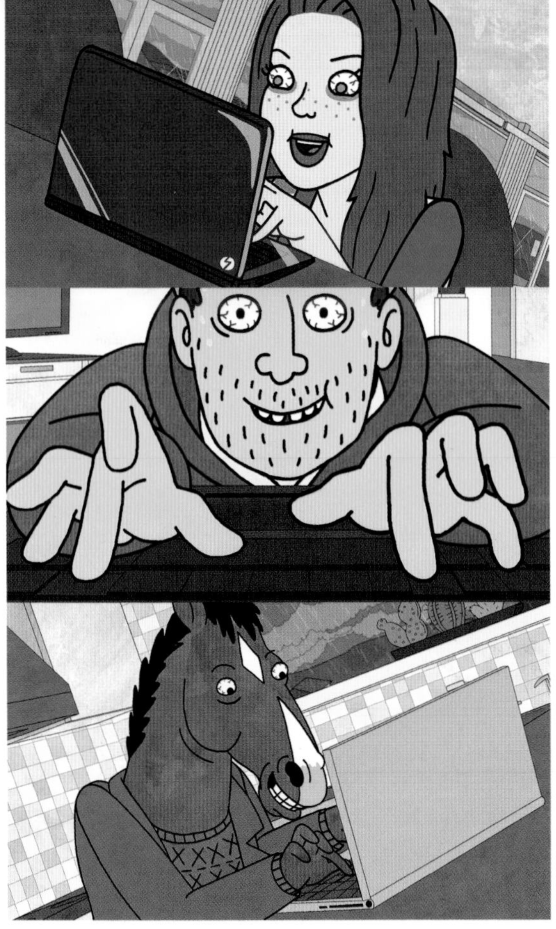

This page: Writers practicing their craft.

Opposite: "Stop the Presses" (S3E07) during the writing process is broken onto sticky notes.

Raphael: So we'll start with episode one. A lot of it is us in a room just kind of talking broadly: "What kinds of things do we want to see in this episode? What are the stories? What's BoJack doing, what's Todd doing, what's Princess Carolyn doing? What's Diane doing, what's Mr. Peanutbutter doing? Is there a special format to this episode? Is there a special way we want to tell this story?"

Mike: Theme—or style.

Raphael: Or what are we trying to communicate with this episode, right? Even when you watch the finished episode, you can't necessarily pinpoint the thing that we said the episode was about at the beginning. For example, this episode is about BoJack feeling like he poisons everything he touches, and that that belief actually poisons things more than him doing it himself. Right? And we say, OK, that's an interesting idea to explore. How can we explore that through this story? And so we try to be very specific about that. It's helpful at the beginning to have an idea of what we want to do.

I really like to empower the writer of the episode to kind of take the lead on running the room when we're talking about his or her episode. And part of that stems from my generosity of spirit, but also it stems from the fact that most of these writers have more experience than I do. Especially when we started, we were getting writers in here that had ten to fifteen years of experience, when I've only worked on a couple shows. So I'm not going to stand in front of the room and be like, "Hey guys, here's how it's going to be." I want to let them craft the story as they know how, better than I do. But I will have my things that I care about. And I'm also running around doing a hundred other things. I'm recording or looking at animatics. So it's helpful to have someone who's in charge when I'm not there. And then I can kind of pop in, and they can talk me through what they're thinking, and I can say, "Oh yeah, I love this. Um . . . this feels a little wonky to me. Can we maybe find a tighter explanation for that? I don't want to do anything involving this. OK, bye, gotta go." So they really, really craft a lot of the episode without me. I just want to give them full credit for that, while also protecting my own ego—I'm important, too. [*Laughs.*]

Lisa: You're very important.

Raphael: I'm very important. When it feels like we're at a good place in the room—when we really understand the episode—I'll ask the writer, "Do you feel like you're ready to go off and outline?" and they'll say, "Yeah," and then they'll go off and write an outline. And we actually do act breaks on this show. Even though it's a Netflix show, so you don't see them as such, there is an act one, an act two, and an act three. I find that's very helpful when breaking the story. It helps you think, "OK, we need something big to happen a third of the way through. And we need something even bigger to happen two-thirds of the way through." I think that's how you prevent the episode from being like one long mush, if you have these kind of goal posts. "OK, by this point in the episode, something needs to happen." That could be seven minutes in, twelve minutes in, fifteen minutes in—doesn't necessarily matter—but we want to know, "OK, we're driving toward something, and then another something that's even bigger."

Mike: It ends up being helpful through the whole project. It's just the way TV shows have been made, for a reason. It's very helpful.

Raphael: So the outline comes back in, and the whole writing staff talks about the outline. I'm usually leading that conversation, and it's kind of like, "Love this; this feels a little wonky still; can we move that?" Or we're all pitching solutions: "Can we tighten this? What are some other ways to do this?" From there, the writer goes off to script; it usually takes about a week to write the first draft. While they're writing the script,

EXT. DECK – MORNING
A GIANT TODD'S HEAD. BJ SLEEPING ON DECK CHAIR. WAKES UP, GOES INSIDE.

INT. HOUSE – CON'T
HOUSE IS OVERRUN WITH CABRA CADABRA. TODD/PB/EMILY THERE. BOXES. EMPLOYEES. "[8] DAYS WITH [NO] WRECKS."

INT. HOUSE – CON'T
BOJACK SEE L.A. TIMES LAND IN DRIVEWAY. "BITCH." DIALS PHONE.

INT. LATIMES – MORNING
CSR ON OTHER END, DEALING WITH BJ. "HOLD PLEASE." GOES TO SUPE. "I CAN'T CALM THIS GUY DOWN." SUPE: "SOUNDS LIKE A JOB FOR THOMAS."

INT. THOMAS'S OFFICE
LUXURIOUS CHAIR. PLAQUES ON WALL, EOM AWARDS PHOTOS. "THOMAS? WE HAVE A SITUATION ON LINE 2." A HAND PRESSES [2]. "THIS IS THOMAS. HOW CAN I HELP"

ACT ONE

EXT. DRIVEWAY – DAY.
THOMAS: "LET'S JUST SOLVE THIS AND GET YOU BACK TO YOUR LIFE. ANYTHING I CAN GET YA?" BJ: "GLASS OF WATER" THOMAS: "NO PROB. A DRONE WILL HAVE THAT TO YOU IN 3..2..1." IT DRIVES IS SHOT OUT OF THE SKY. "YOUR DRONE IS DEAD"

THOMAS: "WHAT HAPPENED"
BJ: "LONG STORY."
THOMAS: "SO YOU'VE BEEN RECEIVING THE LA TIMES FOR A YEAR. WHY DO YOU WANT TO STOP YOUR SUBSCRIPTION NOW?"

EXT. YARD – DAY
BJ: TODD WAS USING THEM... TO MAKE A GIANT PAPER MACHE HEAD... TO PREVENT WHOEVER WAS STEALING OUR FOOD... FROM STEALING OUR FOOD
BJ: CABRA CADABRA TAKES ALL OF HIS TIME NOW.

FB BJ KITCHEN
TODD MAKING A GIANT PAPER MACHE TODD HEAD USING STRIPS OF LA TIMES. (BEHIND HIM A SHADOW STEALS FOOD)

THOMAS: "SMART. I WOULD HAVE NEVER THOUGHT OF THAT."
BJ: "YEAH, WELL IT WAS A LOT BETTER THAN HIS FIRST IDEA."

FB KITCHEN
BJ BEING TRAPPED, HANGING UPSIDE DOWN IN FRONT OF FRIDGE. "GOT YA" BJ: "I'M NOT STEALING FOOD! I OWN THE FOOD!" BJ: "SO WE CAME UP WITH A BETTER IDEA."

BJ: BUT NOW THAT HE'S SO BUSY WITH CABRA CADABRA WORK ON THE BIG SCARY PUPPET HAS STOPPED. AND THE LA TIMES IS STACKING UP.
THOMAS: "WHAT'S CABRA CADABRA?"

FB PB'S HOUSE
DIANE COMES IN SOAKING WET. GOT OUT OF UBER AND WALKED THERE IN RAIN BECAUSE OF CREEPY DRIVER. "THIS WOULD HAVE NEVER HAPPENED WITH A FEMALE DRIVER" PB HAS IDEA!

PB EXPLAINS ENTIRE CABRA CADABRA CONCEPT. "WOMEN ARE GONNA LOVE IT."

FB
TODD MOVING DESK INTO HOUSE. ASKS BJ IF CABRA CADABRA CAN WORK OUT OF HOUSE. BJ: WHY NOT PB'S HOUSE? PB: FILLED WITH SNACKPOT STANDS. DIANE... TODD: HE DOESN'T KNOW WHY HE BOUGHT THEM BUT IT'LL PAY OFF LATER

TODD: YOU REMEMBER EMILY? DISCUSS. WHAT IS IT MAGIC RELATED? NO. EMILY CAME UP WITH IT. CAN'T SAY ANYTHING B/C I DO HAVE FEELINGS FOR HER." YAHOO JOKE
BJ: "OH SURE YOU GUYS CAN USE THE HOUSE.

BJ: "SO I LET THEM USE THE HOUSE 'CAUSE I FELT GUILTY ... THE CAUSE. WEDDING ON FRIDAY"
THOMAS: "WAIT A WEDDING ON FRIDAY?"
BJ: SORRY REHEARSAL DINNER

INT. HOTEL ROOM – NIGHT
BJ EXITS. TODD IS ASLEEP

INT. BAR – NIGHT
BJ SEES EMILY AT BAR. POP TO LAUGHING/DRINKING AT BAR. POP TO HOTEL ROOM (EM'S): BJ & EMILY HAVING SEX

(WHILE SEXING)
BJ: TODD'S GREAT. HE REALLY LIKES YOU. HE'S A FRIEND.
EMILY: I'VE ALWAYS HAD A CRUSH ON HIM.
BJ: I WOULDN'T WANT TO COME BETWEEN YOU TWO SO WE SHOULD KEEP THIS A SECRET!
EMILY: YAHTZEE!
BJ: WHAT?!

THOMAS: BECAUSE YOU WERE GETTING TOO CLOSE TO TODD AND FELT UNCOMFORTABLE AND WANTED TO BLOW THE RELATIONSHIP UP?
BJ: NO NO NO
THOMAS: YOU FEEL LIKE IT'S NEVER ENOUGH? YOU ALWAYS NEED MORE?
BJ: NO NO

T: THEN WHY?
BJ: COULDN'T SLEEP.
T: DO YOU NORMALLY HAVE TROUBLE SLEEPING?
BJ: 'CAUSE OF THE HUSTLE BUSTLE IN MY HOUSE
T: BUT AT THE HOTEL TOO.
BJ: YEAH, I'VE ALWAYS HAD TROUBLE SLEEPING.

FB NIGHT – BEDROOM
BJ GRABS PILLOW & BLANKET AND WALKS TO BOAT

FB INT. LIL BJ'S HOUSE
LIL BJ GRABS PILLOW & BLANKET AND GOES TO PARENTS' BEDROOM. KNOCKS. DAD: "GO AWAY!" DOOR LOCKS. BJ PUTS DOWN HIS PILLOW & BLANKET & SLEEPS AT THE FOOT OF THE DOOR

INT. BOAT – NIGHT
BOJACK FINDS MARGO MARTINDALE LIVING ON BOAT. WE SEE AN RPG. SHE POINTS IT AT HIM. BJ: "YOU'VE BEEN STEALING OUR FOOD?!"

ACT TWO

T: "CHARACTER ACTRESS MARGO MARTINDALE HAS BEEN LIVING ON YOUR BOAT?"
BJ: "DO WE HAVE FULL CLIENT/CUSTOMER SERVICE REP CONFIDENTIALITY?"
T: "OF COURSE."

MARGO HAS BEEN ON THE RUN SINCE YORBA LINDA. CUT TO HER LIVING OFF THE LAND, HIDING. ALSO DID A 3 EP ARC ON "THE GOOD WIFE"
BJ: "YOU WERE ON TV?!"
MARGO: "I DISAPPEAR INTO MY ROLES. IT'S CALLED ACTING"

THOMAS: "I CAN SEE WHY YOU WERE UPSET. NO ONE WANTS A KNOWN FUGITIVE LIVING WITH THEM."
BJ: NOT SO MUCH THAT. I WAS JUST GRUMPY ABOUT THE MARKETING MEETING.

INT. VIGOR – DAY
TWO ADS ARE PRESENTED FOR SECRETARIAT. ONE TRADITIONAL AND THE MIRROR CONCEPT. BJ IS ONLY ONE WHO LIKES THE MIRROR. ANA TAPS HIS SHOULDER (SHUT UP). AFTERWARDS, BJ PULLS ANA ASIDE. "IS THIS ABOUT THE MIRROR ADS OR THE FACT THAT YOU HAND-FELATED ME LAST MONTH"

ANA: "I DON'T WANT TO TALK ABOUT THAT."
BJ: "BUT I DO."
ANA: "I KNOW WHAT YOU WANT. FOLLOW ME TO BATHROOM. AND I'LL LET YOU WATCH"

THOMAS: "YEAH MARKETING MEETINGS ARE WEIRD."
BJ: "NOT AS WEIRD AS HAVING EMILY SKULKING AROUND."
EMILY (O.S.): JIMMY!

INT. LIVING ROOM – DAY
BJ APPROACHES EMILY. MAKE SURE SHE DOESN'T TELL TODD. SHE CAN'T DECIDE. NEEDS TO DO A LIST OF PROS/CONS. BJ: WHAT? NO! PC: C'MON YOU GOTTA TELL HIM. BJ: "WHERE'D YOU COME FROM?!" TAKES HER OUTSIDE. WE'RE NOT TELLING HIM

EMILY: "I DON'T WANT TO START OUR RELATIONSHIP W/ A SECRET." MARGO (O.S.): "NEVER TELL HIM ANYTHING. DON'T BE A RAT!" BJ LEADS HER BACK INTO HOUSE. TODD IS THERE. "TELL ME WHAT?"

THOMAS: "DOES THAT BOTHER YOU, HAVING TO KEEP A SECRET FROM YOUR FRIEND?"
BJ: "NOT ONE BIT. HOW TO KEEP A SECRET IS ONE OF THE 1ST THINGS I LEARNED. MY PARENTS HAD A TON OF THEM."

FB BJ'S CHILDHOOD HOME
BJ'S DAD IS TYPING AWAY CURSING HIMSELF. "YOU SUCK." HE CRUMPLES THE PAPER AND TOSSES IT. LIL BJ UNCRUMPLES IT AND READS IT. HIS DAD'S SHADOW APPEARS. DAD: YOU LIKE SMUT? 'CAUSE THAT'S WHAT

THAT IS. NOT EVEN GOOD SMUT. I USED TO BE A REAL WRITER UNTIL YOU CAME ALONG. NOW I HAVE TO WRITE THIS CRAP JUST TO MAKE A LIVING. THANKS BOJACK.
BJ: "IS THIS WHAT YOU DO TO MOM?"
DAD: "GOD NO"
BJ: 'CAUSE YOU LOVE HER THAT MUCH?

DAD: HA! LOVE? LOVE IS JUST A THING WOMEN USE TO CONTROL YOU. AND SEX IS HOW WE CONTROL THEM. DON'T TELL YOUR MOM I SAID THAT. THAT'S OUR SECRET."

THOMAS: "WHEN'S THE LAST TIME YOU SAW YOUR DAD."
BJ: "IT'S BEEN A WHILE. THANKSGIVING, YEARS AGO. IT'S ACTUALLY PRETTY FUNNY

BJ: THANKSGIVING DAD GOT SUPERDRUNK. IT WAS NO NORMAN ROCKWELL PAINTING. BUT IT WASN'T ROCKBAD EITHER

THOMAS: THAT'S A FUNNY JOKE
BJ: "WAIT." ACTUALLY NOW THAT I THINK ABOUT IT, THE LAST TIME I SAW HIM WAS AT THE NURSING HOME. YEAH. AND I JUST YELLED AT HIM & HE YELLED AT ME. BUT I FINALLY GOT TO GIVE HIM A PIECE OF MIND.

FELT GOOD. CLOSURE, RIGHT?"

FB NURSING HOME – DAY
BJ YELLING AT DAD. DAD YELLING BACK. A NURSE INTERVENES. CHAOS

BJ: ACTUALLY THAT DIDN'T HAPPEN EITHER. NOT EXACTLY.

INT. NURSING HOME – DAY
SAME SCENE AS EARLIER, BUT DAD IS A SMALL, SHELL IN A WHEEL CHAIR. DAD: WANT SOME SOUP? THE ROOM IS EMPTY. BJ: WE NEED TO TALK! DAD: JIMMY? LET'S PLAY A GAME?

BJ: "I COULDN'T YELL AT HIM. IT WASN'T MY DAD. IT WAS A SICK OLD FRAIL PERSON. MY DAD NO LONGER EXISTED. THREE MONTHS LATER HE WAS DEAD."

ACT THREE

T: SORRY ABOUT YOUR DAD. MAYBE THAT'S WHY YOU SLEPT W/ EMILY. FOR SOME SEMBLENCE OF CONTROL. MAYBE YOU COULD GO ABOUT THAT ANOTHER WAY

THE UNIVERSE IS SCARY. TRUTH IS WE DON'T CONTROL ANYTHING. WOULDN'T IT BE NICE TO HAVE SOMETHING YOU CAN COUNT ON. SOMETHING YOU KNOW WILL BE THERE DAY IN/DAY OUT. LIKE

THE LA TIMES?
BJ: YEAH. MAYBE YOU'RE RIGHT.
T: I'LL SIGN YOU UP FOR ANOTHER YEAR. AND BOJACK...

INT. – BJ HOUSE
BJ ON PHONE. MARGO TAPS ON SHOULDER (WHISPERING) "I'M TAKING THE BOAT"
BJ: WHAT?
MARGO: TAKING THE BOAT FOREVER
BJ: I'M ON THE PHONE. SORRY, THOMAS.

BY REACTING TO YOUR FATHER, YOU'RE GIVING HIM CONTROL OVER YOU. STOP REACTING & START ACTING. [END OF CALL]

INT. VIGOR – DAY
BOJACK PUTS HIS FOOT DOWN. DEMANDS THEY GO WITH MIRROR ADS. PC, LT, ANA CONCEDE

INT. LIVING ROOM – DAY
TODD, PB/EM REALIZE MOST CUSTOMERS ARE MALE. B/C OF FEMALE DRIVERS. ARE WE OK? YES. THE REAL IDEA BEHIND THE IDEA WAS WHAT A BIZ TYPICALLY WANTS: TO MAKE MONEY. SO IN THAT REGARD WE ARE NOT DISAPPOINTED"

EXT. LA – DAY
ANA, LENNY, BJ, PC STARE UP AT MIRROR BILLBOARDS. BIRDS, PLANE CRASH INTO IT. IT BURNS SOME PEOPLE. CARS RUN OFF HIGHWAY.
LT: "GOT YOUR WISH!"

Right: Raphael and the writers work on ideas around the table in the writers' room. Photo by Peter Knight.

I usually call Netflix and pitch them the episode. They don't read the outline, but I kind of pitch them through the story, just so they know what to expect. And they'll give their thoughts. They usually say, "Sounds great—can't wait to see it."

Then the first draft of the script comes back in, and again we look at it as a staff. We all give our notes. (I'm kind of giving the most notes.) They go off and spend, like, two or three more days writing a second draft. That second draft comes directly to me, and then I do my pass on it. And that's just to make sure it fits the voice of the show and feels like something that I feel really good about, and I can kind of give it a stamp of "Yes, this is an episode of *BoJack*."

At that point, it goes to Netflix and they read it for the first time. They give their notes on the script; we look at it again as a staff. The writers do another pass, with everyone pitching jokes, everyone throwing stuff in. And then we do a table read, and the actors come in—they're hilarious. We can really hear which jokes are working, which aren't working. "Oh, this scene felt really long." That is a crucial part of the process. It's so important to hear it on its feet, out loud—and you know, our actors are so amazing. And for them, too, it's a great time to hear each other. Because when the actors record, they each record separately, so they find it's really helpful to find that chemistry at the table read, so that they can remember it when it's time to record. After the table read, we do another pass as a room. Sometimes we'll have notes back from Netflix after the table read. And then after that second room pass, it's off to be recorded. That's the writing process, in a very dry, boring nutshell.

Playing with Structure

BoJack's storylines jump back and forth from the 1970s, where we see BoJack's family life (and even earlier to the 1940s in season four), to the 1990s, where we learn about BoJack's rise to sitcom stardom on *Horsin' Around*, to the present day, the late 2010s, where the bulk of the show is centered. Taking advantage of the animation medium, the show is able to time-warp and cut to new locations effortlessly. Raphael's interest in the structure of storytelling itself, practiced during his time with Olde English, results in different narrative devices throughout each season.

Raphael: I am always interested in different ways to tell stories. Obviously the underwater episode came from this idea of, "Can we tell a story without dialogue?" Or "Can we tell a story from the point of view from the 'antagonists'? Can we tell a story from this other character's perspective? Can we tell a story backward? Can we tell a story that just takes place in one room?" That goes back to my sketch comedy background, always looking to find different ways to tell jokes, different ways to tell stories. And we're always looking to steal formats from other shows: "What are some fun gimmick episodes that other shows have done that we can try? What's the *BoJack* version of that—how do we do that? What are some gimmicks that no one has ever tried? Can we do that?" That's something that will always be interesting to me.

Peter: I think it's cool how Raphael will approach [storytelling]. For instance, for that underwater episode, I had breakfast with him in between the seasons and said, "So what's going to happen?" And he said, "Well, we're going to have one episode that's going to be silent. It might be underwater, it might be at a film festival, it might be this or that, but it's going to be silent." So he knows that that's what we're going to do. The gimmicks don't always work—in the first or second season we had one that we tried where every scene was going to be a subsequent day passing you through a month and we tried to break it. You start writing a story that way, and it's not the way you normally break things. But Raphael has certain objectives that he wants to achieve, and doing something as form-bending as a silent episode is going to draw him every time. So then you figure out a way to do it. But even the other ones, like

This page: A photo of the white board in the writers' room illustrating the results of breaking an episode. In this case, "Hooray! Todd Episode!" (S4E03).

COLD OPEN

INT. HOLLYWOO BOWL

FULL ORCHESTRA, EVERYONE WHISPERING, WAITING FOR A PLAYER. TODD RUSHES IN AT LAST MINUTE, PLAYS A, RUSHES OUT.

POST CONCERT BAR

MUSICIANS AFTERWARDS, HANGING OUT LIKE ROCK STARS, TALKING ABOUT ALL THE THINGS THE GREAT + MYSTERIOUS TODD HAS DONE FOR THEM. ONE GUY FEELS BAD

ACT ONE

MR PB'S HOUSE

TODD WAKES UP + DOES MORNING ROUTINE AS KATRINA IS TELLING PB ABOUT FRACKING PRESS CONF. SHE DOESN'T KNOW HIS OPINION YET, BUT RESEARCH WILL COME TODAY BEFORE PRESS CONFERENCE
DIANE IS AGAINST IT, HAS TO GO TO GIRL CRUSH.
TODD HAS TO GET PB'S GLASSES FROM VIM FOR PRESS CONFERENCE. TODD HEADS OUT, RUNS INTO DELIVERY GUY, PB YELLS FOR TODD TO SIGN FOR PACKAGE. TODD WON'T DO IT. HEADS OUT...

STREETS

TODD SKATEBOARDS, HOLDING ON TO BACK OF CARS
TODD NOTICES A SLOW-MOVING VEHICLE FOLLOWING HIM W/ CREEPY GUY. TODD LOSES HIM AND ARRIVES AT...
VIM - PC EXCITED TO SEE TODD, HE CAN SOLVE A PROBLEM
PC TELLS TODD ABOUT COURTNEY, PRETENTIOUS, OUT-OF-TOUCH MOVIE STAR WHO LAST DATED PRINCE. FOR PR, SHE NEEDS TO DATE A REGULAR GUY, + SINCE TODD'S NOT BUSY. TODD TELLS PC HE'S ASEXUAL? PC SAYS SHE'S NOT PROSTITUTING HIM. TODD AGREES TO DATE
? THEY SEE CREEPY GUY SCOPING OUT VIM. TODD GOES TO BRING GLASSES TO PB

PB'S HOUSE

TODD SHOWS UP W/ GLASSES, KATRINA'S MAD. DIDN'T GET FRACKING RESEARCH B/C TODD DIDN'T SIGN. IN FUTURE, ALWAYS SIGN FOR PB! KATRINA TELLS PB NOT TO HAVE AN OPINION. PB TAKES QUESTIONS + MANAGES TO EVADE + PLEASE BOTH SIDES. SOMEONE ASKS TODD IF PB WILL SIGN PETITION, TODD SIGNS FOR PB. TODD SEES CREEPY GUY + FINALLY CONFRONTS HIM. HE'S A P.I. W/ A CLIENT WHO WANTS TO TALK TO HIM.

DINER

HH TELLS TODD SHE'S TRYING TO FIND BJ. SHE'S ADOPTED, 8 GRANDMAS, BUT EVERYONE SAYS SHE LOOKS LIKE BJ, THINKS HE COULD BE HER FATHER. TODD'S NOT SURE IT'S A GOOD IDEA TO GET INVOLVED W/ BOJACK, ANYWAY, HE'S GONE. HH READ BOOK, DOESN'T WANT RELATIONSHIP W/ BOJACK. SHE JUST WANTS TO KNOW. COULD TODD GET DNA?
TODD GUESSES THEY COULD TRY HIS HOUSE.
RICH COW WAITRESS ANNOYED BY TODD'S 20% TIP

BOJACK'S HOUSE

TODD + HH ARE LOOKING ALL OVER FOR DNA

FIND BOJACK ASLEEP. HE'S BACK!

ACT TWO

BOJACK'S HOUSE

TODD WANTS TO GO BUT HH WANTS TO GET BJ DNA, HE DOES SEEM DRUNK, TRY TO PULL HAIR.
BOJACK WAKES UP, CONFUSED. HH SAYS SHE'S THE MAID.
TODD CAN'T BELIEVE BJ'S BACK BUT THEY AWKWARDLY DON'T TALK ABOUT IT. BJ ONLY TOLD STEVEN WEBER.
HH SAYS SHE'LL CLEAN. INDICATES TODD SHOULD DELIVER DNA

DNA LAB

TODD BRINGS HAIR TO SEE [illegible] MATCHES HH, BUT FORGOT TO GET SAMPLE FROM HH. [illegible] GOING TO GO BACK, GETS CALL FROM PC. HE'S LATE TO DATE

SANDRO'S PLACE

COURTNEY'S OUT OF TOUCH, AWKWARD, TODD REVEALS DOESN'T DATE MUCH-ASEXUAL. T RELAYES PHOEBE TO BE W/ A GUY NOT ATTRACTED TO HER.
COURTNEY'S AMUSED BY HIS SIMPLE WAYS. TODD + PHOEBE ARE SURPRISED AT HOW WELL THIS DATE WAS.
TODD LEAVES TO GO TO BOJACK'S. PC SHOWS UP W/ PHOTOGS, ANNOYED TODD'S GONE

BOJACK'S HOUSE

TODD SNEAKILY TALKS TO HH + GETS HAIR. HH SAYS THIS IS GREAT, SHE'S GETTING TO KNOW REAL BOJACK. BJ SEES TODD + SAYS HE'S GOING TO FIRE LAZY MAID IF PLACE ISN'T CLEAN WHEN HE WAKES UP FROM NAP. TODD TELLS HH TO CLEAN BUT HH'S NOT INTERESTED (SHE'S A LOT LIKE BOJACK). TODD STARTS TO CLEAN
- KATRINA CALLS TODD, SHE'S WATCHING MSNBSEA - PB SUPPORTS FRACKING! APPARENTLY HE SIGNED A PETITION + THEY BLAME TODD.
PB GETS ON PHONE + SAYS DIANE WON'T LIKE THIS, CAN TODD KEEP HER AWAY FROM NEWS? TODD GOES TO...

GIRLCRUSH

DIANE WISHES SHE HAD CELEB SCOOP
TODD SHOWS UP + DOES FUNNY DANCE, ETC TO KEEP DIANE FROM LOOKING AT INTERNET. - PC CALLS TODD + SAYS THEY STILL NEED A PHOTO, SO HE HAS TO GO TO FASHION SHOW RIGHT NOW. TODD, DESPERATE, TELLS DIANE HE HAS SCOOP: GO TEST DNA + DON'T LISTEN TO NEWS. CLAIMS IT'S STEVEN WEBER'S. TODD RUSHES OFF TO SHOW...

FASHION SHOW

BIRD MODEL BEAK COVERS "TODD" + TODD SEES "EL ENTRANCE". TODD: GRACIAS! ENTERS. TODD IS RUSHED ON TO CATWALK. HE FEELS PRESSURE TO STRUT HIS STUFF, + IS A SENSATION. TODD SEES COURTNEY + GOES TO HER. PRESS SNAPS PHOTOS. TODD LOOKS AT WATCH + RUNS TO...

HOLLYWOO BOWL

TODD RUNS IN, SEEMS TOO LATE BUT PHONE MAKES CHIME SOUND.
DIANE GOT RESULTS: IT'S A MATCH

APPELS TO JORDANGES
11 | 1

ACT THREE

INT. BOJACK'S HOUSE

TODD GETS BACK. BOJACK: DID YOU KNOW PB'S RUNNING FOR GOVERNOR? ON TV: MSNBSEA - PANEL. ANTI-FRACKERS ATTACK PB - IF IT'S SO SAFE, WHY DON'T YOU FRACK UNDER YOUR HOUSE. PB: OK.
TODD SAYS DIANE WON'T LIKE THAT. HAVE YOU TALKED TO DIANE
TODD: WHERE'S MAID? BJ SAYS HE RECOMMENDED HER TO STEVEN WEBER
BJ: NO, I CAME BACK TO FIX THINGS BUT I DON'T KNOW HOW. I DISAPPOINT EVERYONE. BUILD HOUSES + KNOCK THEM DOWN. I CAN'T LET ANYONE ELSE DOWN. WHICH IS WHY I CAN'T BE FRIENDS W/ WEBER. WILL YOU GO TELL HIM, TODD?

STEVEN WEBER'S HOUSE

HH ISN'T CLEANING AT ALL. CAN TODD HELP CLEAN SO WEBER'S NOT MAD?
TODD SAYS RESULTS CAME IN. IT'S NOT A MATCH. HH DISAPPOINTED.
T: IT'S FOR THE BEST. BJ'S BAD FOR EVERYONE.
DIANE AT DOOR, LOOKING FOR STEVEN WEBER
TODD PRETENDS TO BE WEBER. DIANE REVEALS DNA WAS A MATCH
(WE SEE HH TAKE IN NEWS ABOUT DNA MATCH + PUT 2+2 TOGETHER)
DIANE GETS SUSPICIOUS. TO GET DIANE AWAY, TODD SAYS PB IS FRACKING. DIANE LEAVES ANGRY. TODD SEES HOLLYHOCK IS GONE.
TODD'S PHONE RINGS. PC SAYS TODD'S NOW A FAMOUS MODEL, SO YOU CAN'T DATE COURTNEY. HAVE TO PUBLICLY BREAK UP, SO SHE'LL GET SYMPATHY

SANDRO'S PLACE

PRESS + PC ARE THERE. TODD TRIES TO BREAK UP W/ COURTNEY. SHE FREAKS OUT. HE APOLOGIZES - THOUGHT SHE KNEW. SHE SAYS SHE'S ACTING. BUT SHE KEEPS ACTING SO HYSTERICAL, TODD CAN'T TAKE IT + SAYS HE LOVES HER + WANTS TO MARRY HER. PC FRUSTRATED. TODD HAS TO RUSH OFF TO DEAL W/ PERSONAL ISSUE...

BOJACK'S HOUSE

TODD ASKS BJ WHERE HH IS. SHE HASN'T BEEN BACK SINCE HE SENT HER TO WEBER'S HOUSE. TODD STARTS TO SPIN BUT BJ STOPS HIM. BJ KNOWS SHE'S HIS DAUGHTER; SHE LOOKED + ACTED JUST LIKE HIM. BJ DIDN'T KNOW HOW TO DEAL W/ THAT, TRIED TO PUSH HER AWAY.
TODD IS RELIEVED, HE'S TRYING TO SPIN SO MANY LIES
BJ SAYS HE SHOULD STOP TRYING TO PLEASE EVERYONE.
TODD + BJ ARE GLAD THEY'RE BEING HONEST W/ EACH OTHER + TALKING
BJ WANTS HIM TO STAY, BUT TODD'S NOT READY

PB'S HOUSE

TODD WALKS IN PB + DIANE FIGHTING. LOUD FRACKING STARTING. TODD SLEEPS PEACEFULLY

HOLLYWOO BOWL

TODD DOESN'T SHOW AT CHIME TIME. MUSICIAN IS HAPPY THE MYSTERY MAN ISN'T PLEASING EVERYONE

This page, left to right: Joanna Calo writing on the board, Alison Tafel, Elijah Aron, and Joanna Calo with spoon-eyes. Photos by Peter Knight.

"After the Party" [S2E04], just the way that he jumps around in the timeline in the storytelling so confidently—it makes me tired thinking about it. He goes there. He's eager to explore.

Elijah: Most half-hour comedies are very specifically structured in three acts, and there are rules to where things escalate and where characters change and where they learn lessons, which we all know very well. But even in those episodes that don't seem experimental, we've been happy to throw out some of the rules, because it's a serialized show that can end anywhere, get depressing when things would normally get funny, go to strange places . . . It's just a fun challenge to us as writers to try to help Raphael make an episode the most compelling that it can be by throwing out as many rules as possible.

Raphael: A big running motif of the show is subverting the tropes of traditional television. At this point in our run, the challenge now is: "How do we continue to surprise and subvert when the audience kind of expects certain things from us?" Now that we've established our tone, to a certain extent, we have to find new ways to keep things fresh, and not just be like, "We're not like those other shows." We have to find a new way that we're not like ourselves. What other kinds of stories can we tell? How can we continue to keep people guessing?

Voice Acting

When the script is complete, the voice cast gathers for the table read. This is usually a spirited, energetic meeting, and an exciting one for the writers and artists, who are hearing and seeing their newest episode's lines performed by the cast for the first time.

Paul: We try to get everybody there as much as possible, but you know, careers are chaotic and everyone's got different gigs. A lot of times people are there by phone; it's very rare that somebody is just not there at all, in any way. I've called in from vacation, TV sets, and stuff like that. Aaron Paul, during the second season, I think he was calling in from Italy, and from all over the world—he was working on a movie. So it's rare that every single person on the cast is there at the same time, but even so it's a really wonderful experience. It's the only chance we get to act opposite each other. So we really get to play those moments, those real, sad, or angry moments with each other at those table reads. We always take the same seats and I'm always seated across from Alison Brie, and to be able to do those emotional scenes from their marriage in person like that—you know, even though she's playing a human and I'm playing an anthropomorphic dog—to get to play that relationship, even just that one time face-to-face, is always very exciting to me.

Alison: We get to experience the scenes together, playing off of each other and getting a sense of what the other actors would be doing. So when it comes time to record alone in a booth later, we can recall how it felt to do the scenes together. I think that has been really important for establishing a group rapport. Also I got to meet people I really admire like Angela Bassett, Philip Baker Hall, and Lisa Kudrow, who I probably wouldn't have crossed paths with otherwise.

Linda Lamontagne [casting director]: Even at table reads, everyone is so giving. It's one thousand percent. Nobody is walking through it, and everybody is really connecting. You even see Will turn his head and look to the corner toward a writer who is reading a line [as a stand-in] for a guest actor, and make eye contact and connect. That's so rare. [*Laughs.*] I've been to so many other table reads where it's like everyone's head is just buried in the script and you don't see that reaching out and connecting. It's just great energy, phenomenal.

Amy: When we do the read-through, I'm here in New York on my couch, and I can hear everyone laughing really hard, on a delay, in LA. I'm just so jealous that I'm not there.

Typically, when it comes time to record the dialogue—after final tweaks to the script have been made—each actor comes

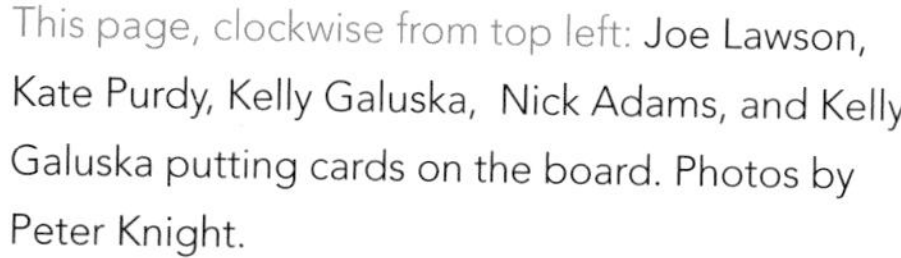

This page, clockwise from top left: Joe Lawson, Kate Purdy, Kelly Galuska, Nick Adams, and Kelly Galuska putting cards on the board. Photos by Peter Knight.

Left: The voice cast sits down for a table read, which is an important opportunity for the entire crew to get their first sense of how the episode flows and works. A table read scene from "The BoJack Horseman Show" (S3E02).

in individually to record all of their lines, as his or her schedule permits. Amy Sedaris records in a sound studio in New York, with Raphael on the phone from LA.

Amy: When I record, Raphael and I will read the scenes together, and I do the Princess Carolyn voice. And then I mispronounce everything, and he has to correct me on everything. And then they have me do these ridiculous tongue twisters. It's so funny because they keep giving them to me.

For one example, see "Hooray! Todd Episode!" (S4E03):

PRINCESS CAROLYN
You are just the guy I need. You know the actress Courtney Portnoy?

TODD
I think so. She portrayed the formerly portly consort in *The Seaport Resort*?

PRINCESS CAROLYN
Courtly roles like the formerly portly consort are Courtney Portnoy's forte. But she's got a new action movie that's supposed to change her image: *Ms. Taken*. You know Mr. Taken, from the *Taken* movies? This is his niece!

TODD
Nice!

PRINCESS CAROLYN
This was supposed to be Courtney's crossover coronation, but that's sort of been thwarted unfortunately, 'cause Courtney's purportedly falling short of shoring up four-quadrant support.

TODD
Makes perfect sense so far.

Raphael: Very rarely do we record people together. We have done it. The paparazzi birds in the first season, those are my good friends Wave [Segal] and Adam [Conover]. We thought it would be fun to bring them in together, and they could riff off each other. The one episode where BoJack and Princess Carolyn have the whole episode in the restaurant, which is, like, one long conversation, Amy called in from New York, and Will and Amy did that together, like it was a radio play, because we wanted to feel that chemistry, and we thought that would be the best way to do it. But usually, everyone records separately.

Amy: Will and I are big fans of each other and [before this show] had always wanted to work together. I love Will's energy; I think we both have fast-paced "up up up" energy, and we play really well off of each other. And who's funnier than Will Arnett?

Unlike the voice recording outtakes sometimes seen in behind-the-scenes clips for other shows and films, in which the actors seem to play fast and loose with the material, the *BoJack* actors stick close to the script.

Raphael: We'll get the take, and then if I have an idea that I can't quite put my finger on, I'll ask the actor, "Oh, do you think there is another way to say this?" And they'll work for a few seconds, and they'll throw stuff out. But you know, the episodes are so tightly scripted, there's not a lot of room for improvisation. Sometimes we'll have alts [alternative takes], and it's good to have those options. Like, "Oh, this joke didn't work, but I think we have an alt for that in the booth." And some actors enjoy thinking on their feet, and others prefer to stick to the script. But again, we're doing it separately. It's not like you can have people riffing in a whole new direction.

Each actor intentionally developed speaking mannerisms for their own character to use during their performances.

This page: Two of Lisa's sketchbook drawings of Paul F. Tompkins, voice of Mr. Peanutbutter, among other doodles.

Amy: When BoJack got picked up, I kind of had the character beforehand. I'd been working on her. I did her in the movie *Chef*, I did her as a character called Pam on *Broad City*, and she's a combination of a lady who runs a post office here with a little pinch of Barbara Streisand in there. And on my own show, *At Home with Amy Sedaris*, the International Wine Lady is a little bit of that character, too.

I like how practical she is. Like the lady at the post office will say things like, "Hey, you pay peanuts, you get monkeys!" And she'll make these statements like, "See you around like a doughnut," or "She thinks two and two is twenty-two!" So that's how I developed Princess Carolyn in my own head, and then merged it with the writing.

Raphael: Linda put together the most incredible cast, and it's inspired us to take creative risks and give all our actors new challenges. Will is amazing at finding the comedy in any line, even if it wasn't written as a joke, but as we also discovered what a great dramatic actor he is, it emboldened us to push the character in new directions. And you could say the same thing about all of our actors: Aaron, Amy, Alison, and Paul all elevate whatever material we give them.

The starring voices on the show even have a strangely similar experience as viewers, experiencing surprises of the series one episode at a time.

Paul: When I read the script of the first episode I thought, "You know, this is a funny show," and I thought it was going to be one of your standard cartoons for grown-ups. And I, as Mr. Peanutbutter, wasn't a regular at that time—I was just a guest star—and I thought, "Yeah, this will be fun; I like the other people involved." But as it went on, I discovered the show in the same way that a viewer would discover it—I didn't know that it was going to take the emotional turns that it took; I had no idea. The arc of the show was never explained to me before I agreed to do it. So I was discovering it week by week as we read the scripts together at the table reads. I experienced this retroactive joy that I was involved in this unique and wonderful project.

When the recording is complete, the voice tracks are edited into the complete radio play version of the episode, and it's ready to be sent down the line to the next team of artists for design and storyboarding, where the visual aspects of the episode begin to take form.

Script Draft: "Prickly-Muffin"

MEHAR

BoJACK HORSEMAN

"Sexy Sex, Sexy Boobs"

BJH #103

Written by

Raphael Bob-Waksberg

SEREALIZATION IDEA

BIGGER IDEA:

BJ & SL take video of themselves having sex w/ SL's phone. It's SL's idea. After they fight & she leaves, BJ says "Shit. I probably shouldn't have let her tape us having sex." Teasing the idea that some day we'll have a sex video scandal.

PRE-TABLE DRAFT
December 12, 2013

BOJACK HORSEMAN "SEXY SEX, SEXY BOOBS"

COLD OPEN

EXT. "HORSIN' AROUND" HOUSE - MORNING

BOJACK (PRELAP)
Whoooo wants chocolate chip pancakes?

INT. "HORSIN' AROUND" KITCHEN - CONTINUOUS

OLIVIA, teenager, and ETHAN, preteen, sit at the table. BOJACK is wearing an apron and chef's hat.

ETHAN
I do! I do!

OLIVIA
Ethan -- didn't you already eat your pancakes?

ETHAN
As Oliver North would say: I don't recall.

An ERUPTION OF STUDIO AUDIENCE LAUGHTER, which leads to CHEERS AND APPLAUSE. The actors all wait a beat for the applause to subside, then:

BOJACK
Hey. Where's Sabrina?

SABRINA (O.S.)
Not hiding under the table, that's for sure!

Audience AWWWWWWs. BoJack gets down under the table where SABRINA, six, is clutching her knees, still in her pajamas.

BOJACK
Why aren't you dressed for school, prickly-muffin?

SABRINA
I'm scared. Olivia told me sometimes at school they have pop quizzes. ~~I don't want to pop~~! (off last look) And I don't wanna pop!

LAUGHTER/AWWWW.

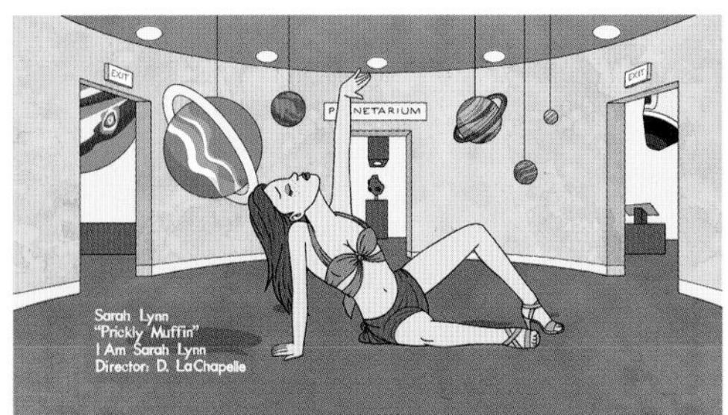

This spread: One of Raphael's prized possessions is an early draft of "Prickly-Muffin" (S1E03), originally titled "Sexy Sex, Sexy Boobs." Each page is followed by additional copies of each page where the writing staff added their own notes to punch up ideas and jokes (circled here in red to indicate where the suggestions were added). This is one way that the writers work together to fine tune and cram in more humor during the process. These pages contain notes from Peter A. Knight, Scott Marder, Joe Lawson, Caroline Williams, and Mehar Sethi.

2.

SABRINA (CONT'D)
(this is her catchphrase)
That's too much, man!

APPLAUSE/CHEERS.

BOJACK
Ha ha, Sabrina. You have nothing to be afraid of. Would I let anything like that happen to you?

SABRINA
No...

← THEY HUG

BOJACK
Sabrina, you stick with me and I promise you everything's gonna be just fine.

SUPER OVER BLACK: "TWELVE YEARS LATER"

INT. E! STUDIO - DAY

A RYAN SEACREST TYPE talks to camera. (A chyron on the bottom of the screen says: "A Ryan Seacrest Type, E! News". In the corner of the screen, a picture of young Sabrina.

A RYAN SEACREST TYPE
Child star Sarah Lynn, who played Sabrina on the popular sitcom "Horsin' Around," has been murdered.
(beat.)
Is the name of Sarah Lynn's debut dance-pop album, in stores now.

IMAGE: AN ALBUM COVER WITH THE TITLE "CHILD STAR SARAH LYNN WHO PLAYED SABRINA ON THE POPULAR SITCOM HORSIN' AROUND HAS BEEN MURDERED"

A RYAN SEACREST TYPE (CONT'D)
The album has already been generating buzz off the suggestive video for the lead single "Sexy Sex, Sexy Boobs."

CUT TO:

INT. MUSIC VIDEO SET

A TEENAGE SARAH LYNN writhes suggestively in a video that recalls Xtina's Dirrty phase.

2.

SABRINA (CONT'D)
I mean (this is her catchphrase)
That's too much, man!

→ felt a little disconnected. Does BJ offer a large plate of pancakes.

APPLAUSE/CHEERS.

BOJACK
Nobody's popping under my watch
~~Ha ha, Sabrina. You have nothing~~ to ~~be afraid of~~. Would I let anything like that happen to you?

SABRINA
No...

A RYAN SEACREST TYPE
FORMER Child star Sarah Lynn, who played Sabrina on the popular sitcom "Horsin' Around," has been murdered.
(beat.)
Is the name of Sarah Lynn's debut dance-pop album, in stores now.

IMAGE: AN ALBUM COVER WITH THE TITLE "CHILD STAR SARAH LYNN WHO PLAYED SABRINA ON THE POPULAR SITCOM HORSIN' AROUND HAS BEEN MURDERED"

Script Draft: "Prickly-Muffin"

3.

TITLE: "SEXY SEX, SEXY BOOBS, DIR. DAVID LACHAPPELLE"

SARAH LYNN
SEXY SEX. SEXY BOOBS. EVERYBODY WANTS TO DO SEX TO MY SEXY BOOBS.

A RYAN SEACREST TYPE (V.O.)
We sat down with the young starlet to discuss the genesis of her new album, and the album's title.

INT. E! STUDIO - DAY

A Ryan Seacrest type sits across from a sexed up Sarah Lynn.

SARAH LYNN
People need to know that I'm not that little girl anymore. I'm a grown-up sophisticated woman now and I have sex and do sexy things. People like sex and since I'm sexy right now they like me. It's a recipe for long-term success. Or should I say succ-sex?

~~A RYAN SEACREST TYPE~~
~~Are you at all worried that when the novelty wears off, audiences will grow bored and abandon you for the next sexy thing?~~

~~SARAH LYNN~~
~~Are you kidding? I'm Sarah [BEEP]ing Lynn. I'm going to be sexy forever!~~

SUPER OVER BLACK: "TWELVE YEARS LATER"

INT. E! STUDIO - DAY

A RYAN SEACREST TYPE
Popstar and child actress Sarah Lynn has committed suicide, sadly making the title of her debut album "Child Star Sarah Lynn Who Played Sabrina On The Popular Sitcom 'Horsin' Around' Has Been Murdered" eerily and tragically prescient.
(beat.)
Is the title of Sarah Lynn's new album --

A RYAN SEACREST TYPE
Are you at all worried that when the novelty wears off, audiences will grow bored and abandon you for the next sexy thing?

SARAH LYNN
~~Are you kidding?~~ When in the history of Hollywood has that happened? I'm Sarah [BEEP]ing Lynn. I'm going to be sexy forever!

SARAH LYNN
People need to know that I'm not that little girl anymore. I'm a ~~grown-up sophisticated~~ woman ~~now~~ ~~and~~ WHICH MEANS I have sex and do sexy things. People like sex and since I'm sexy ~~right now~~ they like me. [It's a recipe for long-term success. Or should I say succ-sex?]

I HAVE BOOBS NOW. BOOBS AND JUNK. AND IF PEOPLE DON'T SEE IT THEY'LL STILL THINK I'M A LITTLE GIRL.

I'M AN ARTIST. SEX IS JUST MY CANVAS.

A RYAN SEACREST TYPE
Are you at all worried that when the novelty wears off, audiences will grow bored and abandon you for the next sexy thing?

SARAH LYNN
Are you kidding? I'm Sarah [BEEP]ing Lynn. ~~I'm going to be sexy forever!~~

I WILL ALWAYS BE SEXY. I'M THE SEXY THING, THE NEXT SEXY THING, AND THE SEXY THING AFTER THAT, AND AFTER THAT, AND THE NEXT 100 SEXY THINGS AFTER THAT, THEN INFINITY THE CAR.

SUPER OVER BLACK: "TWELVE YEARS LATER"

INT. E! STUDIO - DAY

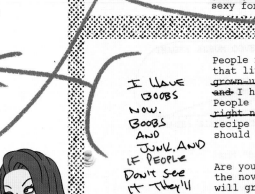

A RYAN SEACREST TYPE
Popstar and child actress Sarah Lynn has committed suicide, sadly making the title of her debut album "Child Star Sarah Lynn Who Played Sabrina On The Popular Sitcom 'Horsin' Around' Has Been Murdered" eerily and tragically prescient.
(beat.)
Is the title of Sarah Lynn's new album --

This spread: Draft of "Prickly-Muffin" (S1E03) continued.

4.

IMAGE: ALBUM COVER: "POPSTAR AND CHILD ACTRESS SARAH LYNN HAS COMMITTED SUICIDE SADLY MAKING THE TITLE OF HER DEBUT ALBUM 'CHILD STAR SARAH LYNN WHO PLAYED SABRINA ON THE POPULAR SITCOM 'HORSIN' AROUND' HAS BEEN MURDERED' EERILY AND TRAGICALLY PRESCIENT"

A RYAN SEACREST TYPE (CONT'D)
Sales of which have been sluggish,
far underperforming her previous
albums--

IMAGE: ALBUM COVER

A RYAN SEACREST TYPE (CONT'D)
"Sarah Lynn Was Caught Shoplifting"

~~IMAGE: ALBUM COVER~~

~~A RYAN SEACREST TYPE (CONT'D)~~
~~"Sarah Lynn Has A Penchant For~~
~~Misleadingly Declarative Album~~
~~Titles"~~

IMAGE: ALBUM COVER

A RYAN SEACREST TYPE (CONT'D)
And "Sarah Lynn's Disappointing
Follow-Up To Her Breakout Debut
Album Is Not Selling Very Well,"
her sophomore album from 2004,
which sold very well. The
performer's new single, however,
has not been finding traction on
the charts.

CUT TO:

INT. MUSIC VIDEO SET

Sarah Lynn writhes suggestively in a video that recalls present-day Miley Cyrus.

TITLE: "HOTT BUTT, DIR. TERRY RICHARDSON"

SARAH LYNN
I GOT A HOTT BUTT. I TWERK A LOT,
WHAT. ALL THE BOYS AND ALL THE
GIRLS WANT TO TOUCH MY HOTT BUTT.

A RYAN SEACREST TYPE (CONT'D)
Sales of which have been sluggish,
~~far underperforming her previous~~
~~albums--~~

COULD END HERE IF Feels TOO LONG.

IMAGE: ALBUM COVER

A RYAN SEACREST TYPE (CONT'D)
"Sarah Lynn Was Caught Shoplifting"

"SARAH LYNN DRESSES TOO SEXY FOR A 12 YEAR-OLD."

IMAGE: ALBUM COVER

A RYAN SEACREST TYPE (CONT'D)
"Sarah Lynn Has A Penchant For
Misleadingly Declarative Album
Titles"

IMAGE: ALBUM COVER

A RYAN SEACREST TYPE (CONT'D)
And "Sarah Lynn's Disappointing
Follow-Up To Her Breakout Debut
Album Is Not Selling Very Well,"
her sophomore album from 2004,
which sold very well. The
performer's new single, however,
has not been finding traction on
the charts.

"SARAH LYNN'S STORY WILL END TRAGICALLY & LA.

CUT TO: THE GIRL WHO PLAYED KIMBERLY ON "DIFFERENT STROKES"

INT. MUSIC VIDEO SET

Sarah Lynn writhes suggestively in a video that recalls present-day Miley Cyrus.

A RYAN SEACREST TYPE (CONT'D)
And "Sarah Lynn's Disappointing
Follow-Up To Her Breakout Debut
Album Is Not Selling Very Well,"
her sophomore album from 2004,
which sold very well. The
performer's new single, however,
has not been finding traction on
the charts.

CUT TO:

INT. MUSIC VIDEO SET

Sarah Lynn writhes suggestively in a video that recalls present-day Miley Cyrus.

TITLE: "HOTT BUTT, DIR. TERRY RICHARDSON"

SARAH LYNN
I GOT A HOTT BUTT. I TWERK A LOT,
WHAT. ALL THE BOYS AND ALL THE
GIRLS WANT TO TOUCH MY HOTT BUTT.

"A story all too familiar"

per netflix note:
Seacrest guy: Perhaps it's time for Sarah Lynn to wander back into... then pick up the snarky speech on 6

feigning sympathy in that crocodile tears

Script Draft: "Prickly-Muffin"

5.

A RYAN SEACREST TYPE (V.O.)
We've assembled a panel of bloggers and comedians with zero combined expertise on the matter to speculate about Sarah Lynn's recent fall from grace and just generally be dicks.

We've assembled a team of bloggers and comedians who were milling around after improv practice.

INT. E! STUDIO - DAY

A Ryan Seacrest Type is now sitting at a desk surrounded by THREE SNARKY GEN-Y-ERS (two animals and a human).

A RYAN SEACREST TYPE
Panel, what happened?

HIPSTER GOAT
What happened is Sarah Lynn sucks now. A. She's not sexy anymore. B. She's old. C. I hate her.

D. Check please.
E. As if!

SNARKY HUMAN
I have to agree. No one is a bigger supporter of Sarah Lynn than I am. ~~I love her unconditionally. But her new album is boring and she makes me puke.~~

But she's turned into a talentless shit and I have never supported her.

LIONESS BLOGGER
You know, I keep waiting for her to surprise me. Where's the new "Sexy Sex, Sexy Boobs"?

~~SNARKY HUMAN~~
~~Where's the new "My Clitoris Is Ginormous"?~~

~~HIPSTER GOAT~~
~~Oh I loved "My Clitoris Is Ginormous."~~

~~LIONESS BLOGGER~~
~~"My Clitoris is Ginormous" is a modern rock masterpiece beyond reproach, that's not up for debate.~~ But we have to face facts -- that Sarah Lynn doesn't exist anymore.

A RYAN SEACREST TYPE
So where does the singer go from here?

5.

A RYAN SEACREST TYPE (V.O.)
We've assembled a panel of bloggers and comedians with zero combined expertise on the matter to speculate about Sarah Lynn's recent fall from grace and just generally be dicks.

I turn it over to you, Andy Dick.

INT. E! STUDIO - DAY

A Ryan Seacrest Type is now sitting at a desk surrounded by THREE SNARKY GEN-Y-ERS (two animals and a human).

A RYAN SEACREST TYPE
Panel, what happened?

HIPSTER GOAT
What happened is Sarah Lynn sucks now. A. She's not sexy anymore. B. She's old. C. I hate her.

~~I don't mean to sound harsh but...~~

I can't tell if it's that her hooks haven't evolved with the rest of the post-pop slash dubstep slash emo core revolution or if it's that she's old, ugly and I hate HER.

SNARKY HUMAN
I have to agree. No one is a bigger supporter of Sarah Lynn than I am. I love her unconditionally. But her new album is boring and she makes me puke.

LIONESS BLOGGER
You know, I keep waiting for her to surprise me. Where's the new "Sexy Sex, Sexy Boobs"?

SNARKY HUMAN
Where's the new "My Clitoris Is Ginormous"?

HIPSTER GOAT
Oh I loved "My Clitoris Is Ginormous."

The dancing in that video was like Bob Fosse meets Martha Graham.

LIONESS BLOGGER
"My Clitoris is Ginormous" is a modern rock masterpiece beyond reproach, that's not up for debate. But we have to face facts -- that Sarah Lynn doesn't exist anymore.

Pitchfork wasn't wrong.

A RYAN SEACREST TYPE
So where does the singer go from here?

This spread: Draft of "Prickly-Muffin" (S1E03) continued.

5.

A RYAN SEACREST TYPE (V.O.)
We've assembled a panel of bloggers and comedians with zero combined expertise on the matter to speculate about Sarah Lynn's recent fall from grace and just generally be dicks.

MUCH LESS SUCCESSFUL

INT. E! STUDIO - DAY

A Ryan Seacrest Type is now sitting at a desk surrounded by THREE SNARKY GEN-Y-ERS (two animals and a human).

A RYAN SEACREST TYPE
Panel, what happened?

HIPSTER GOAT
What happened is Sarah Lynn sucks now. A. She's not sexy anymore. B. She's old. C. I hate her.

NOTHING HAPPENED. IT WAS JUST TIME TO START TEARING HER DOWN SO WE CAN CHEER HER ON AS SHE PULLS HERSELF OUT OF THE GUTTER.

SNARKY HUMAN
I have to agree. No one is a bigger supporter of Sarah Lynn than I am. I love her unconditionally. But her new album is boring and she makes me puke.

BUT HER LAST ALBUM WAS JUST A BUNCH OF MUSIC AND ~~ALL MUSICALLY~~ ~~AND PRETENTIOUS~~ SONGS AND SINGING. POP SINGERS ARE SUPPOSSED TO BE PSEUDO-STRIPPERS, NOT MUSICIANS.

LIONESS BLOGGER
You know, I keep waiting for her to surprise me. Where's the new "Sexy Sex, Sexy Boobs"?

HAVE SEX ON CAMERA

SNARKY HUMAN
Where's the new "My Clitoris Is Ginormous"?

HIPSTER GOAT
Oh I loved "My Clitoris Is Ginormous."

OR

LIONESS BLOGGER
"My Clitoris is Ginormous" is a modern rock masterpiece beyond reproach, that's not up for debate. But we have to face facts -- that Sarah Lynn doesn't exist anymore.

A RYAN SEACREST TYPE
So where does the singer go from here?

"MY CLITORIS IS GINORMOUS" IS THE "IMAGINE" OF OUR GENERATION. SONGS LIKE THAT ONLY COME AROUND ONCE EVERY 40 YEARS.

EXACTLY, SOMETHING PERSONAL AND REVEALING. I HEARD THAT SONG WAS ABOUT TORTURE IN ~~THE~~ GITMO

HIPSTER GOAT
What happened is Sarah Lynn sucks now. A. She's not sexy anymore. B. She's old. C. I hate her. D. All of the above.

SNARKY HUMAN
I have to agree. No one is a bigger supporter of Sarah Lynn than I am. I love her unconditionally. But her new album is boring and she makes me puke.

LIONESS BLOGGER
You know, I keep waiting for her to surprise ~~me.~~ Where's the new "Sexy Sex, Sexy Boobs"?

SNARKY HUMAN
Where's the new "My Clitoris Is ~~Ginormous~~"?

HIPSTER GOAT
Oh I loved "My Clitoris Is Ginormous."

LIONESS BLOGGER
"My Clitoris is Ginormous" is a modern rock masterpiece beyond reproach, that's not up for debate. But we have to face facts -- that Sarah Lynn doesn't exist anymore.

could cut

A RYAN SEACREST TYPE
So where does the singer go from here?

6.

SNARKY HUMAN
~~You know where she should go? She should go~~ Wherever famous people go when they're done being famous and nobody cares about them anymore.

CUT TO:

EXT. BOJACK'S HOUSE - DAY

DOORBELL RING.

INT. BOJACK'S HOME OFFICE - DAY

BoJack and DIANE sit in his office.

→ ~~BoJack playing Cole Porter record for her & crying~~

BOJACK
(cheerful)
Who could that be?

END OF COLD OPEN

Script Draft: "Prickly-Muffin"

ACT ONE

SUPER OVER BLACK: "FIVE HOURS EARLIER"

EXT. BOJACK'S HOUSE - MORNING

TODD (PRELAP)
Whoooo wants chocolate chip pancakes? I do! I do!

INT. BOJACK'S BEDROOM - CONTINUOUS

BoJack is in bed. TODD's in his doorway.

BOJACK
What?

TODD
I thought maybe if I said that, you'd make me chocolate chip pancakes.

BOJACK
Ugh. Don't we have a rule about you talking to me before ten?

TODD
Daylight savings, bro. Todd beats the system again! Take that, Arizona!

BoJack MOANS, hides his head under his pillow.

TODD (CONT'D)
Oh, come on, buddy. It's a beautiful morning. The sun is shining. Birds are chirping --

Two BIRDS (human-sized, clothed) are standing outside BoJack's window, looking in.

BIRD 1
Hey, what's up. What's up.

BIRD 2
What's up.

BIRD 1
What's goin' on in there?

B1: Hey the sun's out.
B2: It's morning. We might mate later.
B1: I'm hungry for breakfast.
B2: I hope our friends hear us!

TODD
I thought maybe if I said that, you'd make me chocolate chip pancakes.

BOJACK
Ugh. Don't we have a rule about you ~~talking to me~~ making eye contact before ten?

BIRD 1
Hey, what's up. What's up.

BIRD 2
What's up.

BIRD 1
What's goin' on in there?

- THERE'S NO BIRDSEED IN THE BIRD FEEDER.
- HEY ASSHOLES, REFILL THE BIRDFEEDER.
- BUY SOME BIRDSEED, ASSHOLES.
- WHO DO YA GOTTA FUCK AROUND HERE FOR SOME BIRDSEED.

TODD (CONT'D)
Oh, come on, buddy. It's a beautiful morning. The sun is shining. Birds are chirping --

Two BIRDS (human-sized, clothed) are standing outside BoJack's window, looking in. Maybe like flying papparazzi w/cameras hunting him...

BIRD 1
Hey, what's up. What's up.

BIRD 2
What's up.

BIRD 1
What's goin' on in there?

Bird 1 | Hey, Bojack. Got any plans this weekend? That shit on our troops?
Bird 2 | Are you gonna eat all their muffins for breakfast?
Bird 1 | Or just light an American flag on fire?

INT. BOJACK'S BEDROOM - CONTINUOUS

BoJack is in bed. TODD's in his doorway.

BOJACK
What?

TODD
I thought maybe if I said that, you'd make me chocolate chip pancakes.

BOJACK: I wouldn't make you chocolate chip pancakes if... (beat) Um... (beat) Hold on. (beat) If you asked me for them. (beat) This is why my Match Game reboot never made it out of development

BOJACK
Ugh. Don't we have a rule about you talking to me before ten?

TODD
Daylight savings, bro. Todd beats the system again! Take that, Arizona!

BoJack MOANS, hides his head under his pillow.

TODD (CONT'D)
Oh, come on, buddy. It's a beautiful morning. The sun is shining. Birds are chirping --

Two BIRDS (human-sized, clothed) are standing outside BoJack's window, looking in.

BIRD 1
Hey, what's up. What's up.

BIRD 2
What's up.

BIRD 1
What's goin' on in there?

I second the pitch to make paparazzi

This spread: Draft of "Prickly-Muffin" (S1E03) continued.

8.

TODD
-- Let's do something fun today.

BOJACK
Like what?

TODD
Like a cannonballlllll!

He jumps on the bed, which immediately breaks.

TODD (CONT'D)
(sheepishly)
Like a buying you a new bedddddd!

EXT. FANCY FURNITURE STORE - DAY

A few BIRDS fly by.

INT. CROFT HOUSE - DAY

Todd and BoJack walk through the store passing oddly shaped furniture made out of reclaimed wood.

TODD
Wow, everything in this store is made out of old train tracks and a reclaimed pier.

BOJACK
Oh great, for ten thousand dollars, I can sleep like a hobo.

TODD
Hey, BoJack, do we need letter openers made out of Confederate bayonets? It says here they're stained with authentic Yankee blood.

Todd grabs a couple bayonets and puts them in his basket.

which already has a bunch of useless shit in it. Old-timey clock. Typewriter. Globe.

BOJACK
No, Todd, put those back. My house is not a theme park. It is my temple, for moments of quiet reflection.

TODD
Hey, BoJack, do we need letter openers made out of Confederate bayonets? It says here they're stained with authentic Yankee blood.

Todd grabs a couple bayonets and puts them in his basket.

See back in lieu of flashback

BOJACK
No, Todd, put those back. My house is not a theme park. It is my temple, for moments of quiet reflection.

Maybe BoJack sees a bed.
BJ: This one looks good.
BJ goes into a pantomime of air fucking the bed violently, switching positions, "finishing" ~~then calmly hops off the bed. BJ:~~ "lighting a cigarette."
Then, to Todd: "Not bad."

bayonets? It says here they're stained with authentic Yankee blood.

Todd grabs a couple bayonets and puts them in his basket.

BOJACK
No, Todd, put those back. ~~My house is not a theme park. It is my temple, for moments of quiet reflection.~~

I don't waste money on alleged historical merchandise with no authentifications.

<Cut to Flashback>
Bojack in Hollywood Pawnshop:
a ten speed bike with a pricetag that says $5000.89
Bojack to clerk:
"So Kelly Ripa had it for 2 years?"
The clerk nods. Bojack sniffs the seat, then
"I'll take it."

This page: Lisa's design notes on specific clothing design elements to apply across the show.

3: Designing Horses

BoJack's Character; Background and Prop Design

Production designer Lisa Hanawalt's many interests are on display in her personal zines and sketchbooks. Familiar, funny, animal-headed characters like She-Moose and He-Horse are there, but so are detailed drawings of southwestern woven fabrics draped over leather couches in hotel lobbies, and studies of curious desert and tropical plants. There are interiors and exteriors of buildings and pool patios, and characters sporting funny graphic T-shirts, leggings, and sweaters. Her keenly observant design and fashion awareness also comes with a large helping of humor. Whether the year in a *BoJack* episode is 1997, 2007, or 2017, Lisa's designs expertly skewer laughable fashion trends differentiated with laser precision—from dad jeans to velour tracksuits to artfully distressed denim.

Lisa Hanawalt [production designer]: For me, designing the show has allowed me to dip into my interest in graphic design, interior design, and fashion in a way that I didn't before, because I'm always looking for new things to do—to differentiate backgrounds or characters from each other. So that's been really fun for me. I just have tons and tons of folders on my desktop.

When designing the animal characters, I like thinking about what kind of animal they are when I'm designing their clothes. I might use a pattern with something that they would choose. Princess Carolyn, of course, would choose a fish dress. And Mr. Peanutbutter has bone shorts.

Raphael Bob-Waksberg [series creator]: And doesn't Mia the mouse have a little cheese necklace?

Lisa: Yeah. Stuff like that is really fun. When we were designing Mr. Peanutbutter's house, I drew butts all over the walls because I was like, that's what a dog would have.

Mike Hollingsworth [supervising director]: Diane likes butts, too. Mr. Peanutbutter has got a great butt.

It Takes a Studio

In an animated series, every single character, prop, and background has to be imagined, sketched, and refined. *BoJack*'s world needs an entire studio full of people to produce the

Left: The hand-drawn, inspired-by-reality aesthetic of Lisa's production design extends to the carefully executed asymmetry of Tina the bear nurse's bosom.

Opposite: Character designer Samantha Gray created this animalized image of the character design staff and Lisa (front and center) as a personal piece.

volume of designs needed for a season of episodes, and the trick is figuring out how to do it cohesively.

Mike: I have to remind the artists a lot that the initial thing was that we were going to create a graphic-novel look, so that it looked like a DIY zine.

The DIY zine tradition doesn't call for any one aesthetic per se, but digitally approximating the look and feel of a zine can often be achieved by including black outlines (to mimic having been photocopied) and messier, more idiosyncratic pen strokes (to seem hand-drawn, rather than slick and clean, like most Hollywood cartoons). *BoJack* designers work almost entirely digitally, from the first concept designs for characters all the way through to the final effects. Programs like Adobe Flash and After Effects offer advantageous presets, effects, and techniques that might fly on another show but are considered forbidden fruit for the *BoJack* designers.

Mike: A lot of times on the show, artists will want to put in really clean, cinematic special effects. As an example, I always remind everybody of our camera flashes. Our camera flashes, which we see all the time and take for granted, are drawn graphics. So when artists want to put crazy lens flares on them and the lights and stuff, I point out, "How does this lens flare live in the same world as those camera flashes?"

Lisa: It's really hard to get that hand-drawn feel into a show made in Flash and animated by so many different people.

Raphael: I think there's a little asymmetrical and wobbly aspect to Lisa's art, and we try to keep that.

Lisa: Originally, in the backgrounds, the lines were going to be wobbly to kind of mimic that, but it just took too long. We ditched that. [*Laughs.*]

BoJack backgrounds are designed with mechanically clean lines filled with flat, bright colors.

Mike: But we still have our wobbly, asymmetrical characters! I will direct you to the bear nurse's bosom.

Lisa: Yeah, one of her tits is higher than the other. It's lovely, my favorite. [*Laugh.*] It's way realistic.

Noel Bright [executive producer]: We also have the watercolor look because that was something that excited us about Lisa's art in the beginning, and one of the things we asked Mike was "How can you preserve that?" It just looks like nothing else.

The watercolor textures are scans of washes that Lisa creates on paper, which are then adjusted to overlay parts of every character and background.

Mike: It was very trial and error. But I had worked on a bunch of Playhouse Disney stuff where I used this similar technique to create texture, to create a chalkboard feel, so I knew straightaway how to do it. Lisa and I work a lot on how much texture to add to each element.

Lisa: Sometimes it's too much. Sometimes the textures look kind of blown out [overlaid on certain colors]; sometimes the relative scale [difference between the texture and the item] is too much. So it's a customized extra step to make sure that every background looks spot on.

Despite being viewed on a glowing, light-emitting screen, the subtle wash and paper-like texture humanize the crispness of the computer-generated lines and temper the saturation of the colors, lending the sense that you are viewing artwork on a printed page—like a zine.

Right: Especially for human designs, Lisa found that each variance in eye size or placement, shape of jaw, or head to body proportion, changed the perception of who the character was because of how attuned to the human face, even in cartoon form, human audiences are. Todd's design was the most difficult to settle upon, with Diane being a close second. Here, even as Todd comes closer to the final design (far right), Lisa's experiments with his features still suggest a wide variety of character range and expectations, from childish goofball to stoned hobo.

Animals: Easy. People: Hard.

A constant reality for Lisa since the early development of the show has been the relative ease of drawing animals compared to human characters.

Lisa: With animals, it's sort of like you can draw any horse, and it kind of just looks like a horse. But with humans, every little tiny detail—how far apart the eyes are, how big the nose is—is under much finer audience scrutiny. Each variation looks like a specific person because we're just so finely attuned to the human face.

Lisa's early presentation designs for BoJack, Princess Carolyn, Mr. Peanutbutter, Tom Jumbo-Grumbo, Lenny Turteltaub, and Neil the Navy Seal all felt right within several conceptual drawings, or sometimes even a single drawing. Todd and Diane required many more iterations to get them right.

Lisa: The human characters were really, really hard for me. I was used to drawing animals. I would have these conference calls with Raphael and Noel and Steve, and they were really frustrating because we'd just be talking in circles. I wasn't getting a lot of specific direction. It was kind of just like, "This isn't quite working, but we're not sure why." But I'm glad that we had the time to work on them, because I think we landed in a good place. Todd went through many variations—he wasn't even in his finished form in the presentation pilot. Todd was a primary reason the pilot footage had to be redone.

Lisa: There's one Todd incarnation where he was a surfer dude. We were trying anything. There's one where he kind of looks like Seth Rogen, but he's, like, a drum-circle dude. [*Laughs.*] Diane was so hard for me because she was supposed to be attractive, but also bookish, and it's like, how do you just draw, like, a hot person? We had some debate over clothing items, too, but I pretty much just designed different outfits, and then we just liked one of the ones I came up with. For Diane, the jacket with the little red arrows was just a fun design I came up with, not based on anything real. The little boots . . . It's funny, because now, to me, her outfit looks slightly dated. Like, there's something about it that looks 2012 to me, instead of 2017. Maybe it comes down to my personal taste and how that's changed.

Diane's jacket, though nonspecific in its origins, does visually recall an army-surplus-type jacket, and her character seems to be the kind of person who might wear one—or at least used to in high school.

Lisa: Which is very *Daria.* Which is definitely an inspiration. There aren't a lot of female characters in animation that I could reference for Diane, but Daria is definitely one. She's just kind of a tomboy. . . . She was hard to design because she's a tomboy, but she had to look sexy, you know? She is a love interest. Originally, I was thinking, "This character doesn't exist in real life." And I had that problem with her. And then I think as the show progressed, she became more of a real person.

Part of Lisa's early character-design efforts included populating the world with background characters.

Lisa: I just drew a bunch of people, thinking, "Oh, these could be background people." We were working on the main character designs, but I just added in some extras. And then with one of the designs, we had a long conversation. It was just like, "He's got a skinny snake head, but then his body is large. So what is under his clothes?" I was like, "You guys, it doesn't matter. It's just a human body." Everyone got hung up on that one in a way that I would never worry about while drawing in my sketchbook. When you're working on a project of this scale, you do have to explain your decisions to people. I'd never really experienced that before, beyond doing small illustration jobs. Yeah. The design still makes sense to me.

This page: Lisa's familiarity with animal drawing and horses in particular meant that these explorations of dog-fashion and difficult views of horse heads flowed smoothly from her drawing tools.

As the show found its tone, the rules of its universe (such as the fact that animal characters don't have tails, with few exceptions, like the scorpion DJ at Penny's prom in "Escape from L.A." [S2E11]) began to make more sense to everyone.

Lisa: It's funny. I do feel like I have a lot of freedom there. There is a certain realism that the show is tied to. We don't get too surreal. The characters don't get too cartoony, or kind of noodle-y. Part of that is just the fact that it's done in Flash, so the characters have to be puppeted, and they don't have a lot of stretch and pull in the animation. But I also think Raphael just wanted it to be kind of anchored by a lot of real-life rules.

Human or Animal?

The script doesn't always designate the new slate of characters needed for each episode.

Lisa: Sometimes it says that a character could either be a duck or a lizard or whatever, and sometimes it's super specific.

Raphael: "It's a goat, but it's a goat that looks like the goat I saw on a field trip in fourth grade."

Lisa: Or "It's a dolphin version of that girl who was in our fifth-grade math class." [*Laughs.*]

Mike: Right around season four, we introduced an important new character, Yolanda. The script didn't say whether she was a human or anything.

Raphael: Maybe we just talked about her being a lizard.

Mike: And then one of our directors, Anne Walker [Farrell], pitched that Yolanda was an axolotl, which is this beautiful lizard that you really need to be a kind of animal nerd—it's a deep cut, a deep animal cut—to know. When it first came up in the room, Steve was like, "What is this? Is this an alien?" And our director was like, "No, actually, this is an axolotl, which can be found in the area around Mexico City. It is this kind of animal, and blah blah blah blah," and he was like, "OK . . ." [*Laughs.*]

Kelly Galuska [writer]: Sometimes we'll ask Lisa what kind of animal she hasn't drawn yet that she wants to draw, and we can create characters that way. Or we'll tell her about a character that we are creating and she'll help us decide the best way to represent that character on-screen.

Lisa: Though that happens pretty rarely. I'm actually pretty shy about going into the writers' room because they're busy, and I'm like, "Oh my God, they're writers!" [*Laughs.*] I sneak past them to get a LaCroix out of the fridge and hope they don't notice me. But yeah, once, Raphael called me in and he was like, "Hey, Lisa! Should it be Quentin Tarantulino, Quentin Tarantuna, or Quentin Tarantoucan?" And I was like, "Hmm, I've been drawing a lot of birds and fish recently so let's make it Tarantulino because that sounds like a challenge." So I got to choose that one with the writers.

Joe Lawson [writer]: For one character, we just incidentally wrote in the script that it was a "sexy eel," and we didn't say anything else about it. We just wanted to see what would come back with "sexy eel."

Eyebrows, or No Eyebrows?

Designing a bird, fish, insect, arachnid, or crustacean face presents its challenges, including whether or not to add extra humanizing elements to the design.

Raphael: BoJack is very expressive, but he's less expressive than a real, live person. We can project a lot of different

This spread: Ants (from "Underground" [S4E07]), spiders (Quentin Tarantulino, first appearance in "Say Anything" [S1E07], and Jill Pill, first appearance in "Start Spreading the News" [S3E01]), an axolotl named Yolanda Buenaventura, eels, and snakes—all are fair game for the anthropomorphic *BoJack* design treatment.

ROCK
BAND
UNKLE HANKY!
HI-HO!
Busy Bee

Opposite: A fraction of the total amount of characters that have been designed to populate the *BoJack* world. These are Lisa's concept drawings before being passed on to the character design department.

Below: Called "crayon people" in the production, these low-detail, small, colorful extras are the type of designs that are seen on screen in the distant background, often on a city street for example.

feelings based on just his mouth shapes, his eyes—it's amazing how many different emotions you can convey with a limited number of expressions.

Adam Parton [animation director]: A lot of thought goes into the eyes when designing *BoJack* characters, as it can be such a dark and restrained show that sometimes we will have a scene where the character is basically motionless and we have only the eyes to sell the emotion or feelings behind the scene. So we will decide at an early stage if this character is going to be overly expressive, in which case we might go for bigger eyes in the design so we have a bigger emotional canvas to work with when acting. If a character is going to be intense or menacing, we might go for thinner or smaller eyes to put that at a base level of their character design. It's something that when done properly really helps enhance the atmosphere and characters of *BoJack*'s world.

Lisa: You have to give the animals eyebrows—otherwise you're extremely limited. [*Laughs.*] Eyebrows are really an important thing for expressions—to make them more human. So some of the animals don't have them, and they're less human. I always default to no eyebrows, and then I have to add them. . . .

Raphael: Well, I feel like we do have characters who don't have eyebrows, and then just for one shot, you'll see their eyebrows appear.

Mike: But we try not to do that. Lenny Turteltaub does not have eyebrows. Tina [the bear nurse] does not have eyebrows—

Lisa: Because Tina is . . . a less-human animal.

Mike: Yeah, that's true. It gives them a more blank expression with no eyebrows. Tina is our biggest character that kind of talks in an animalistic way.

Raphael: She's like, "*Rrrngrnngh!*"

Character Lineup

After Lisa completes concept art for each new character, the drawings are handed over to the character design department, where artists extrapolate them into a cleaned-up character model (composed of a series of "turnaround" images that show each figure fully rotated in space). The result is something like a police lineup. Designers also use horizontal guides to make sure that the top of each brow, bow, or button lines up across all poses.

BoJack's character turnarounds—designed in the same software that they will be animated in—are dynamic. Double-clicking each head symbol reveals a timeline of fully articulated mouth shapes, also referred to as "mouth packs." Each limb is also sectional, on its own layer, and ready for posing—like a jointed paper doll puppet. Tracking the details of a character design at every angle is key.

Artists use combination drawing tablet/monitors to ink the final line art in Flash with the brush tool, which provides a clean black line with the slightest wiggles and variation—the human element that contributes to the show's zine-like DIY aesthetic. They do try to ink as cleanly and smoothly as possible, however, to achieve a consistent show-wide look.

Adam: One of the most labor-intensive yet effective things about the character design in *BoJack* is how we use textures on certain animals to show that they have leathery skin or fur. It really helps with characters like Hank Hippopopalous, making their "skin" look old and lived-in and a little bit creepy—which certainly fell in line with his character. Similarly, with BoJack's fur, the texture we used there makes him look patchy and mottled, which adds to the feeling that he is no spring chicken and definitely a flawed character. On the downside, using the textures can create difficulties during the animation process—making sure the textures line up in a way that doesn't create obvious seams, for instance—but it's a price worth paying for that extra level of detail.

Annette Huckell [character designer]: For most shows, you tend to design a front view, a three-quarter view, and a side view. We often will also do a seven-eighths view and a five-eighths view. And on the main series cast, like BoJack, if you look at his lineup—oh my God, he has so many poses. Because they want that ability to have really subtle motion.

Big Mouth (Packs)

Mouth pack design is a large part of the character design department's work. The script-driven, celebrity-guest-voice-heavy show

Continued on page 148

Below: Wanda Pierce's design went through some minor changes from Lisa's initial sketch below, including larger eyes, feather tufts, and a more refined outfit.

This spread: Character designers must consider how each character looks and also how that character relates to the others. Some related groups of characters are designed simultaneously, such as the Clown Dentists, Ralph Stilton's family, and Hollyhock's eight dads.

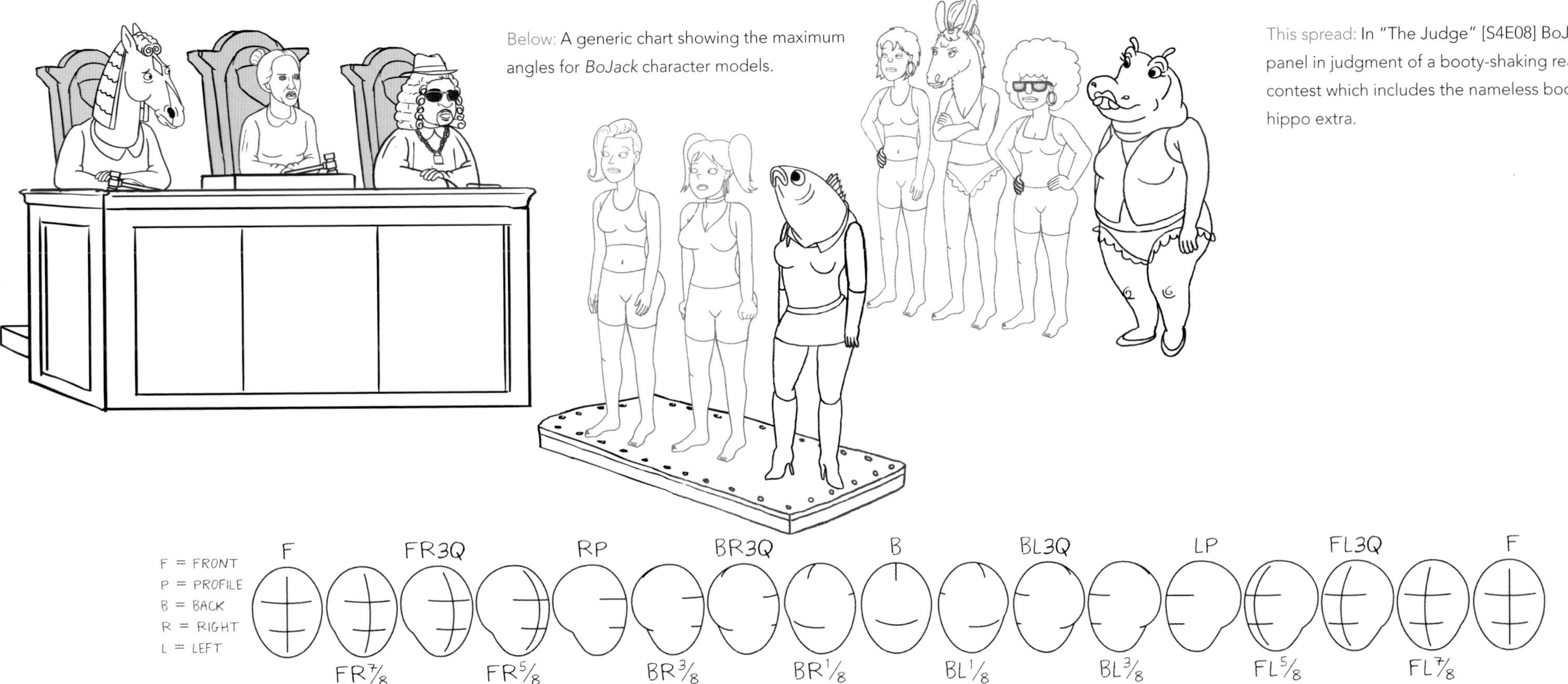

Below: A generic chart showing the maximum angles for *BoJack* character models.

This spread: In "The Judge" [S4E08] BoJack joins a panel in judgment of a booty-shaking reality show contest which includes the nameless booty-shorts hippo extra.

is full of dialogue, and therefore extra effort goes into making sure that the characters look as natural as possible while talking.

Lotan Kritchman [character design supervisor]: I've worked on a lot of shows and a lot of mouth packs. No one does as many mouth syllables or the amount of angles that we do.

Adam: Most characters that need to do any sort of acting have two full sets of mouth shapes: one "happy" and another "sad." Occasionally they're even given a third "neutral" mouth chart. We combine these mouths with a number of custom eye expressions—as many as we feel we need—to fulfill the acting goals for any given character.

Phylicia Fuentes [character designer]: A lot of the emoting in the animation phase comes from the eyes. I think Princess Carolyn in particular has great eyebrows for a range of expressions. There's a lot to work with for her to show attitude as well as sadness.

The designers can reuse some human body and head shapes, as well as mouth packs, for new human characters. But every animal design needs its own original mouth pack because of their variety.

Lotan: Animal mouths don't really move like ours do, so we get to take some pretty fun liberties. Sometimes we just indicate mouth movements, such as for some of the weird maggot or worm-type characters you see, and other times we do extreme overshoots, such as for the catfish characters in season two ["Yes And" (S2E10)]. It's really fun to see what you can get away with.

Adam: Gregory Hsung, Hollyhock's lizard dad in season four, had one of the more extreme mouth packs I've designed on the show. He has a very long and narrow head, most of which is jaw and mouth. This means that there's a huge difference between his widest and narrowest mouth shapes. When he makes an *oo* sound, his lips contract almost halfway down the length of his face, and when he makes an *ee* sound, his entire jaw and lips pull back. In both cases, the facial features of this character needed to distort in a way that shouldn't be anatomically possible.

Lotan: I loved working on the ant warriors in season four. Anyone looking at those designs alone could think you were working on a completely different show. They could be ancient warriors or futuristic space aliens. I love the range of this show.

Samantha Gray [character designer]: My favorite design I worked on was a booty-shorts hippo in season four. She may only be a background character, but I felt there was a body-positivity message that applied. Wearing only a sports bra and short shorts, she is unabashed about her full figure and is *rocking* it! I was delighted that when I turned in the first draft to Lisa, her only note was, "Make the shorts shorter."

Special Poses for Special Action

The character design department is also responsible for all key drawings that fall outside of the standard rotations of any character and their happy, sad, and neutral mouth shapes.

Lotan: If there's any sort of special pose—let's say a character gets punched in the face, and then his head swings upward—we do that here.

Adam: If the Korean animation studio [Big Star Enterprise, Inc.; see pages 198–200] is drawing anything at all, it's something like an in-between drawing to keep the smoothness of the animation. So if a character were to do some extreme thing, like fall down a hill rolling over and over, we draw the special poses.

This spread: In "See Mr. Peanutbutter Run" (S4E01) a skiing contest required Lotan Kritchman and the team of character designers to create many special poses for all of the action unique to this episode.

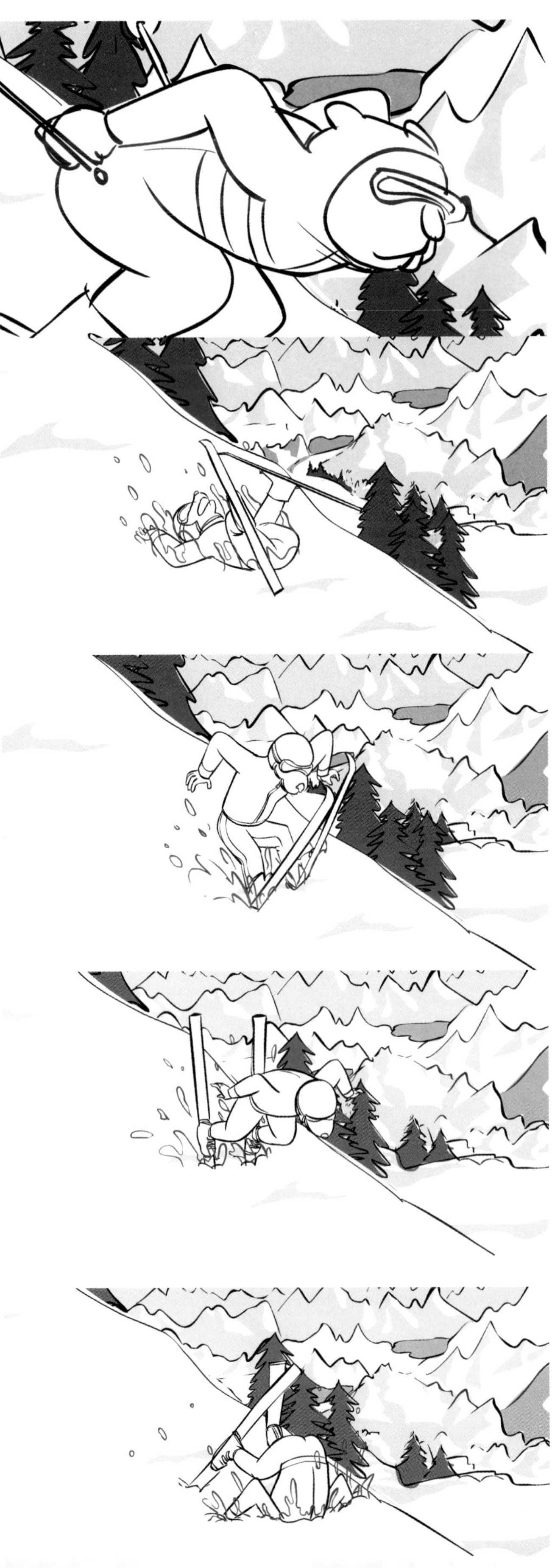

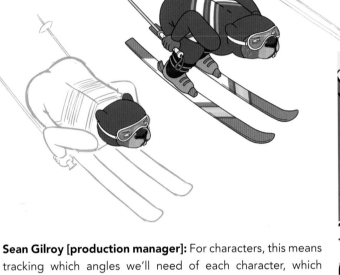

Sean Gilroy [production manager]: For characters, this means tracking which angles we'll need of each character, which angles need which mouths (happy or sad), eyes, or special poses. For backgrounds, it means tracking how many different angles we need to draw, how the environments function, how wide we go or how tight we go so we can make sure that the textures hold up in every shot. If someone opens up a drawer in the kitchen, we need to make sure that kitchen has both a drawing of the drawer shut and open. Similarly, with props, if someone opens a beer, tilts it up, take a swig, then smashes the bottle on the ground, we'll need to draw a key frame of every single iteration of that moment.

Punny Animal Gags

It's hard to find an establishing shot or piece of background art from the series that is not crammed full of animal jokes. Every crowd full of extras, every bookshelf or store window is an opportunity—gleefully seized by the entire crew—for visual puns and animal goofs. The Mike Hollingsworth influence is nowhere more evident than in this aspect of *BoJack Horseman*, as it is his guiding vision that oversees all visual layers of the show. Not surprisingly, in his spare time, Mike also makes animal gag cartoons on his personal blog, *Stuffed Animals*.

Mike: Something that Lisa and I love—and it's a continuation from *Looney Toons* and Tex Avery cartoons—is coming up with punny names for Hollywood institutions. In Tex Avery cartoons, they would go to all these Hollywood places, and Bugs

Bunny was always mixing with celebrities, and they constantly had Brown Derby jokes, and—

Lisa: Carrotmount Studios, like that . . .

Mike: Yeah . . . [*Laughs.*] There certainly is a long history of "animalizing" Hollywood.

Just to sample a few, *BoJack* backgrounds have featured the Swine Within Reach Modern Furniture store, Chipmunk Cheek Storage, and Chateau Marmoset Hotel.

The background extras also get into the act. There's the cow waitress at the diner who nonchalantly milks herself on the spot for a milk refill but gets a bit grumpy when serving a steak. There's the sheep lawn service worker who mows the grass clippings directly into his mouth; the bloodhound cop sniffing along a crime scene; a Seeing Eye dog walking with a blind guy, their arms linked; a mosquito sipping blood from a woman's arm as they share a cafe table; and the fly waiter serving soup with his thumb dipped in it.

In a southwestern shout-out to legendary *Looney Tunes* director Chuck Jones from season three, a roadrunner runs down a suburban street, followed shortly by a coyote jogger.

The background jokes aren't always animal gags. See Sextina Aquafina's pregnancy test brand of choice, "DTF," for example.

Background Department

Kelly Wine [background designer]: We are given a rough image, usually from the storyboard, to start each BG, or background. This is particularly helpful when it's a new location in the series. Lisa has definite ideas for the show's aesthetic; she usually shares these ideas with us as we proceed on BGs. For the longtime BG designers on the show, I feel there is an earned sense of trust that Lisa has in our ability to create BGs that meet her design ideas, but she also gives us space as designers to put our own personalities into our work. The main objective is that the BGs are believable and work together within the *BoJack Horseman* world.

Using the rough image, the background artist will establish the perspective of the shot using a horizon line and vanishing points plotted along it. The new background is drawn in gray scale at first, using the line and pencil tools in Flash. Any parts of old BGs that can be reused are placed into the scene, such as plants, bushes, pieces of buildings, or street infrastructure.

Colleen Police [background designer]: A lot of these trees [in a season four forest background] are elements that have been in some other episodes, so I was able to reuse them, and I'm making little changes to them. These trees are from season two. The show has gotten a little more refined and detailed as

This spread: Visual jokes including plenty of animal puns permeate the series.

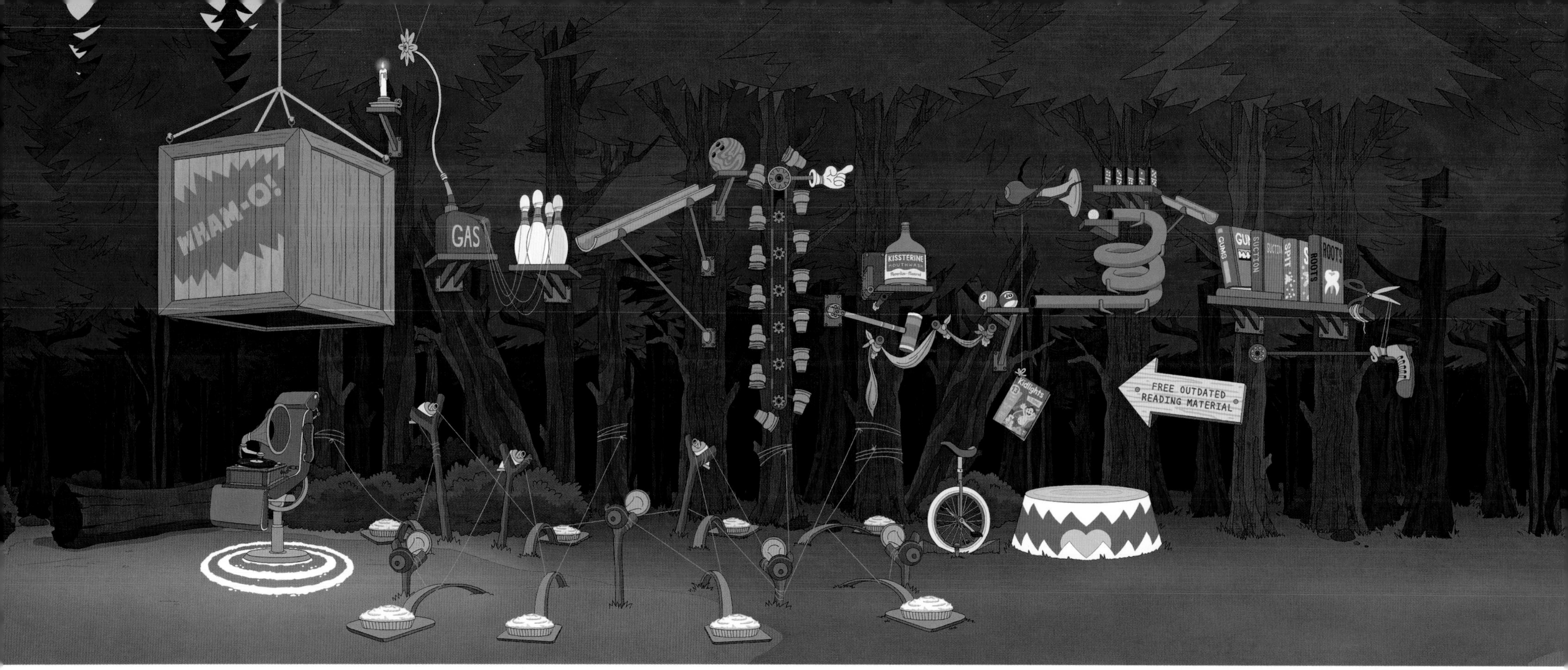

Free Outdated
Reading Material

Opposite: Todd's contraption in "What Time Is It Right Now" (S4E12) goes haywire.

This page: Lisa's art direction based on observation of reality extends to the plant life in the show.

the seasons have gone on. For a lot of the older elements, we go in and we spruce them up a little bit.

Sometimes background elements are animated. These must be placed on their own layers and prepped for motion by the designers.

Kelly: If there's an animating element in the background and it's not a prop that the characters are going to come into contact with, then we are responsible for it, as background designers—or at least for doing key frames of it, and then the Korean studio will fill in the in-betweens.

In the season four finale ("What Time Is It Right Now" [S4E12]), Kelly Wine was tasked with drawing the artwork for Todd's insane mechanical contraption in the woods that gets destroyed before ever having to function on-screen.

Kelly: [*Laughs.*] It's fairly complicated, just because there are a lot of parts, you know? The good thing is that the contraption itself doesn't actually work as a Rube Goldberg machine. So, in that aspect, it's good. Before I worked here, I worked at a company doing animated greeting cards. And so I did a bunch of Rube Goldberg animated greeting cards, and those actually did have to work. All that happens here is that Todd runs through it backward, and it all goes crazy and falls apart.

Mad Props to the BGs

The prop department is a smaller, distinct group of artists responsible for producing multiple angles of objects that often work their way into backgrounds at a later date.

Elizabeth McMahill [lead prop designer]: If a character picks up an item, then it typically goes to the prop department to design. If it's an item that already exists in a background but is handled in the animatic, then we'll often take the work that the background department has done and add the necessary angles and functionality for that artwork. The same occurs with the character department when a character takes off their hat or clothes. In that instance, we match the designs in the character art but draw new angles of the object for when it's being handled or thrown on the floor. While background designers do all the set dressing for their backgrounds, they do often pull the more generic assets from our prop library to help fill things out.

As each episode is completed, a new crop of props is created and eventually added to the digital library of prop assets accessible on the studio server.

Continued on page 170

Right: Lisa's notes detailing some of the required designs from a meeting at the beginning of season four production. Both in notes and on the model sheet from the end of season three, Hollyhock is referred to as "BoJack's daughter" (in quotation marks). Harper, BoJack's daughter from his imagined life with Charlotte the deer in Maine, is also mentioned in the notes.

Below: Hollyhock's design started with Harper, then evolved.

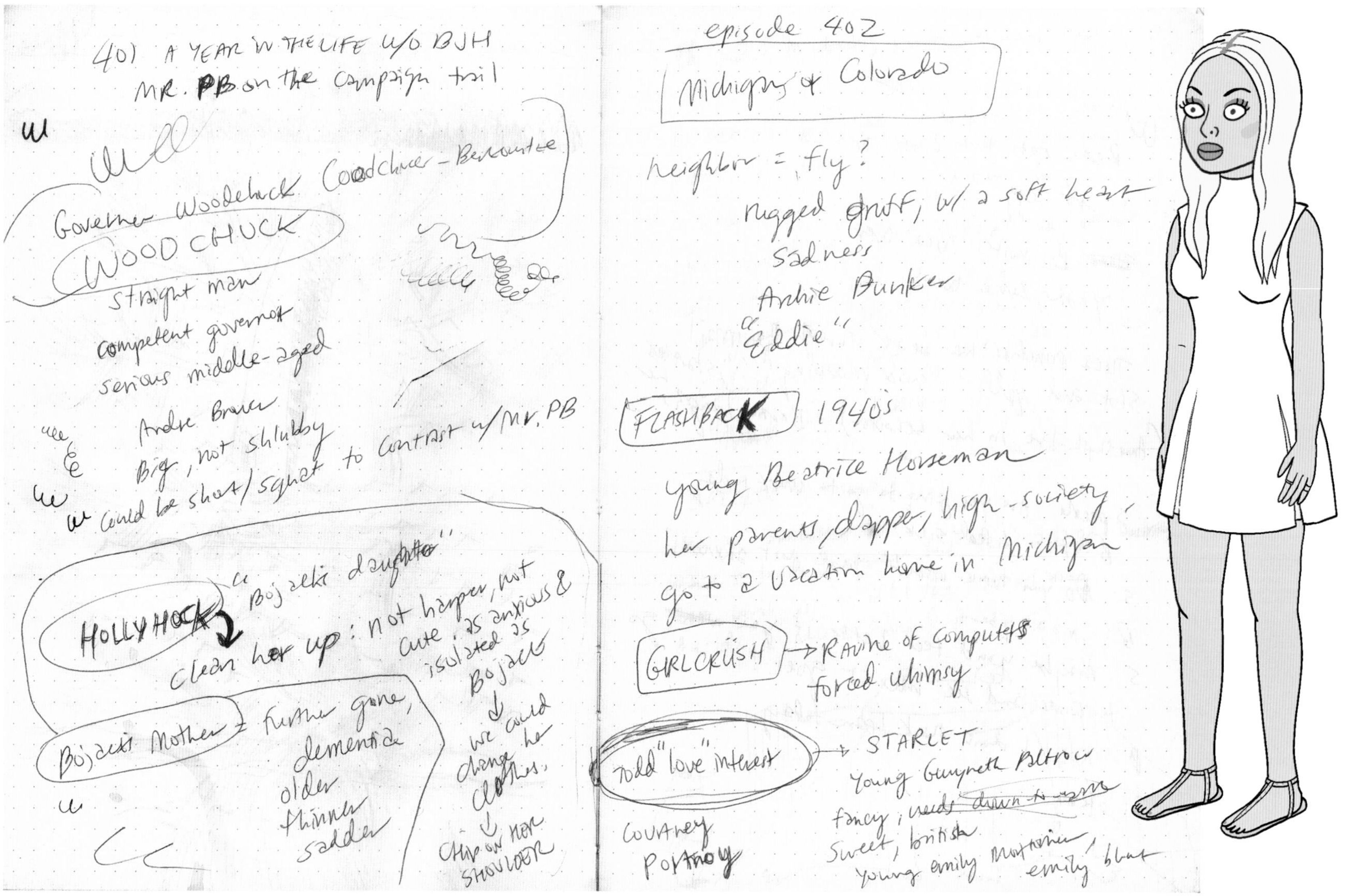

401 A YEAR IN THE LIFE W/O BJH
MR. PB on the campaign trail
Governor Woodchuck Coodchuck-Berkowitz
WOODCHUCK
straight man
competent governor
serious middle-aged
Andre Braugher
Big, not shlubby
could be short/squat to contrast w/ MR. PB
HOLLYHOCK
"Bojack's daughter"
Clean her up: not harper, not cute, as anxious & isolated as Bojack
we could change her clothes.
CHIP ON HER SHOULDER
Bojack's Mother
Further gone, dementia
older
thinner
sadder
episode 402
Michigan & Colorado
neighbor = fly?
rugged gruff, w/ a soft heart
Sadness
Archie Bunker
"Eddie"
FLASHBACK 1940's
young Beatrice Horseman
her parents, dapper, high-society
go to a vacation home in Michigan
GIRLCRUSH → Ravine of computers
forced whimsy
Todd "love" interest → STARLET
Young Gwyneth Paltrow
fancy, needs down to earth
Sweet, british
Young emily Mortimer, emily blunt
Courtney Portnoy

7
6 1/2
6
5 1/2
5
4 1/2
4
3 1/2
3
2 1/2
2
1 1/2
1
1/2
Character: "Bojack's Daughter"
Episode: 312
Date: 02/25/16
BOJACK HORSEMAN
DEFAULT
THINNER
THINNEST

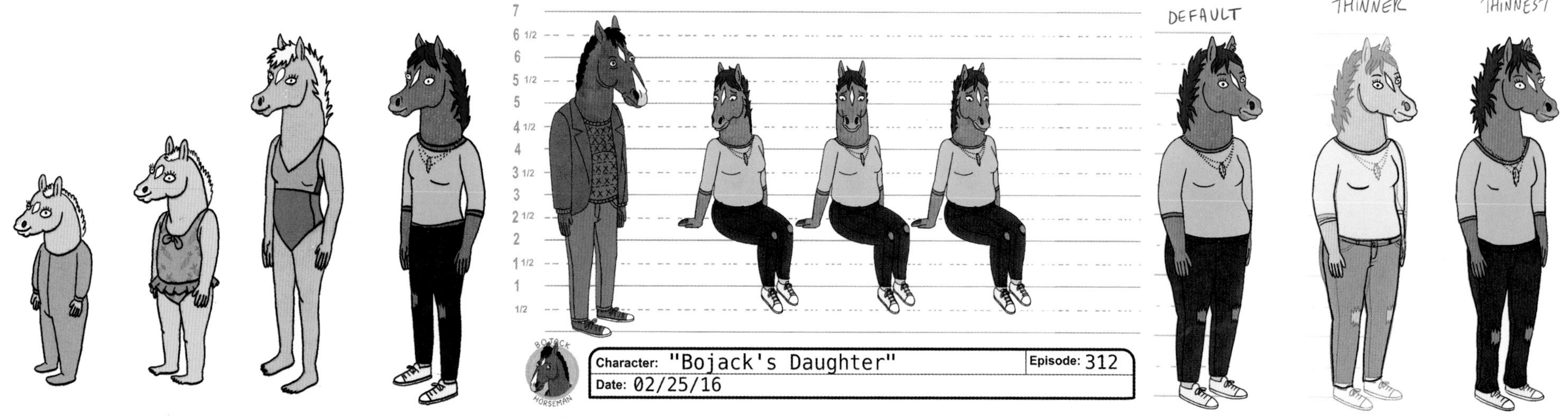

Below: Kelly Wine designed the pristine and destroyed versions of the Sugarman vacation home.

Following spread: The Girl Croosh office background art designed by Sarah Harkey with a wall of inspirational quotes illustrated by Lisa.

Girl
CROOSH
JOOSH
BAR
CLEANSE
DIGEST

PERFECTION IS A MICROAGGRESSION
TODAY WILL BE POWERFUL
BE KIND & DRINK MORE WATER
CROOSH IT!
Open your mind
But not too much
CHANGE THE WORLD & LOOK CUTE ♥
HONESTY, HUMOR AND DEATH TO ALL HATERS
IT'S OKAY TO BE A LITTLE BIT CRAY
CROOSH, GIRL. CROOSH.
LOVE YOUR SELFIE
Don't talk to me until I've had my green juice
WELCOME: OVER-THINKERS & TIME-WASTERS
CLICKBAIT?

BoJack's House

This spread: A blueprint of BoJack's two-level home with some views of the interior.

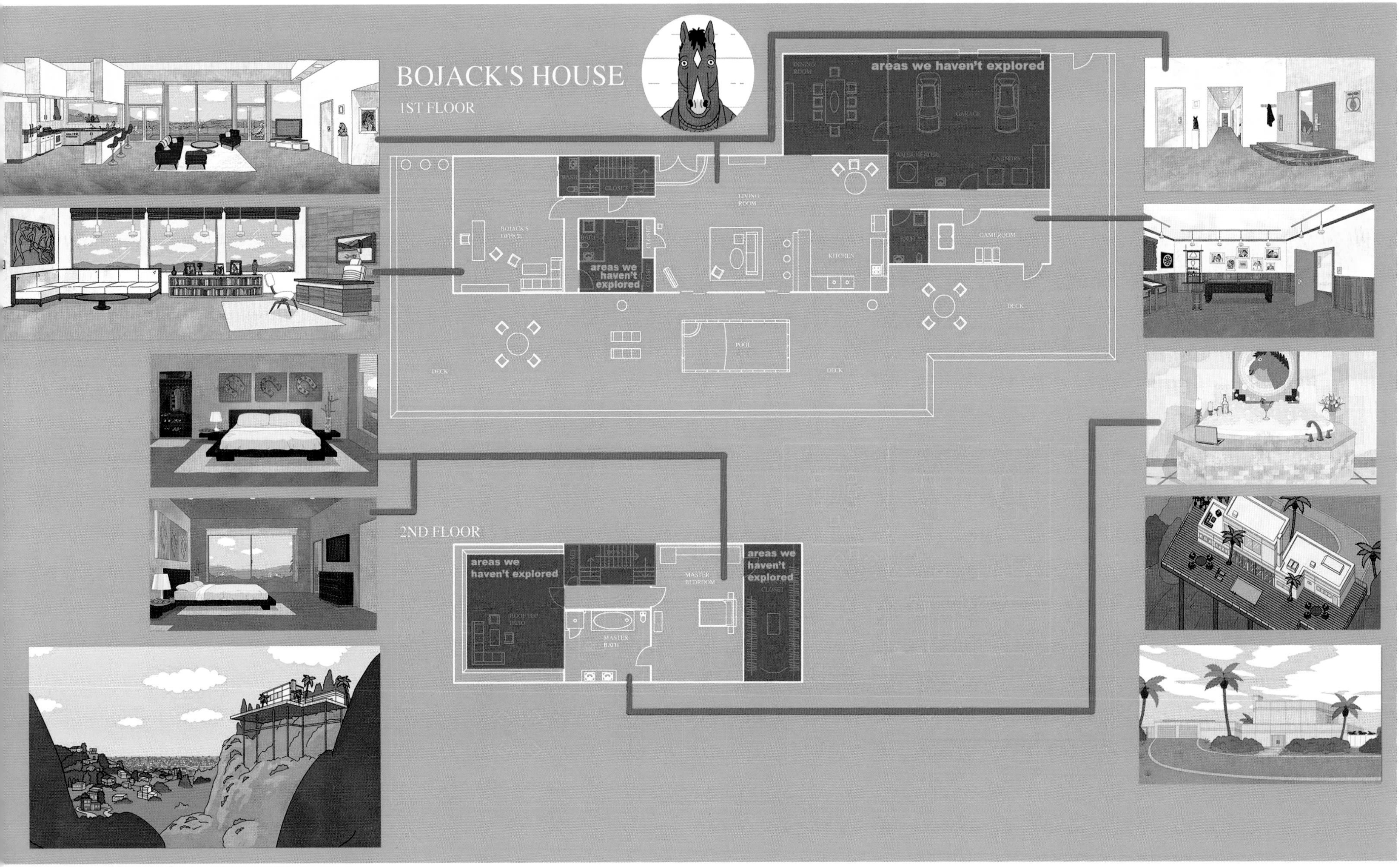

BOJACK'S HOUSE

1ST FLOOR

areas we haven't explored

areas we haven't explored

2ND FLOOR

areas we haven't explored

areas we haven't explored

CAMELPARI
Sliced Beets
APPLE
BUTTE
MUSTARD

Backgrounds

Below: Alison Dubois [background designer]: Drawing Meryl Streep as topiaries [in "Stupid Piece of Sh*t" (S4E06)] was a dream.

Right: Background art designed by Megan Willoughby.

Backgrounds

Right: Background art designed by Alison Dubois.

DINO WORLD
Parking ahead on right
AND GIFT SHO
SPACE ROCKS!
NOSAUR

Backgrounds

This spread: Colleen Police [background artist]: I loved, loved being able to harken back to my fine art roots to do a couple of awesome landscape pans at the beginning of "The Old Sugarman Place" [S4E02] (the sunset over the red rocks, and the pan with the anthropomorphic cow skeleton).

BUCK BEER
PIGARONI PIZZA
PIZZA PIES PIZZA

This spread: Lana, Langdon, Larry, Leon, Les, Liam, Linus, Lisa, and Lola Lemur are among these party lemurs that always like to show up for a party.

This spread: Similar to designing a "real" logo, designing logos, packaging and marketing material for things that exist in a fictional world is an involved process, with the artist creating many options to solve the design problem.

Elizabeth McMahill [lead prop designer]: I'm really proud of the logo work I got to do in seasons two and three. I designed the logos for Chicken 4 Dayz, Gentle Farms, Seaborn Seahorse Milk, Freshwater Taffy, and the Pacific Ocean Film Festival.

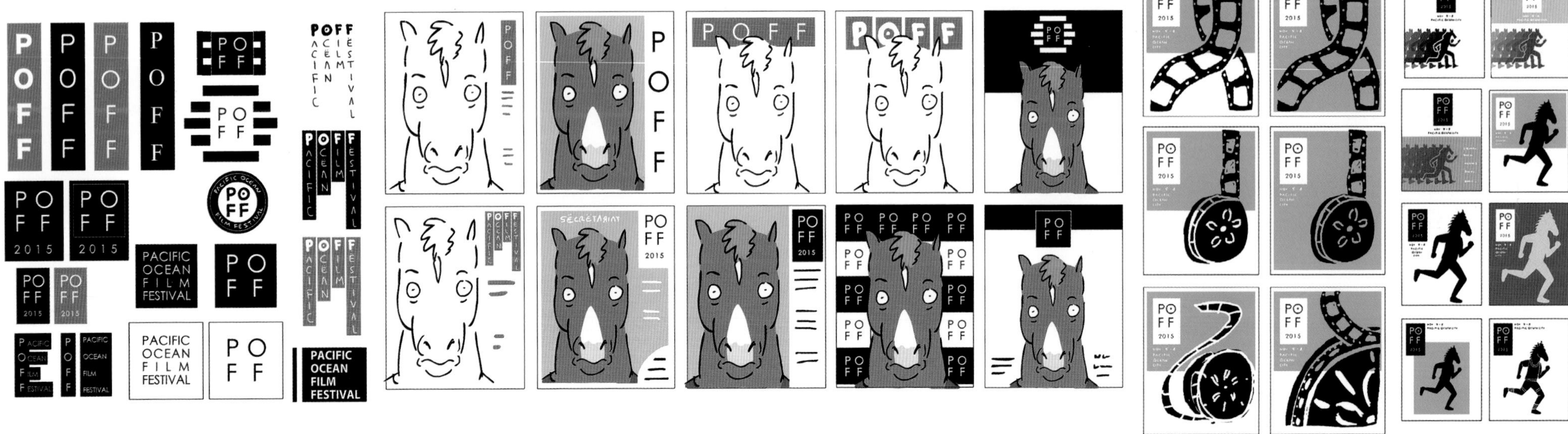

Sarah Harkey [background supervisor]: It was Elizabeth's idea to create the prop archive. Artists from both the prop and background departments are invited to submit to the library, but the busy schedule often results in the library becoming neglected during production. The libraries get their biggest overhauls at the beginning or end of a season.

Elizabeth: We get a lot of mileage out of reusing old props on this show, but we often have to update them for new scenes if they need to look a little different or if a character is handling an object in a new way. Certain things show up a lot like plates, cups, silverware, beer bottles, and cans.

Alison: I know the "Alcohol" library is separate from the "Food/Drink" library, which is probably no surprise to anyone who has seen the show.

Colleen: Some of my favorite asset libraries are the "Drugs/ Alcohol" and "Accessories/Clothing" collections. They're treasure troves.

Elizabeth: Whenever there was time I would consolidate art and make a clean turnaround of particular high-use objects. On the bridge episode—the Christmas special ["BoJack Horseman Christmas Special"]—I did turns and tilts of silverware, and we've been reusing them ever since. When Diane gets depressed, moves in with BoJack, and builds beer towers ["Yes And" S2E10], we needed a lot of cans in a lot of angles with different brands and label rotations so they didn't all look like the same thing just copied and pasted. For that, I did a master can prop with forward and back tilts, open and unopened versions, and new and crushed versions, with several different label wraps applied to the drawings. I don't think we've had to draw a single beer can since. It's hard to make a master prop for everything that might be useful, though, because an object has to really show up a lot to warrant that use of time on it. There's tons of stuff we're only drawing once. Even though we now reuse most of our drawings of magazines, we still draw new cover graphics for them—especially if they're featured. No one wants a rerun gag! The definite one-offs tend to be very episode-specific things, like the choke-off [autoerotic asphyxiation] kit. I doubt that one will make a comeback any time soon.

Sarah: The prop library was so helpful that we've also created a library of cars that contains many angles of the main characters' cars and random vehicles for populating streets. Despite this, somehow we always end up not having the angle we need, and someone has to draw more cars. The many vehicles in BoJack's world have led the background department to become less than enthusiastic about drawing them, and we've even drawn straws to see who has to draw backgrounds that require extensive new angles. [*Laughs.*] . . . And it was me. I pulled the short straw.

Casting Extras

In the normal production of a given episode, Lisa, production manager Sean Gilroy, and design coordinator Allison Morse will spend some time combing through folders of characters and "casting" extras that populate each scene as needed.

Sean Gilroy [production manager]: We always have a million things going on, on-screen. Like, if we're at a restaurant, there are people in the background eating. But we try to be efficient and reuse things we've already built all over the place. The conversation is literally like, "All right. All these little things in the background of the boards that we've kind of been ignoring for a little bit, now it's time to cast them, bring them to life." And so we pitch everything to Lisa, and she says, "Yeah, no, change that, great." And in an additional way that our show is heavily based in continuity, sometimes there are extras that have certain side stories, or really subtle things that have been going on in the background. So during this casting meeting, someone might say, "That guy wouldn't be at this restaurant, because the last time we saw him, he was at the whale stripper club."

Continued on page 174

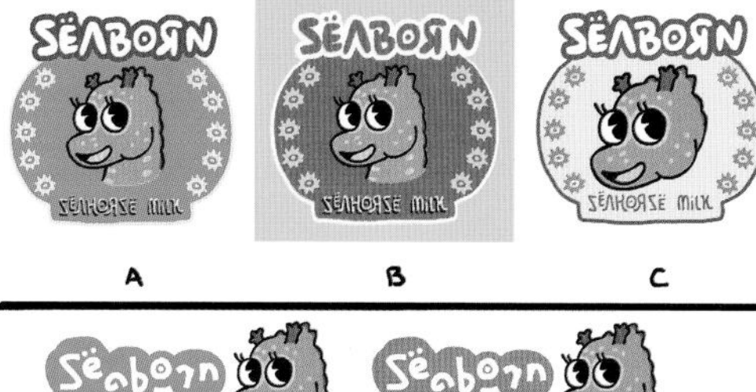
A B C

4
A B

A B

5
A

A B

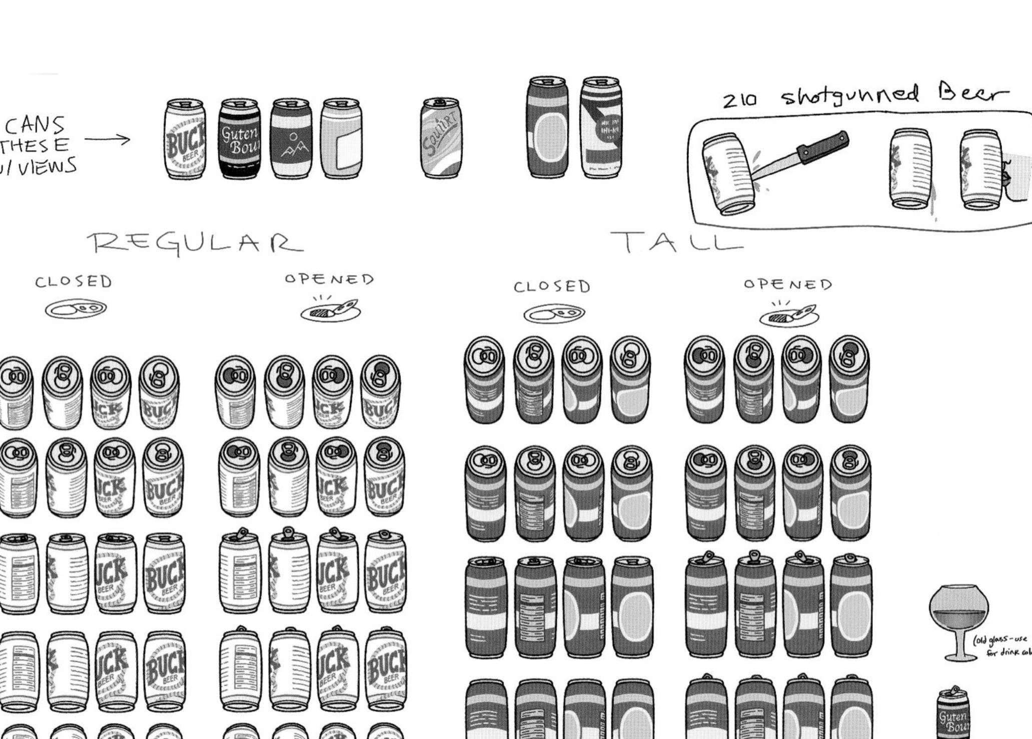
CANS THESE W/VIEWS
210 shotgunned Beer
REGULAR
TALL
CLOSED
OPENED
CLOSED
OPENED

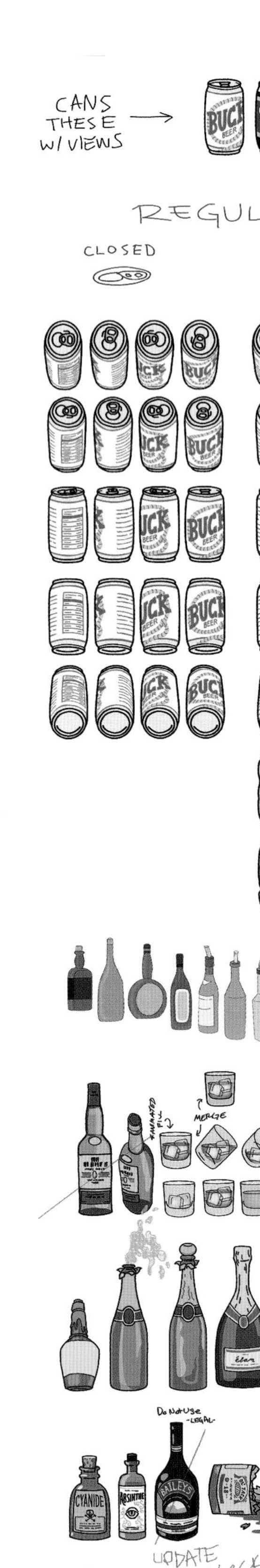

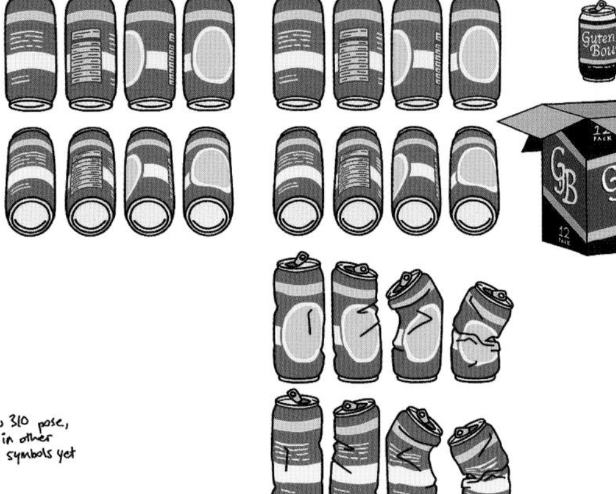

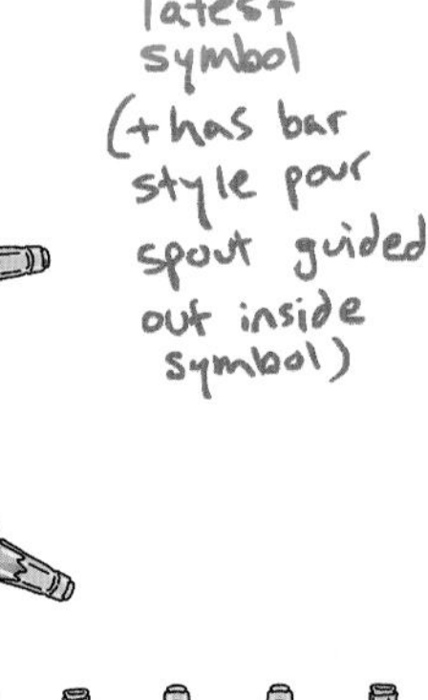
latest symbol (+has bar style pour spout guided out inside symbol)

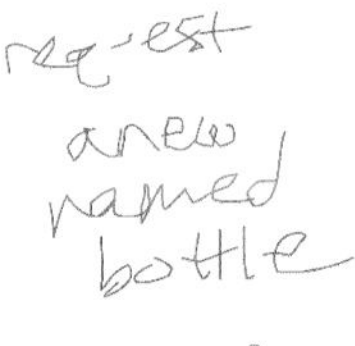

New 310 pose, not in other can symbols yet
LIQUOR
CLEAN +whiskey/ scotch pun name
301 animated pour
UPDATE
BEER
request anew named bottle
OPENED
UNOPENED
BUCK NEW COLORS

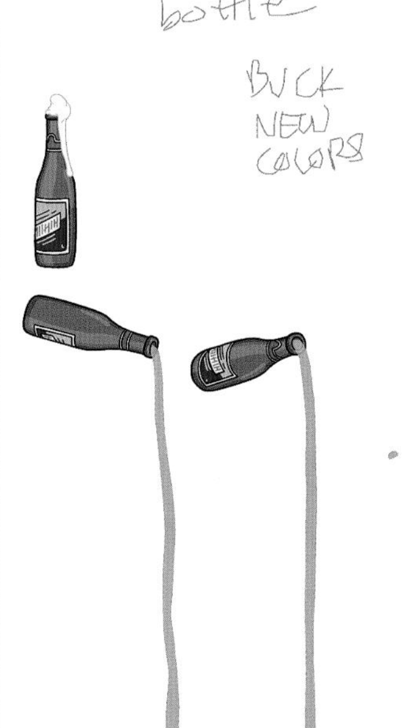

This spread: A selection of reusable drawings from the alcohol section of the *BoJack* prop library.

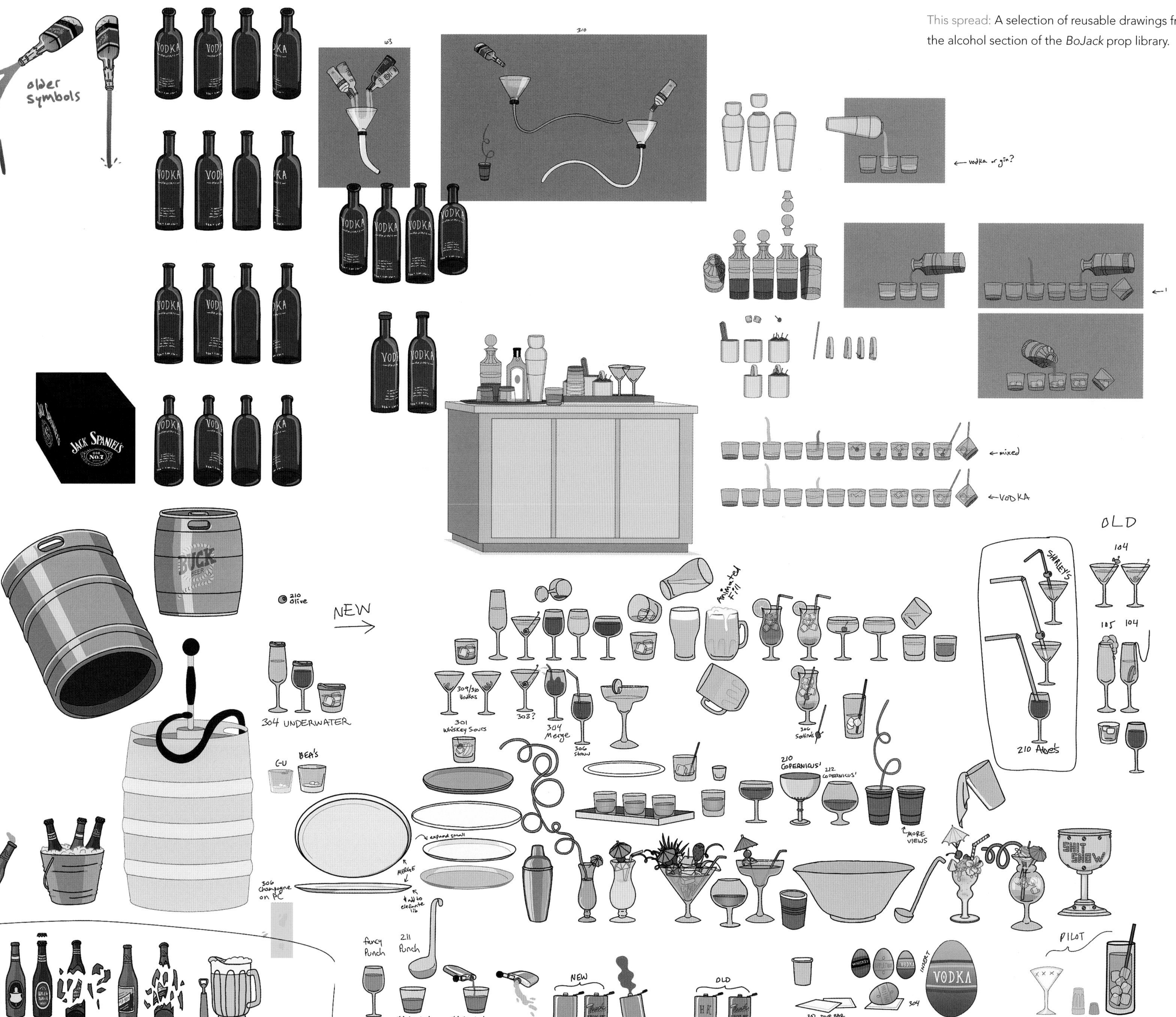

This spread: A selection of creepy crawlies and critters that populate *BoJack*'s world.

Lisa: And we have certain extras who we like bad things to happen to. There's this one extra I've named Barf, because BoJack barfs on him in the first episode, and he also falls in a hole. And, like—

Sean: He gets pushed in a fountain of cheese [in "It's You" (S3E10)]—

Lisa: Yeah. And then, later, he starts going on dates with this bird who keeps getting slammed in doors and stuff. [*Laughs.*]

Barf was also a "mark" for the same telephonic girlfriend scheme Todd was falling for in season one. To be fair, Barf also seems to often be gainfully employed as a sound tech on sets, or out and about enjoying himself on the town in the background of many scenes where he is not being barfed on. Like so much else on *BoJack*, Barf's ups and downs, deep in the background, are one more element that we can all relate to.

Paul F. Tompkins [voice of Mr. Peanutbutter]: The show is so beautiful. And the designs that Lisa has for the characters—not just on this show but on her other art—she's a wildly imaginative person but makes everything feel . . . familiar, you know? Like the postures in the characters, no matter what they are—even if they're not human beings—you just feel like you know them. I think that she has really done something so special with this world.

This page: Special pose designs of Vincent Adultman and a buck-naked BoJack.

4: Horse Moves

Storyboarding and Animating BoJack

Animation technology has made leaps and bounds over the past two decades. The ease with which thirty minutes of footage can be created now relative to the old way—pencil drawings animated on paper, inked onto celluloid, painted with cel paint, and individually photographed to film on top of a background painting, one frame at a time—is a colossal advantage for the studio and individual artist alike. Hand-drawn animation can now be storyboarded and animated directly into a computer on a drawing tablet–monitor combination. Scenes can now be reviewed instantly (no more waiting for days for the film to come back from the lab just to see your pencil test!), and episodes can be shipped around the globe in just seconds via file transfer to partner studios that complete the animation.

Modern animation software is full of tempting shortcuts and effects that can simplify animation even further. Used unwisely, however, these tricks can produce an undesirable, overly manufactured result. "Tweening," for example, is the process of using the program Flash to automatically create positions for a drawing in between two set key frames. The effect is that the static drawing—maybe a head, arm, or leg—smoothly glides from position A to B, without having to be redrawn. The resulting movement looks a bit like an animated paper doll. While a shortcut like this sounds fantastic, it can't replicate the art of hand-drawn animation, in which an artist can theoretically draw anything from any angle and animate it doing anything—given enough time. And there's the key factor: time. Animation is a laborious process, and every production's schedule and the related budget concerns are major influencers in the decision to build a pipeline around a particular set of tools.

A production like *BoJack* will find the efficiencies of Flash advantageous, especially considering that the show's strong writing and performances of the actors are at the core of the entire series. The dialogue-heavy style of the show makes it a perfect candidate for using digital puppet characters with reusable mouth shapes and expressions.

The puzzle facing every digital animation director is how to apply the technology available as tastefully as possible, without sacrificing the vitality and human touch of traditional animation—all within undoubtedly tight schedules and

budgets. In every department, the *BoJack* crew has developed methods and put in the extra effort to make the animation as special as every other element of the series.

Flash Relationship Status: It's Complicated

The software used for *BoJack* from storyboards through animation is popularly known as Flash (though it was renamed Adobe Animate in 2015). The program dates back to 1996, when it debuted as FutureSplash Animator. Used for many purposes over the years, including dynamic web design, interactive web applications, and mobile app development, it has also been employed to create animation for internet and television broadcast.

Flash was the best tool with which to deliver cartoon animation over the internet during the primarily dial-up modem days of the late 1990s and early 2000s, when limiting the kilobyte size of each file was an important concern because viewers had to wait for minutes as the crude cartoons preloaded to their computers at fifty-six kilobytes per second. Flash files use vector graphics (which create pictures out of points and the vector curves between them). Generally, vector graphics have smaller file sizes than raster graphics (which store information about every single pixel that makes up a picture). Thus, Flash cartoons led the way for entertainment on the internet, especially since streaming video was not yet practical for "Web 1.0" users (and since YouTube didn't even exist until 2005).

Even as bandwidth increased and broadband became standard, Flash never developed a reputation as a tool that could replicate the work of traditional animators who worked on paper. Instead, the advantages built into the program for those early internet animators—which include vector graphics, the ability to "tween" art objects, and a library that allows elements to be reused easily—made the program a popular choice for limited animated television shows that could use the program efficiencies to their advantage.

Flash was also widely available as consumer software, both legitimately licensed and rampantly pirated. As bandwidth concerns fell away during the later 2000s, many amateur artists continued to use Flash, creating a new wave of internet animation that also took advantage of the program's shortcuts, uploading homemade cartoons of all sorts to video websites like YouTube and Newgrounds. Over the years, "looking like Flash" became shorthand to connote digital animation that may have any combination of flat, puppetlike character designs, characters that are animated in extra-smooth sliding motions but without many original drawings, and animation that is limited in scope and/or drawn and produced amateurishly in general.

This reputation is unfair, as Flash is merely a tool, and the quality of work produced with it depends entirely on the artist or artists who wield it. This is proven again and again by directors producing incredible works of animation with the program all over the world.

Mike Hollingsworth [supervising director]: Flash is a tool that democratized the ability to animate. When Flash came along—a program created to build web banners—it suddenly gave me the ability to create tiny animated worlds around my dumb jokes. In Flash I could knock out a finished cartoon in a week and slap it up on Newgrounds, where it would get a million views. I just started banging out shorts! My first substantial one, "The Mustache Contest," was accepted into the Annecy Animation Festival, which is, like, Cannes for animation. I had found my software!

Notably, the *BoJack* crew uses the program's advantages while adding layers of custom hand-animated work, in a hybrid approach.

Mike: I've worked on many shows and projects using Flash, but in my opinion, *BoJack Horseman* is the most exquisite example of the software's capabilities.

This spread: BoJack's extensive turnaround is loaded with ready-to-be-animated mouth packs.

Below: A few bizarre Flash character errors that director Aaron Long has encountered.

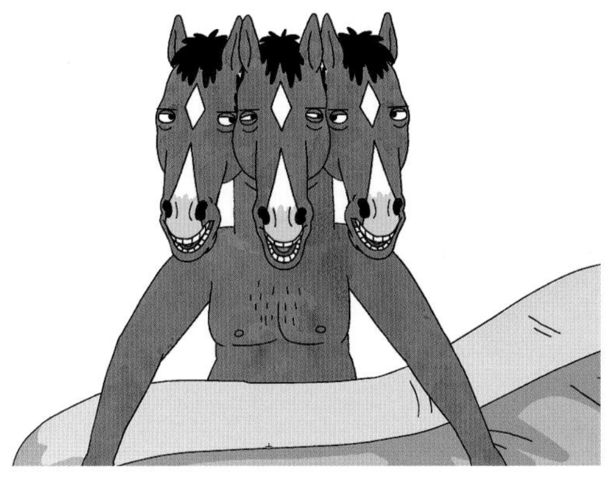

Below: A selection of pre-thumb images from director Aaron Long's pre-thumb meeting materials for "Hooray! Todd Episode!" (S4E03). These previsualized scenes were for a special montage with illustrated stills inspired by men's adventure magazines from the 1950s.

Opposite: Lisa and Alison Dubois's finished images for the episode created in an illustrative style.

The *BoJack* production's most impressive animation is evident when physical action is the focus on-screen. "Fish Out of Water" (S3E04) is the standout example from season three, as the majority of the cartoon takes place at an underwater film festival in the Pacific Ocean. Land creatures, like horses and humans, attend with clear diver helmets that muffle their voices unless used properly. BoJack does not use his properly, so the entire time he is underwater, he is unable to communicate vocally and relies on pantomime and broad gestures. Add to this the script calling for an extended chase involving BoJack, a baby seahorse, an angry shark, bioluminescent anemone, and security guards, and you've got a tall order for animation. The visual gags climax with BoJack and the baby seahorse navigating through a freshwater taffy factory, bringing to mind the comic action from films such as the Daffy Duck and Porky Pig cartoon *Baby Bottleneck* and Charlie Chaplin's *Modern Times*, among others.

The work of the *BoJack* storyboarders, directors, and animators also shines visually whenever there is the opportunity for any action beyond the typical dialogue. When one of Todd's schemes involves a gigantic contraption exploding, or BoJack is running over a deer-man with his car, or Sextina Aquafina's latest music video features coat-hanger spaceships blasting a space fetus with lasers, the artists use the language of film to choose the most effective sequences of shots to sell the comedy or drama—or dramedy.

Pre-Thumbing Before Thumbing

After the script is written and the actors have recorded their dialogue, but before the storyboard is drawn, there is a pre-thumb meeting, also sometimes known as a breakdown meeting.

Mike: Once we get our hands on a script, the director will just sit with the script for a week and come up with all their concepts, as well as thumbnails of different backgrounds, different locations, and how they would approach each scene. And then, at the end of that week, we sit down and have a pre-thumb pitch with RNS—Raphael [Bob-Waksberg], Noel [Bright], and Steve [Cohen]—and pitch all these ideas.

Amy Winfrey [director]: At the pre-thumb meeting, we go over the script, ask questions, show reference materials, and share our ideas about staging and about what we can reuse and what needs to be created new.

Eric Blyler [line producer]: Previsualization is the time to explore new ideas and methods, and also to work out the best way to tell the story of each particular episode. In the pre-thumb meetings and during the thumbnail stage, we're working with roughly drawn images that are quick to draw and redraw. We like to encourage the directors to shoot for the stars and this is the best time for that. As Mike Hollingsworth likes to say, "Working in animation is like working with cement"—in that the more time you spend on something, the more solid it becomes as the cement dries, so to speak, and it becomes more difficult to work with and make changes. Once we move into the final clean storyboards, we are primarily focusing on acting and blocking and usually not still working out the bigger concepts of an episode.

Next, the thumbnail board is created, which is the first complete (but roughly drawn) visual version of an episode. It is loosely sketched directly in Flash or another program like Photoshop if preferred by the episode director and storyboard artists. Because the show is script-driven, the dialogue has already been recorded and edited into a radio play. An advantage of this process is that the thumbnail boards can directly reference the intonation of the actors' final dialogue.

Matt Garofalo [director]: We go into thumbing the episode for a week. The thumbs are just "keep 'em loose," so we can focus on acting, get the pace of everything.

Continued on page 184

Pre-Thumbs

This spread: A selection of pre-thumb images from director Tim Rauch's pre-thumb meeting materials for "What Time Is It Right Now" (S4E12). Tim's initial direction suggestion was to style this sequence in stark black, white, and red graphics with a nod to the design and illustration work of Paul Rand, Saul Bass, and UPA's short 1953 animated horror film *The Tell-Tale Heart*, directed by Ted Parmelee.

Dialog
I went to every hospital and county clerk house in LA.

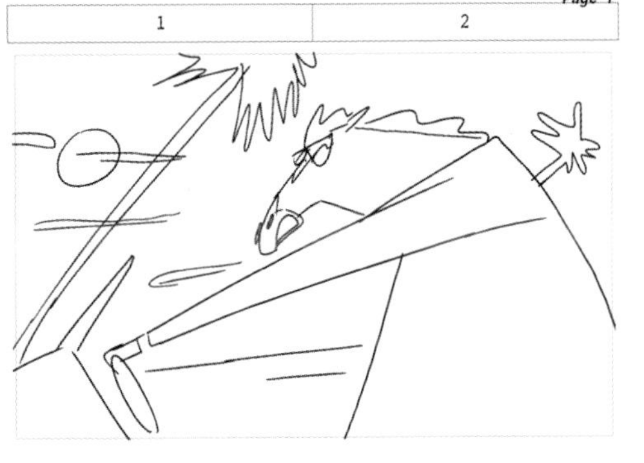

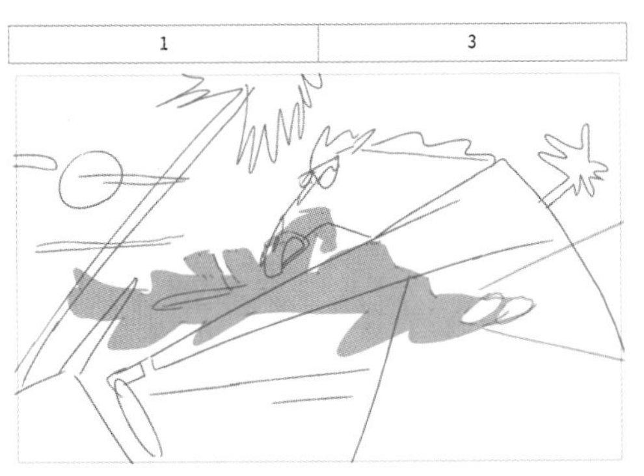

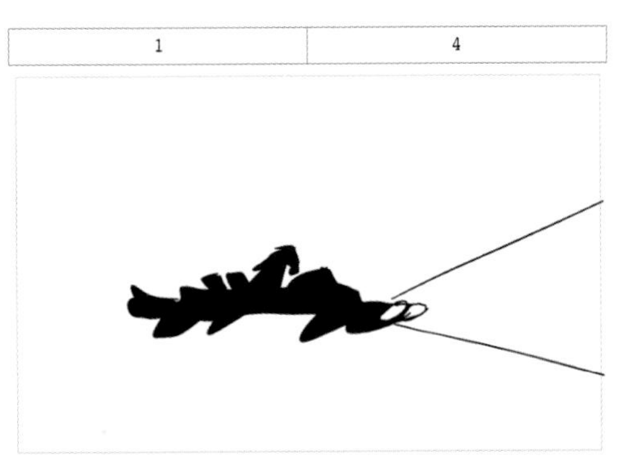

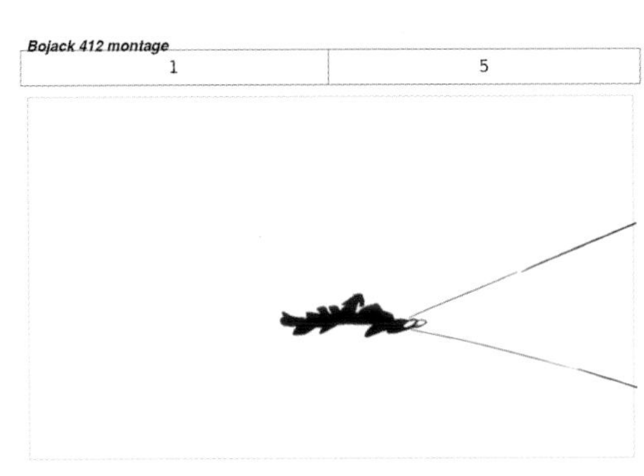

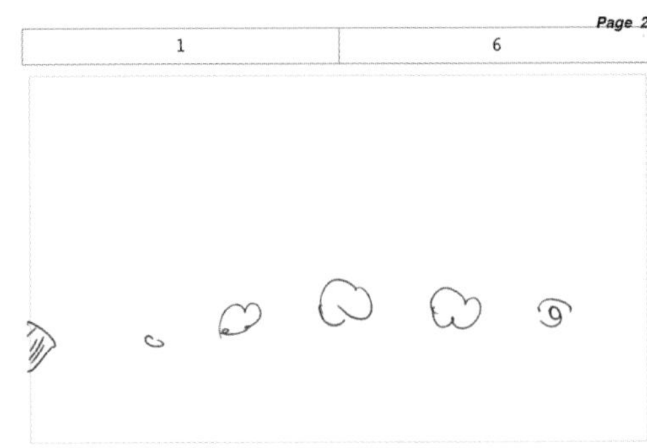

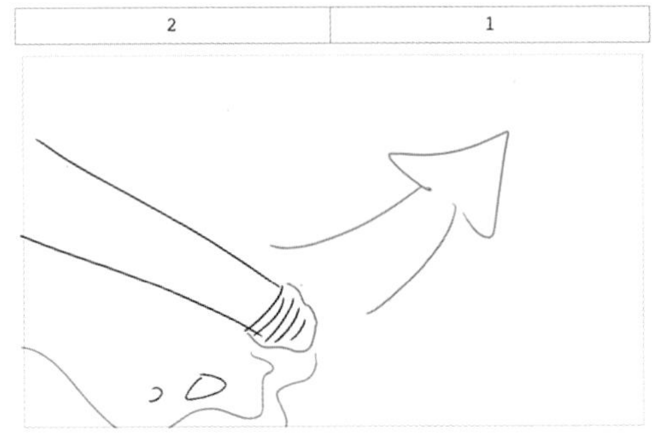

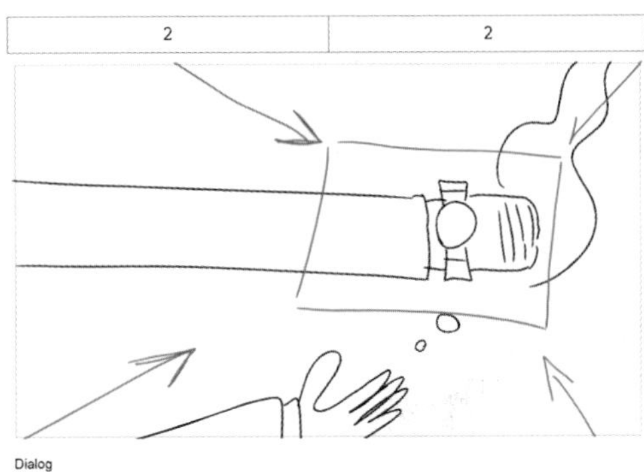

Dialog
I waited in lines.

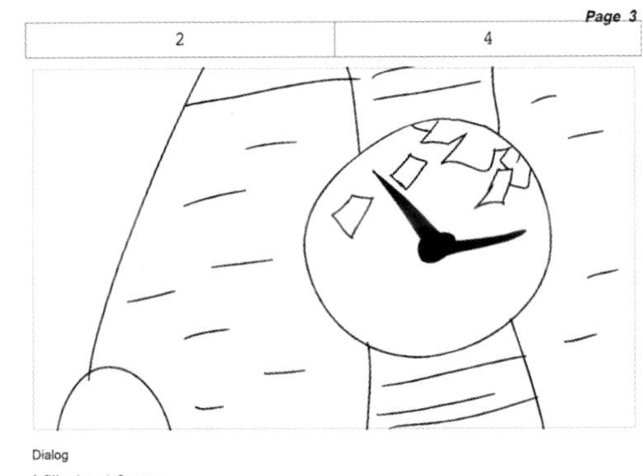

Dialog
I filled out forms-

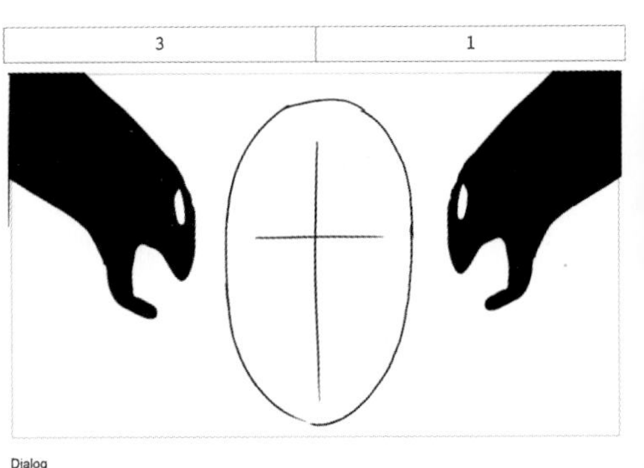

Dialog
talked to anyone who would talk to me-

3	2

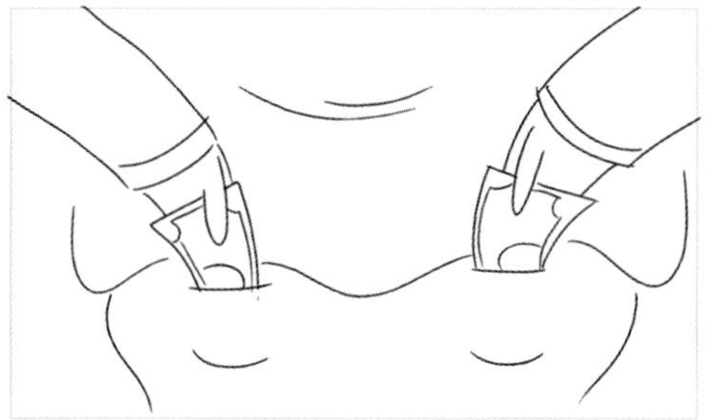

Dialog

bribed anyone who would take a bribe.

3	3

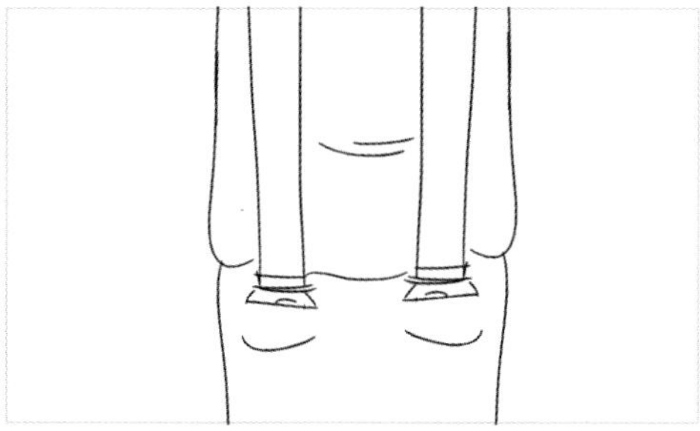

3	4

3	5

Dialog

I wouldn't rest until I knew I'd done everything I could.

3	6

3	7

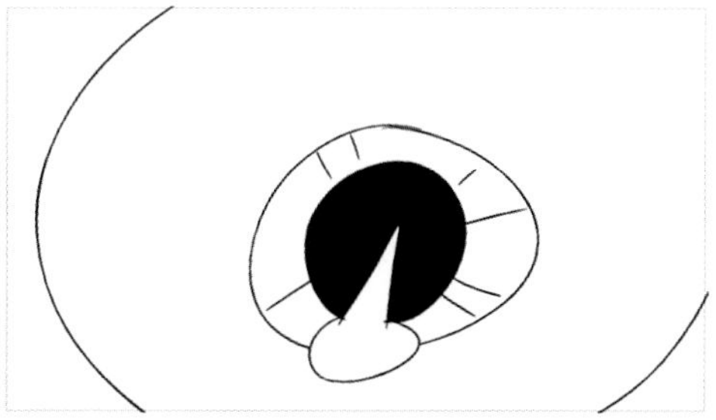

Dialog

I didn't want to be-

3	8

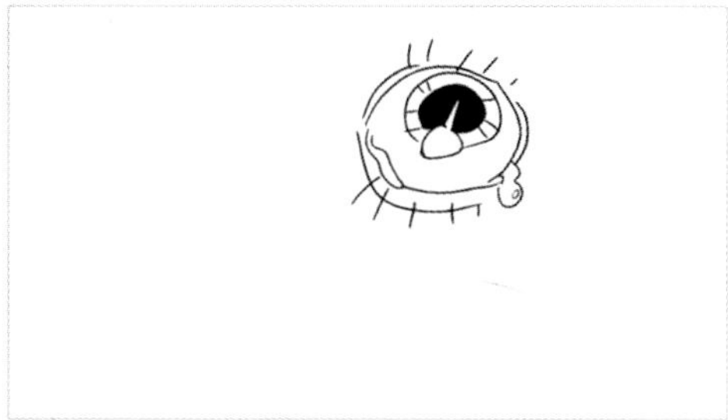

Dialog

like the guy at the end of Chandler's List.

- Did you say Chandler's List?

3	9

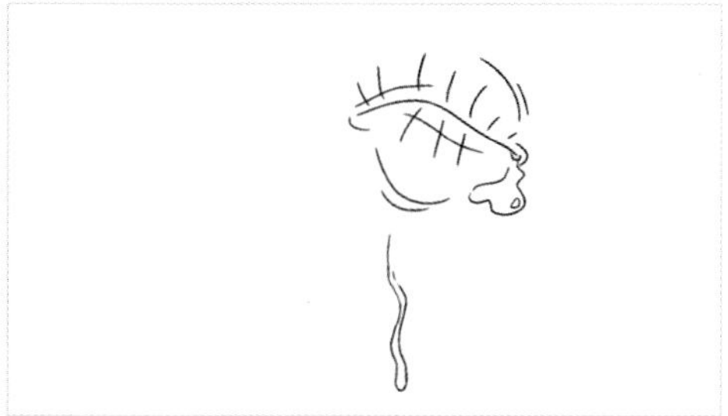

Dialog

But there was no record of a little horse girl born on Hollyhock's birthday.

3	10

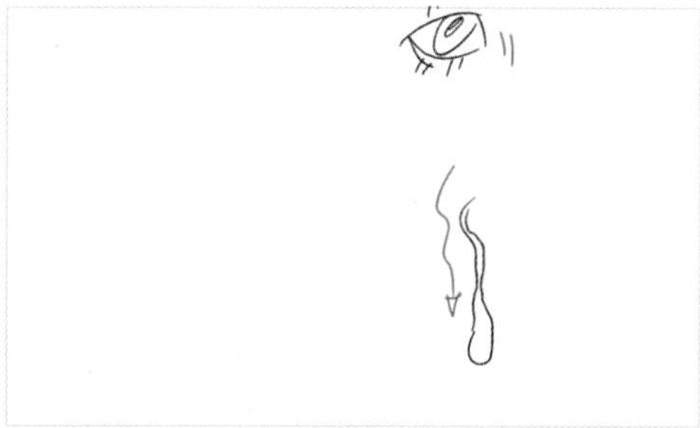

Dialog

-Okay so-

3	11

Dialog

In LA. Because Hollyhock wasn't born in LA. She was born in San Francisco.

3	12

Dialog

I got a little bug in my brain-

3	13

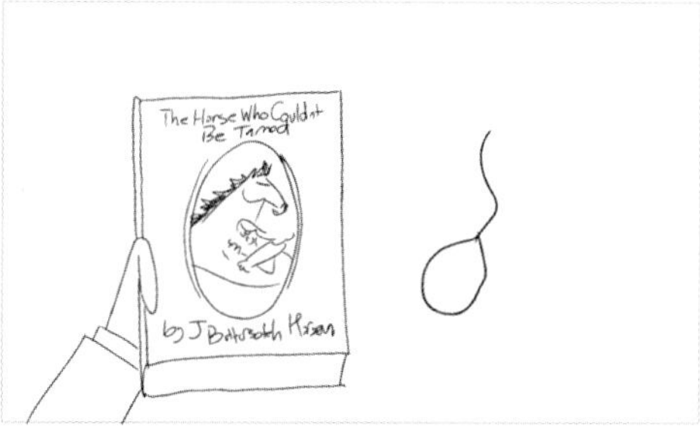

Dialog

-hat my father knocked up the help.

3	14

Dialog

So I went up there-

3	15

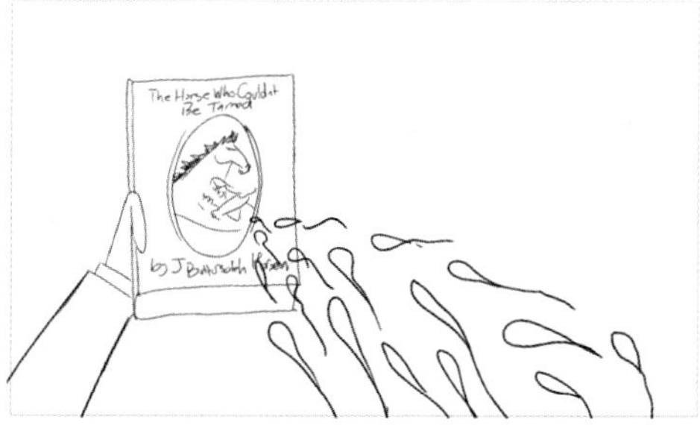

Dialog

did the whole thing again--

3	16

Dialog

and-

3	17

Dialog

I found it.

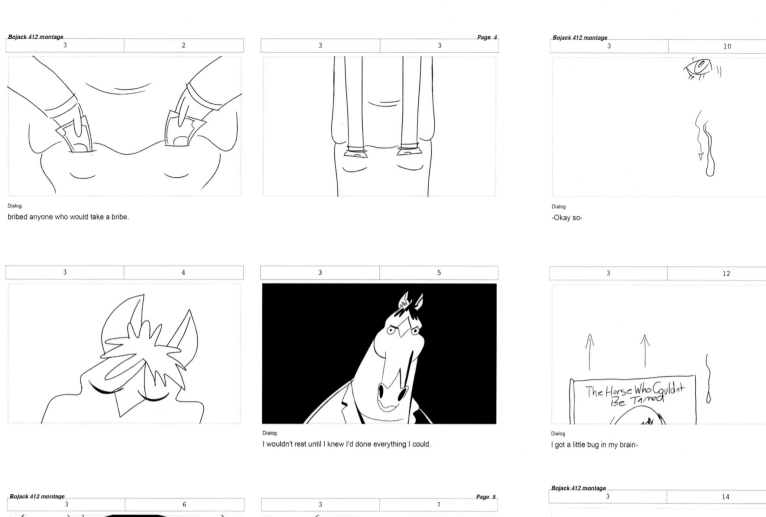

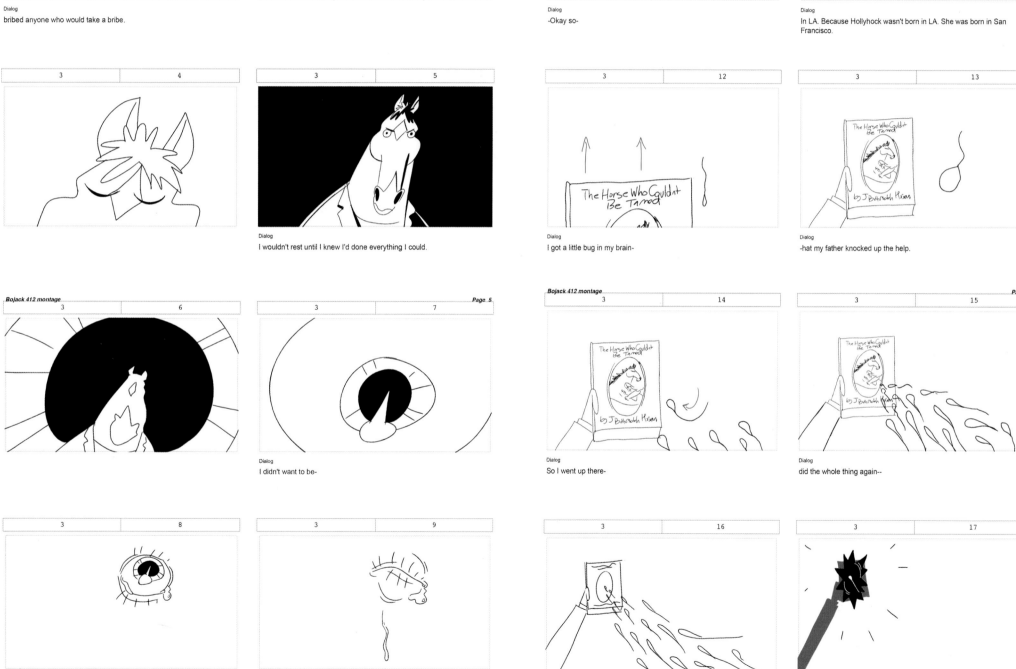

Amy W.: While some thumbnails are worked out in preparation for the pre-thumb meeting, we typically work with a team of two storyboard artists and an assistant director for a week on thumbnails. During this week, the boards are also timed to the radio play.

I like to start the thumbnail process off by going over the script with my team, showing them reference material and talking through sequences so that we can all contribute ideas. We tend to spend a lot of time coming up with animal gags and funny store names.

Anne Walker Farrell [director]: I learned this process from Amy and use it in my own episode directing. While I understand the appeal of thumbing everything yourself, it's ultimately a ton of work, and it's kind of unnecessary. Sometimes I'll take on a sequence myself, like the cold open from "The Old Sugarman Place" [S4E02], but generally I feel the episode is much stronger when you can come together with a team you trust and all bring ideas to the table. When everyone feels like they're contributing to the final product, everyone's way more excited about working on it and helping it come together.

Then the crew reviews the animatic, which consists of thumbnail storyboard images paired with the recorded dialogue and played back as a complete, rough version of the episode. The review meeting lets the team make any important structural adjustments before proceeding further, though the changes here don't generally affect the writing.

Final Storyboard

Next, the directors and their storyboard crews create the final storyboards in Flash. Some older backgrounds are reused, and those panels have the final artwork in place, while others are sketches of scenes that the background department is working on finishing. At this stage, the "chicken scratch" thumbnail characters get replaced with the final on-model puppet characters set up in their key poses for each panel. This provides the clearest blueprint possible for the Korean animation studio to follow when they are tasked with animating each scene.

The detailed character puppets have many angles and built-in head options to choose from, especially for the main cast. The majority of the storyboard poses can be created with these existing puppet options. However, the director and storyboard artists still have to do a substantial amount of custom work.

Matt: We do a lot of redrawing of hands, and if there's any crazy facial expression or special poses. We draw a lot of the torso movement. Even though we have a ton of stock hands that we can reuse over and over, there's still a lot of redrawing of arms—you know, moving around in space. You can't rely too heavily on the puppets, but you take advantage of them when you can.

Amy W.: Mike Hollingsworth always insists on us keeping characters busy in novel ways, and so we are constantly coming up with new poses for everyone. Next time you watch a *BoJack* episode, watch the background characters! No one is standing still. People with drinks have to sip them. People at restaurants have to be eating. Passersby on the street are on phones, looking at things, talking to each other. Sometimes it's normal; other times it's crazy and surreal, like a couple of seagulls harassing a neighboring table at a restaurant, trying to steal fries. Mike is a stickler about this but I think, again, it makes the world we're building richer and crazier.

Storyboard Theories

Directing and storyboarding an episode of *BoJack* requires being disciplined, starting simply, and knowing when to occasionally break out of the mold and draw an intense sequence of psychedelic horror-show hallucinations.

Matt: As a board artist, you always want to be conservative about background usage. If we can reuse a background by

This spread: A fraction of the psychedelic chaos from "Downer Ending" (S1E11), including Diane's mutating flesh sequence, an apparent tribute to the climactic scene in Katsuhiro Otomo's *Akira*.

designing a master shot and just punching in on it a number of times for the medium and close-up shots, that's probably going to go over really well. I just focus a lot on the character acting, because that's going to sell it.

Amy W.: We don't tend to use more than one or two angles in a sequence. However, there are always stylish exceptions to those rules. We are not shy about finding moments for more cinematic staging.

Aaron Long [director]: The directors are encouraged to bring bold ideas when we start an episode. We're always trying things we haven't done before, new ways to tell the stories. It all gets filtered through Mike Hollingsworth's sensibilities of timing, acting, and visual storytelling, as well as Raphael's. We generally lean toward staging things simply, partly for the comedy and partly because, in the beginning, there was an effort to make it feel like a three-camera sitcom—but that's largely fallen away as the show's become more ambitious with each season.

Amy W.: For "Downer Ending" [S1E11], there was originally a part in the script during BoJack's drug trip when BoJack is running through his own brain that just said, "Weird things happen." I viewed this as a great opportunity to add more fun drug trippiness! I worked with my storyboard team to come up with some interesting additional shots for BoJack to run through, such as Herb turning into a skeleton and BoJack encountering a diner full of Mr. Peanutbutters and a giant Mr. Peanutbutter. Unfortunately, they didn't budget for using Paul F. Tompkins, the voice of Mr. Peanutbutter, in this episode, since it wasn't originally in the script, so we had to use a big weird laugh for giant Mr. Peanutbutter instead of his actual voice.

In "Escape from L.A." [S2E11], there was a late decision to add a sequence set to music of BoJack coming back to Los Angeles atop his towed yacht. For the animatic, I put together a sequence that was inspired by the opening credits, and that showed the passage of time through changing sky colors. I used some stock photos mixed with photos of the sky from my own vacations to Greece and Peru. Raphael, Noel, and Steve liked the look of the photos, so we ended up using them in the final episode.

In "That Went Well" [S3E12], I asked Anne what sequence she would like to work on. She instantly said she wanted the final sequence of BoJack driving and finding a herd of wild horses. She knew what she wanted for that sequence and thumbed it so beautifully that I had absolutely no notes on it. Sometimes my job as a director is to know when to just let my board artists shine.

My assistant director Peter Merryman did a great job with the ski sequences in season four, episode one, "See Mr. Peanutbutter Run." For inspiration, we watched *Downhill Racer* and the ski sequences in *The Spy Who Loved Me*, and Peter really managed to re-create the great dynamic POV shots from those films for Mr. Peanutbutter, Woodchuck, and Todd.

In season four, episode nine, "Ruthie," we made a fun, photo-collage style for Princess Carolyn's ancestors. I spent a lot of time looking in the Library of Congress database for tenement photos, and I solicited cat photos from the crew! I used a photo of my pet chicken as a captain of the boat headed for Ellis Island. I also photographed arms and hands holding some of my mother-in-law's old silver so that we could use more arm poses on the characters. The final sequence was boarded and animated in-house by Peter Merryman.

Aaron: For the nonverbal episode, "Fish Out of Water" [S3E04], the emotional content of the story was completely locked in the script, but a lot of the action was necessarily vague in places. The process for that episode wound up being different from any other, since the show is usually so dialogue-based. It was a fun challenge where the artists were able to take the lead on many things. It felt like we had freedom to try almost anything we wanted if it truly served the story, and as a result,

Continued on page 196

"Downer Ending"

This spread: Thumbnail storyboards by Natasha Kline from "Downner Ending" (S1E11).

SOME STORYBOARDING NOTES

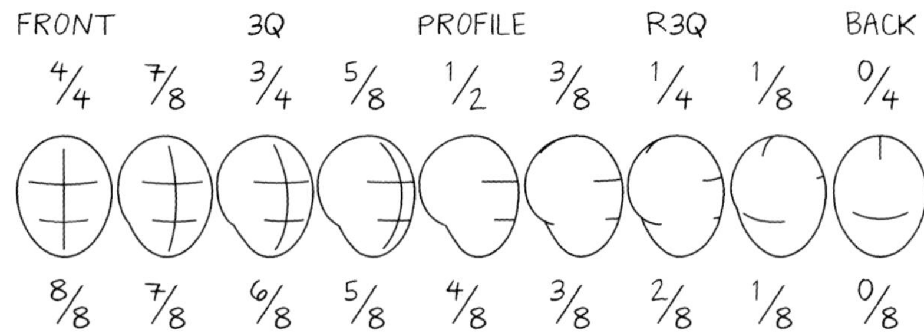

- Work clean! You're not the only one who will have to open your file. Create masters (BG and character layout) in symbols then find your shots and create your camera moves on the main stage with that symbol.
- Use high quality (not high file size) screen grabs for BGs instead of the actual line work from the BG's flash file.
- Don't break the 4th wall. Only show three angles in one setting at a time. Noel wants the camera to be used like it would be on a sitcom like Seinfeld. What was in front of Jerry's sofa? Who knows?
- Start sequences with your master shot (wide shot). Noel always wants to see where everyone is and what's going on in the room before we get into the action.
- CUT DON'T PAN. Yes we make small adjustments for characters entering the shot and an occasional joke reveal, but on BoJack we favor cutting around over panning around.
- Make sure you don't have too many singles in a row. A typical shot flow should be Master - Medium - Single - Single - Medium - Single - Single. NOT Master - Medium - Single - Single - Single - Single- Single - Single - Etc.
- RESPECT LIQUIDS!!! If a character is holding a drink make sure they're not gesturing with it in a way that would cause the drink to spill or splash. ALSO, if a charcter is holding a drink they should -- drink it.

V.06 09/28/17

SOME STORYBOARDING NOTES

FILM MAKING STUFF -- CONT'D

- Don't go directly from the Master to a Single. It's too jarring. Going - Master - Medium - Single - is more comfortable.
- SCALE! Watch that the scale of your characters is correct in relation to each other and correct in relation to their environment.
- EYE LINES! Make sure the characters are looking where they're supposed to be looking -- at the other character, at a prop they're about to pick up, at the TV, etc.
- Avoid looking straight into the camera.
- Give characters business like texting, drinking, cleaning their glasses, etc. They can't just be standing around talking all the time.
- 4th wall entrances and exits should be suggested but then hidden with a single on another character.
- Do everything you can to keep characters in their 3/4 poses while they're acting, especially the humans because they look weird in profile. The exception to this is BoJack, who has a particularly pleasing profile that can be used liberally. So turn that snout!
- Try to stay away from "indicating." If Todd says, "I'm here because you need me," he doesn't need to point to himself and then point to BoJack.
- DO NOT CUT ON A LINE OF DIALOGUE — the person who is talking needs to be onscreen. Unless director tells otherwise.
- Keep the extras alive!
- Avoid closing characters eyes for acting in your boards. It doesn't look right when the animation comes back.

V.06 09/28/17

This spread: A selection of pages from the series bible, a document that codifies best practices for the production.

SOME STORYBOARDING NOTES

FILM MAKING STUFF -- CONT'D

- BoJack's living room is always cluttered with Todd's stuff (clothes, blanket, backpack, etc).
- When characters shake hands it should always be with their right hands.
- MAKE SURE ALL REFERENCES TO ANIMALS SHOW THEM IN THEIR HUMANOID FORM.
- Don't use the actual names of magazines or stores. Make up a joke or use something similar. For example, "Best Buy" becomes "Beast Buy." We are not afraid of animal puns.
- No fan art. None of the characters should be designed to look like existing characters (i.e. Snoopy, Bugs Bunny, Kermit the Frog) unless that is a specific joke in the script.
- No robotic clapping, laughing, etc. in group shots. Separate levels and stagger motion so they don't move in sync.
- WE CAN ADD TIME TO THE RADIOPLAY - Cut it up! The editors don't always leave time for physical business so we frequently need to add time.
- PROPS ARE CHARACTERS TOO!!! Track their storyline through a sequence just like you'd track BoJack's storyline. If a character is holding a plate one second and then it's gone the next we'd better see him put it down or head to the kitchen where it's logical that he probably put it in the sink.

DON'T PULL US OUT OF A CHARACTER'S BUTT!

V.06 09/28/17

FINALLY, AND IN CONCLUSION, AND IN SUMMARY

FRESH EYES!!! Show your scene to your assistant director or to your neighbor. You'll be amazed what they can spot just because they're looking at your scene for the first time.

CHECK THESE THINGS BEFORE YOU TURN IN A SCENE:

- ARE THE CHARACTERS SCALED CORRECTLY?
- IS THE TIMING OF THE ACTING CORRECT?
- ARE THE PROPS BEING HANDLED CORRECTLY?
- ARE THEY OVERACTING?
  - Mike tends to strip poses out of the file, we don't have to hit every beat.
  - A shrug goes a long way!
- NO UNDERPOSING.
  - Does everyone have their arms glued to their sides?
  - Give characters something to do.
- CAN THESE BOARDS BE ANIMATED?
  - If the character hits a new pose on every line, when animated, they're going to look like a moth caught in a bug-zapper.
  - Make sure walking is properly paced.
- BE AWARE OF THE FRAMING OF THE SHOT.
  - A lot of boarders will pose stuff out inside the scene symbol and lose focus of the actual shot flow. So you end up boarding for a wide but in actuality you're in a single. This leads to a lot of lopped off finger tips on the bottom of the screen.

- IF YOU GET the BEACH BALL of death on your computer, PLEASE CONTACT TECH

V.06 09/28/17

Thumbnail Storyboards

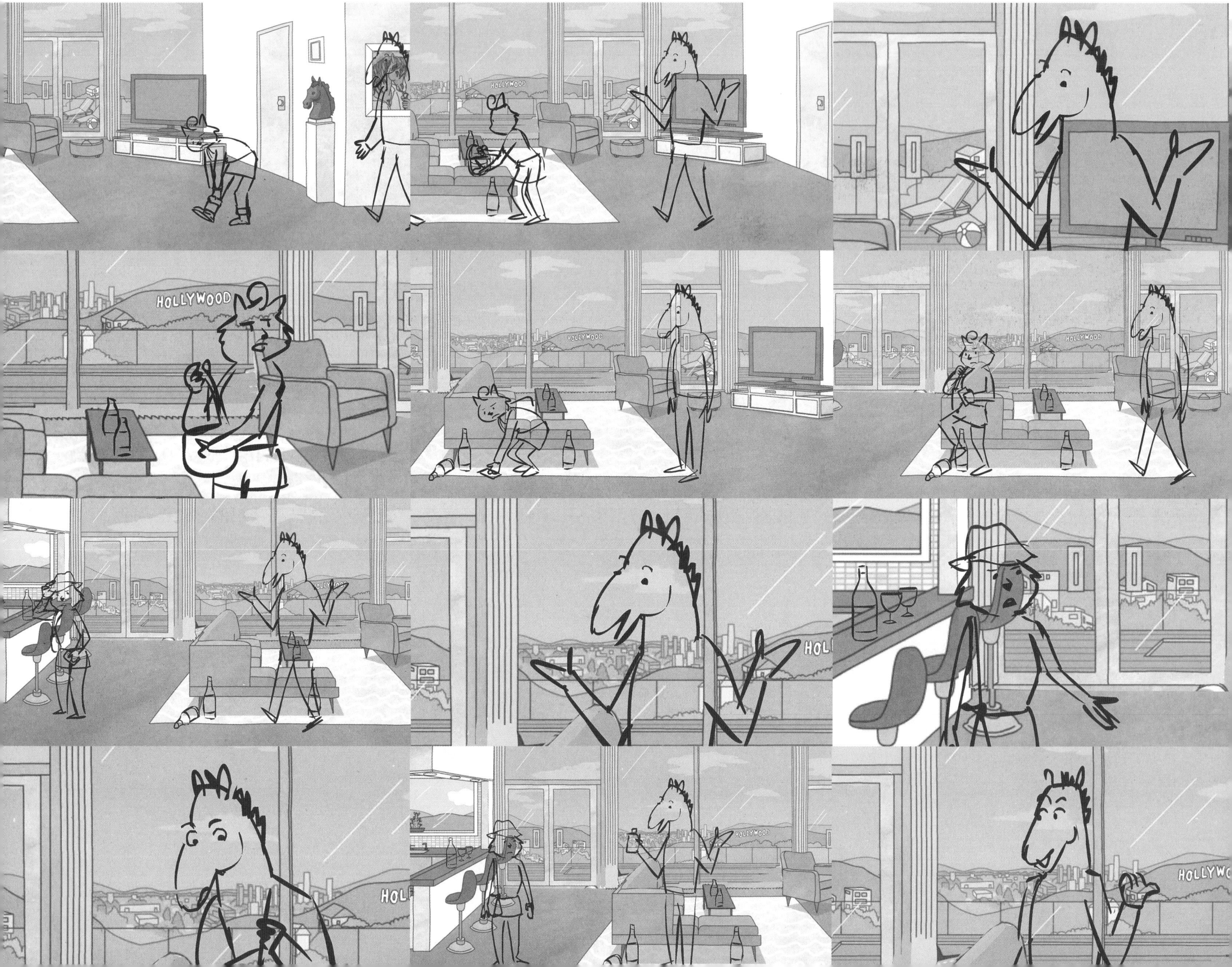

This spread: The same opening scene of "The BoJack Horseman Show" (S3E02) thumbnail storyboard versions 9B and 11. Though the location changed, in both boards the artists keep the characters busy with lots of "business" to do while talking, and hit a rhythm of medium and close-up single shots.

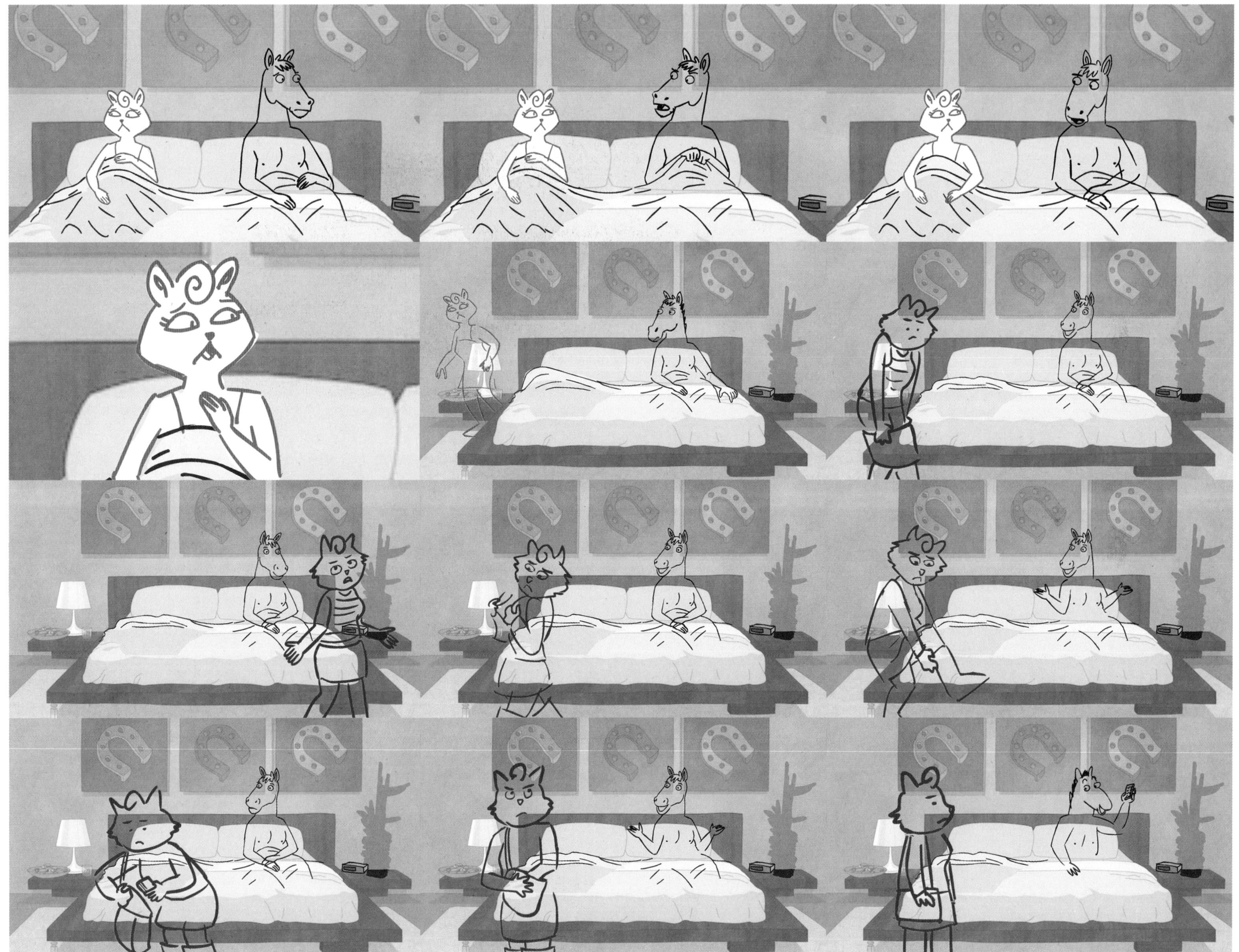

THUMBS —TO→ BOARDS —TO→ FINAL ANIMATION

THUMBS THUMBS

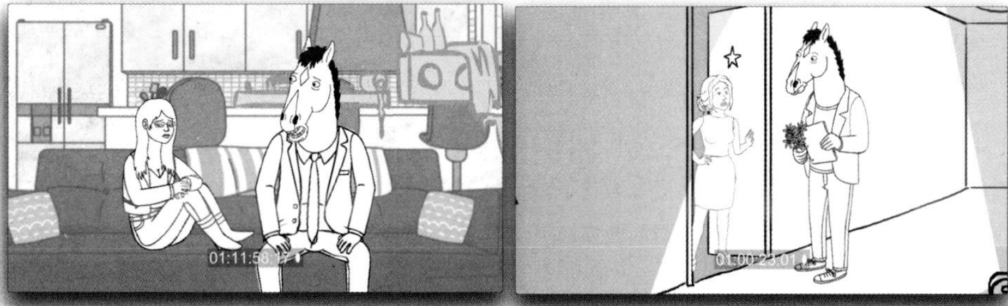

STORYBOARDS STORYBOARDS

FINAL ANIMATION FINAL ANIMATION

V.06 09/28/17

BOJACK HORSEMAN STORYBOARD TECHNIQUES

HOW ON-MODEL SHOULD MY DRAWINGS OF THE CHARACTERS BE?

WE ALL LOVE NICE CLEAN DRAWINGS IN THE STORYBOARDS. UNFORTUNATELY THE SCHEDULE DOESN'T ALWAYS PERMIT US TO WORK THIS CLEAN.

YOU CAN WORK LOOSER AS LONG AS THE SCALE IS CORRECT AND THE ANATOMY IS ON POINT.

YOU CAN AND SHOULD WORK LOOSER IN ACTION SCENES.

YOU DON'T ALWAYS HAVE TO DRAW DETAILS LIKE BOJACK'S LAPEL AND COLLAR.

JUST DON'T GET TOO LOOSE.

V.06 09/28/17

This spread: Pages from the series bible with specifics on the process of and how to approach storyboarding.

BOJACK HORSEMAN STORYBOARD TECHNIQUES

HOW DETAILED SHOULD MY DRAWING OF THE BACKGROUND BE?

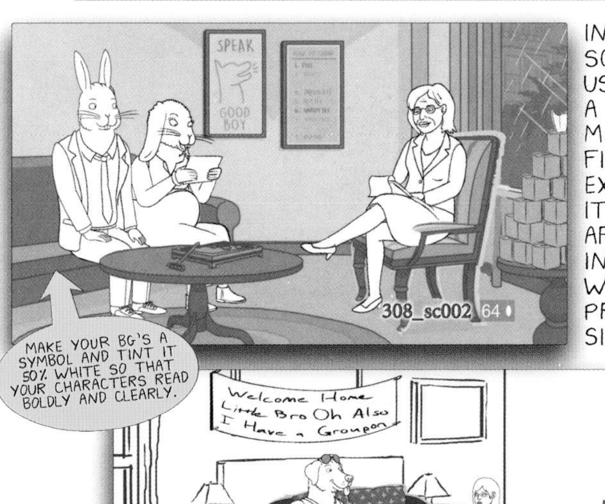

IN MANY INSTANCES THE SCENE WILL CALL FOR THE USE OF A BACKGROUND FROM A PREVIOUS SEASON. PLEASE MAKE SURE TO ALWAYS FIND AND USE THESE EXISTING FILES. ALTHOUGH IT'S REUSE, DON'T BE AFRAID TO ALTER THE BG. IN THIS EXAMPLE THE CHAIR WAS SCOOTED UP AND NEW PROPS WERE ADDED TO THE SIDE TABLE.

THE DRAWING CAN BE PRETTY SIMPLE AS LONG AS THE PERSPECTIVE IS SOUND AND IT CLEARLY SUGGESTS THE PROPER LOCATION.

BUT IF YOU REALLY NEED TO SELL A VISUAL GAG OR AN ATMOSPHERIC FEELING YOU'LL HAVE TO GET IN THERE AND ADD WAY MORE DETAIL TO THE BACKGROUND.

IN THE PAST WE'VE ALSO BOARDED OVER SKETCHUP MODELS AND PHOTOGRAPHS.

V.06 09/28/17

BOJACK HORSEMAN STORYBOARD TECHNIQUES

HOW SHOULD I APPROACH BOARDING EXTRAS?

EXTRAS WILL BE "CAST" AFTER THE BOARDS ARE LOCKED BY OUR DESIGN COORDINATOR. UNLESS YOU HAVE A PARTICULAR REASON TO DRAW A DETAILED EXTRA WE SUGGEST YOU KEEP THEM GENERIC. WE'D RATHER YOU TAKE THAT ENERGY AND PUT IT INTO THE EXTRA'S ACTING.

WE HAVE CREATED MALE AND FEMALE "EXTRA" STORYBOARD PUPPETS FOR YOUR USE. THEY HAVE LOTS OF POSES BAKED IN! ESPECIALLY HELPFUL ARE ALL THE EATING AND DRINKING POSES AS WE FREQUENTLY HAVE TO POPULATE RESTAURANTS AND BARS.

SOMETIMES IT'S FASTER TO JUST NOODLE IN A BUNCH OF EXTRAS. THIS IS GREAT TOO! JUST MAKE SURE YOU KEEP THEM ALL ALIVE.

EXTRAS DON'T NEED TO BE PRETTY THEY JUST NEED TO TELL OUR STAFF AND THE OVER-SEAS STUDIO, "THERE'S MEANT TO BE A CHARACTER HERE AND SHE'S CLAPPING."

V.06 09/28/17

This spread: When the script calls for action, it usually requires unique key poses of the characters to be drawn in the storyboards that the standard puppet characters could not accommodate. Princess Carolyn and BoJack's fight in "Best Thing That Ever Happened" (S3E09) is an example of a scene that needed extensive original poses.

Anne Walker Farrel: The scene—which runs around twenty seconds in total—took me a solid week to board. I was tracking whose claws were in whose mane, who was shoving who away, and who knocked over what in the restaurant. We mostly stick to pretty simple staging, so turning these characters—who are fairly stylized, with a lot of textures and patterns and details to track—360 degrees and upside down and forward and backward was a challenge. Princess Carolyn is one of my favorite characters in the show, though, so it was fun to kind of break the rules with her and get some crazy action stuff in.

This page: "Commence Fracking" (S4E04) features a generous amount of cleverly obscured on-screen sex which resulted in one of the funnier special pose models created: the disembodied under-the-blanket legs model (far left).

the storyboarders really got to "own" their sequences—particularly James Bowman, who did several standout sections, like BoJack bouncing after the baby through the tunnels.

"Time's Arrow" [S4E11] was the most exciting episode for me so far, because of the surreal, time-traveling nature of the story. Just about every scene has some weird visual element, most of which came from Mike Hollingsworth and me. We tried to find unique transitions between scenes, as well as constant visual cues to remind the audience that this wasn't a conventional biopic-style life story, but hopping through faded memories. Things like pictures on the walls changing, characters without faces because Beatrice can't remember them, et cetera. I storyboarded the climax montage, where Beatrice and Henrietta give birth. It seemed like it was going to be a tough sequence to crack, but it became much easier when I realized I could visually link their stories through screen direction, showing them in the same angle as their babies are taken away from them.

Anne: "Stupid Piece of Sh*t" [S4E06] is the episode I think I'm proudest of. We dive into BoJack's head, and my assistant director Otto Murga and I decided we wanted to do something crazy and unexpected. We decided on a United Productions of America style. BoJack is impatient and immature and hedonistic—how appropriate that he would see the world like an angry five-year-old, scribbling with crayons! The storyboard team (and animation team) ran with it, creating these quick-cut, laugh-out-loud, insane sequences as we follow BoJack around his mind and ultimately into the darkness of it. I boarded the last dive into BoJack's mind the week after the 2016 election. I was in a dark place—I've struggled with depression and anxiety my whole life—and being able to scream a lot of what I was feeling into the art I was making helped. I love this episode for many reasons, perhaps most of all because, in true *BoJack* fashion, it doesn't feel the need to tell the viewer it's all gonna be OK in the end. The final sequence of the episode, on BoJack's deck (storyboarded by Tristyn Pease), is this quiet, still moment following a tornado of color and shape and scribble—but it's not a resolution. It gave me goose bumps when I saw it all put together. As Amy said, sometimes the best part of directing is letting my board artists be amazing.

Matt: Season four, episode four ["Commence Fracking"] was pretty straightforward. Tons of sex, and us trying to hide that tons of sex. At first, we were going in a pretty graphic direction with the sex scenes and showing some skin . . . fur? It ended up being more shock than humor. I believe it was written that BoJack and Marcie were having sex up against one of the shelves, and we covered them up with an end table and lamp. It was funny in its own way, but too graphic and not really in the comedic style of the show. We decided to put BoJack and Marcie behind a couch and have them pop up for their lines.

Jokes on Jokes on Jokes

Imagine *BoJack*, for a moment, without the constant visual gags and animal puns that reliably land in every establishing shot and live in the backgrounds through most scenes. The tone of the series would be entirely more serious. These constant mood-lighteners are shepherded carefully into shot after shot by Mike Hollingsworth and the entire crew throughout the process.

Raphael Bob-Waksberg [series creator]: The idea is that the story comes first. We avoid stepping on what's important in the scene and what we're focusing on. We want jokes that complement that, service that, as opposed to drawing focus or distracting from that. I think that's the challenge.

Mike: We have to act as a helping hand, not a tripping foot. As far as animal jokes, I just love them so much. I was raised on *The Muppets* and Chuck Jones and Tex Avery. In the studio,

This page: Plant people exist in Lisa's sketchbook, but that line is yet to be crossed in the *BoJack* universe.

This page: Some personal artwork from lead prop designer Elizabeth McMahill.

there's a note up on the wall that reads, "Mike says no more goddamn giraffe jokes!" [*Laughs.*] When you think of these animal jokes, you think of the tallest, the biggest, the fastest—so that's, like, the first thing everybody keeps going to, and I'm like, "Guys, we hit giraffes hard, HARD, in seasons one and two. We have *explored* giraffes." You have to really make a case to get me to approve a board with a giraffe. It's got to be some kind of giraffe that I could have never imagined. Because I have had it up to HERE [*laughs, groans*]. A lot of times I may push an animal joke too far, and when viewing the animatic, Raphael, Noel, and Steve will be like, "What is going on?" And I'll be like, "Well, if you don't know, an aye-aye is this lemur that has one long finger, soooooo, it's funny that he's doing one extra-long line of coke with his long finger!" And they're like, "Okaaaaaaay."

The Right Tools for the Job

An experienced eye will notice the occasional three-dimensional element in the largely two-dimensional world of flat characters and background artwork. The most literally upfront example is the signature opening credit sequence that was specially directed by Mike Roberts, with the theme music by Patrick and Ralph Carney. While the character art in the opening titles is made of flat, drawn pieces, the rooms of BoJack's house are three-dimensional sets that give a sense of depth as the virtual camera pans through and over them with BoJack's head fixed front and center.

More 3-D elements pop up throughout the show, including some cars, the backgrounds that recede into the distance during a driving shot, and Todd's giant papier-mâché head—but their use within the episodes proper is strictly a practical matter in this intentionally flat cartoon world.

Mike: When we first started, I was very excited about the concept of basically making a show that looked like a zine, an indie comic. I'm a really big fan of the show *Mission Hill*. That show really looked like a graphic novel come to life. But then, when you're creating this world, you can kind of get yourself into a pickle where you're like, "We need a 3-D element to make this look proper; otherwise it's just going to look too bumpy." The writers are just writing what's compelling, and sometimes that involves a car coming to a screeching halt—

Raphael: Right. Or swerving.

Mike: And if you kept it 2-D with clunky in-betweens, then that would kind of take you out of the moment.

The strategy for visually integrating a 3-D element, like a swerving car, into the flat 2-D cartoon world is usually achieved by shading the car with flat colors and a black outline, mimicking the drawings around it.

Raphael: And so we don't want things to look too polished or 3-D, either. You know, the goal is whatever serves the story, and the best way to tell each story beat.

Mike: Yeah. I remember the first time I started seeing 3-D in *The Simpsons*. It was the episode where all of the people were in a big ball that was rolling and destroying the town, and I was like, "That looks really weird." [*Laughs.*] It was too smooth, too textural—like, a 3-D texture of people applied to a sphere. So yeah. We do what we can to keep to Lisa [Hanawalt]'s aesthetic.

Animating Mouths

Big Star Enterprise, Inc. is the Korean animation production studio that takes the completed animatic files with all the character puppets and special pose models and completes the animation in each scene. Given the importance of the dialogue in *BoJack*, syncing the character mouth shapes to the audio track is first completed in-house at ShadowMachine.

This page: Some visual gags, including the one strangely frog-like musician, the "twin" scientists, and a few costumed extras.

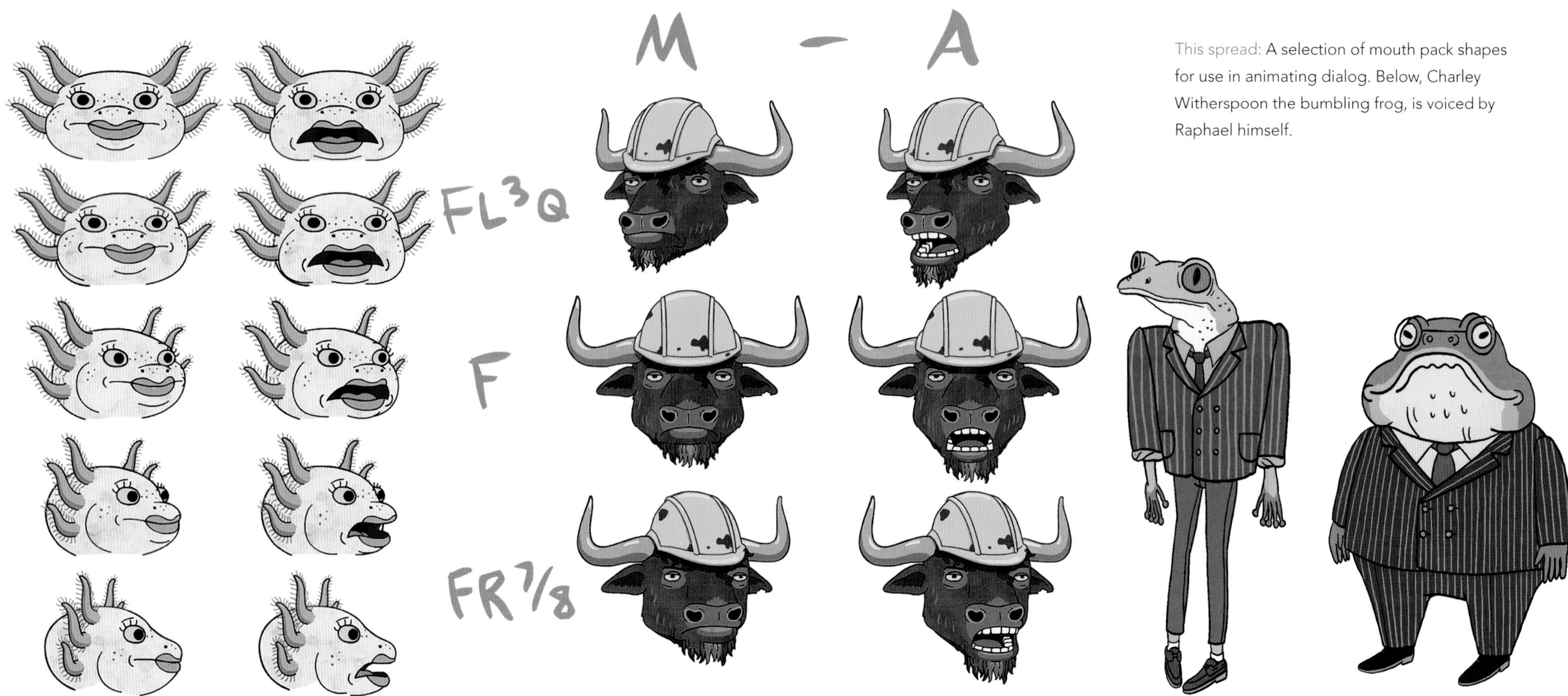

This spread: A selection of mouth pack shapes for use in animating dialog. Below, Charley Witherspoon the bumbling frog, is voiced by Raphael himself.

Anthony Ananian [lip-sync animator]: We take the puppet head that we need for a specific shot, animate it, and send the completed lip sync to Korea, and they incorporate our animated puppet heads into their work.

Alex Linares [lip-sync animator]: BoJack himself has a very unique speech pattern. At times it feels that he is racing through his words. Instead of trying to hit every single letter and word, we have to figure out which shapes we can leave out to allow the mouths to flow together most naturally. When it comes to lip sync, most of the time less is more.

Anthony: Usually we end up with around ninety unique mouth shapes for the important characters, which include happy and sad versions. If we feel like we need some extra mouth shapes to really deliver the dialogue for a particular scene, we ask the designers and they help us out.

The rest of the facial animation is done at Big Star based on the blueprints of the animatic.

Animating Animation in Animate

When the artists at Big Star receive the episode to work on, the assets are all neatly contained within the Flash/Animate files and already set up to be animated. Each scene will have the background on a layer, and any other background props or overlays (like furniture or foreground elements) on layers above the characters. The characters themselves are the puppets from the character design team at ShadowMachine, which contain all of the stock angles, expressions, and pre-animated lip sync. The primary animation that happens in Korea is the tedious work of making the puppets move between the set key poses. Additionally, the artists draw any custom animation that the scene requires.

The character puppets are animated from pose to pose with the previously mentioned "tween" effect, creating a smooth, slick movement style. The episode director in the *BoJack* studio will massage these movements back into the chunkier, clunkier rhythm of traditional animation, where drawings usually are held for two frames at a time. An unaltered tween would move art on every frame, making things look too smooth.

Aaron: In theory, everything comes back to us with tweened animation, but we break almost everything apart and tweak it by hand, if not outright animate it frame by frame. The overseas studio has been improving over the course of the series as they (and we) have come to understand the visual style better.

Anne: Tweens are used, but they're a shorthand that works well only when utilized by skilled animators. A scene with a lot of tweening will look mushy and almost have a slo-mo sort of appearance, so, like Aaron said, we usually break the tweens apart and put things on twos [hold a drawing for two frames at a time], as well as change up the timing so not everything's moving at an equal pace.

After the episode animation arrives back stateside in a digital instant, it is reviewed and any further notes are compiled into spreadsheets. Retake animators at ShadowMachine then tweak elements here and there.

Matt: We'll get the animation files back from Big Star, and our animation directors will review them. Raphael gives rounds of notes as well, and he'll say, "Well, we want to see *this* expression here," or, "This acting isn't working; let's try something different." There are a lot of eye fixes—eye-acting changes that we make.

Anthony Rollins [retake animator]: A lot of the time it's just plussing [enhancing] the acting. So it's largely facial changes.

Adam Parton, a director at ShadowMachine on previous

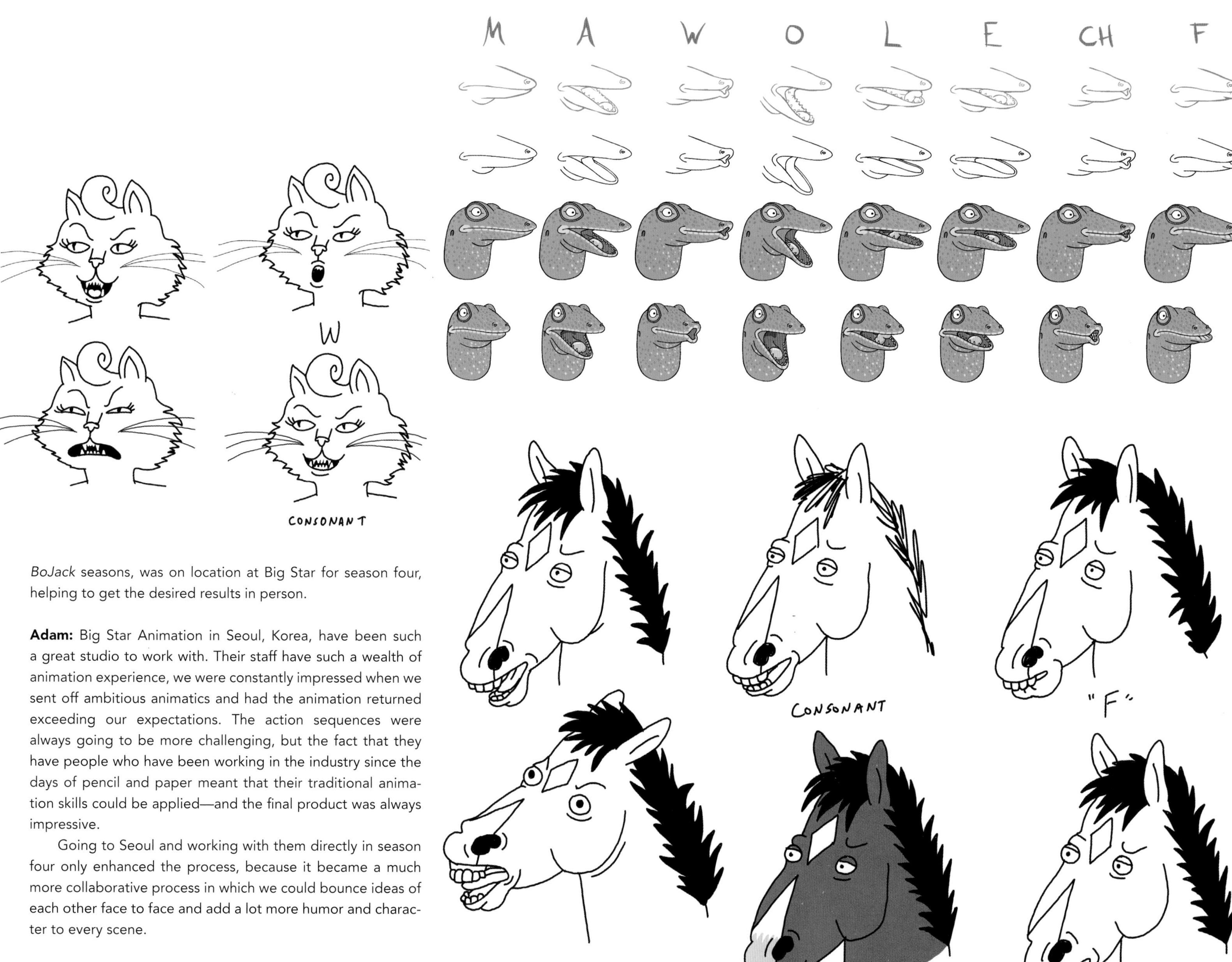

BoJack seasons, was on location at Big Star for season four, helping to get the desired results in person.

Adam: Big Star Animation in Seoul, Korea, have been such a great studio to work with. Their staff have such a wealth of animation experience, we were constantly impressed when we sent off ambitious animatics and had the animation returned exceeding our expectations. The action sequences were always going to be more challenging, but the fact that they have people who have been working in the industry since the days of pencil and paper meant that their traditional animation skills could be applied—and the final product was always impressive.

Going to Seoul and working with them directly in season four only enhanced the process, because it became a much more collaborative process in which we could bounce ideas of each other face to face and add a lot more humor and character to every scene.

“That Went Well”

This spread: **Anne Walker Farrell:** The last sequence of "That Went Well" [S3E12] was a sequence I saw in my head when I read the script. *BoJack* is unique for an animated show in that it allows you, and really almost invites you, to push the drama. Amy was gracious enough to let me run with it and it was awesome to be able to go all out in terms of staging and shot design. When I had the opportunity to direct my first episode, "The Old Sugarman Place" [S4E02], the cold open was a direct hookup to the last sequence of "That Went Well," and I knew instantly I wanted to do something similar. I storyboarded BoJack's dreamlike journey across the country and into his past; the beautiful animation from Adam Parton and the team in Korea, and the music from Michelle Branch and Patrick Carney, brought the sequence together and made it something really special.

Stylization

Below: Anne Walker Farrell designed this stylized sequence from "Stupid Piece of Sh*t" (S4E06), drawing inspiration from the mid-century design work of United Productions of America.

Opposite: Background designer Alison Dubois worked on the Wayne Thiebaud/United Productions of America mash-up-inspired backgrounds in this special sequence for "What Time Is It Right Now" (S4E12), while episode director Tim Rauch designed the characters as extensions of the stylized designs from director Anne Walker Farrell's episode (below).

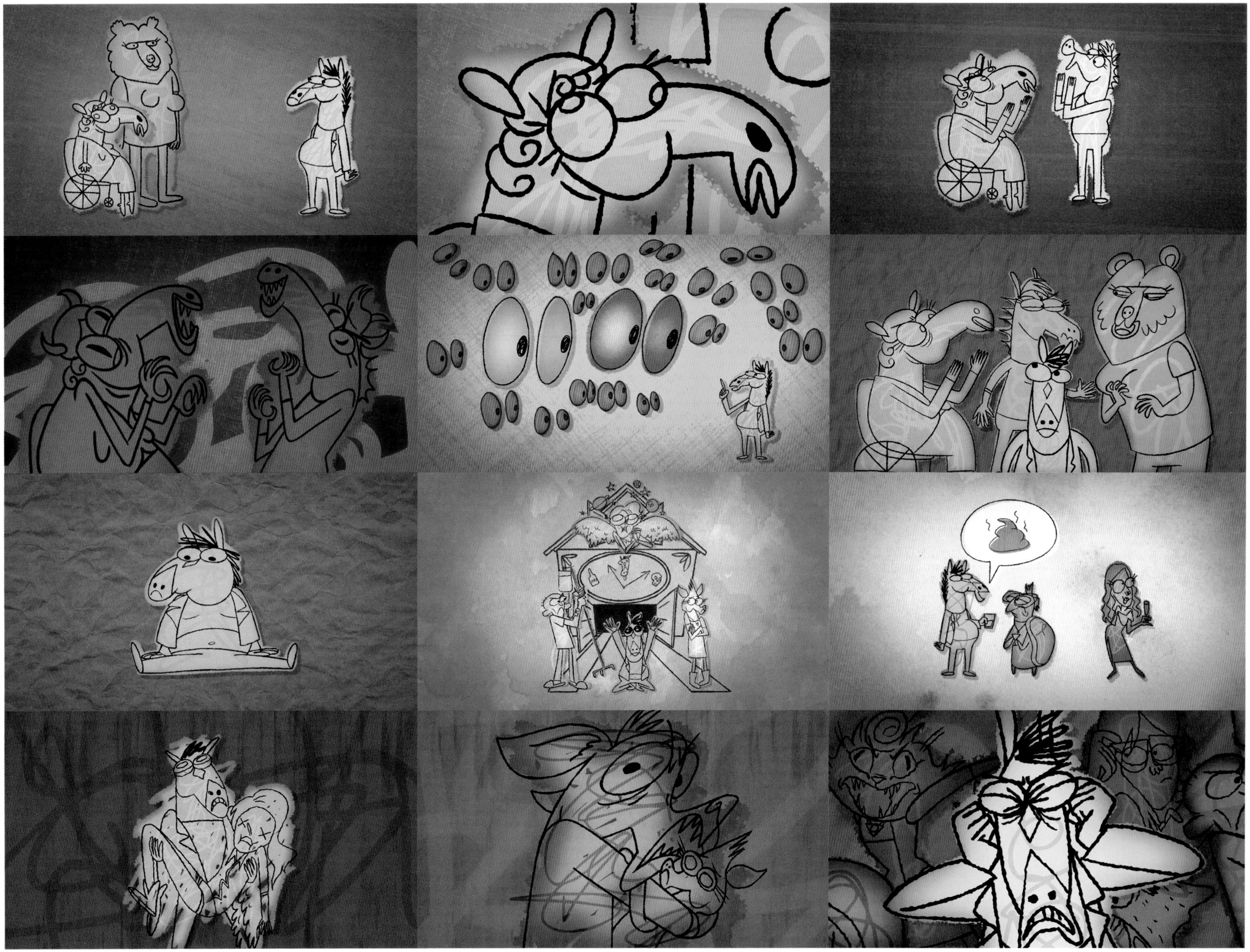

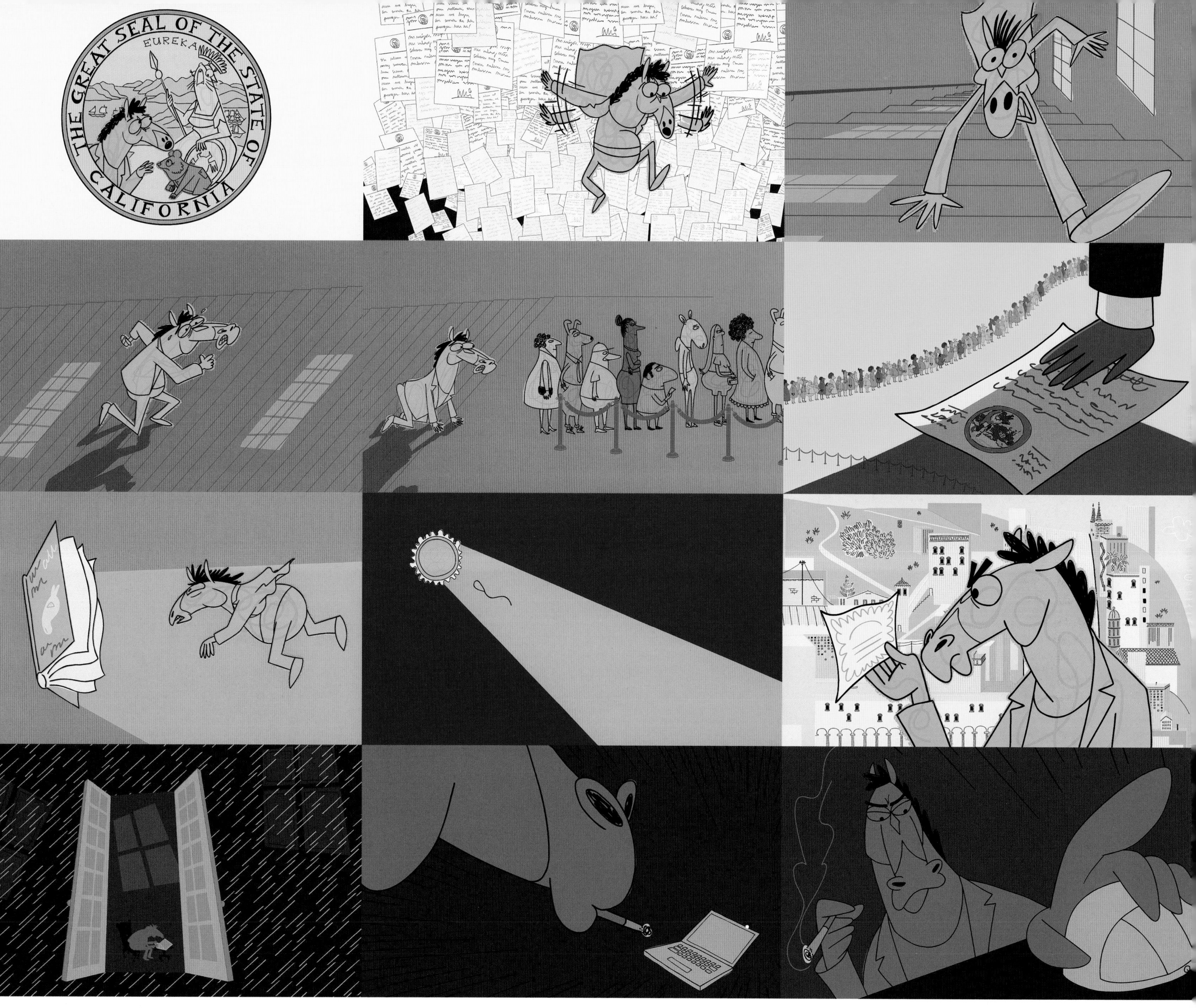
THE GREAT SEAL OF THE STATE OF
EUREKA
CALIFORNIA

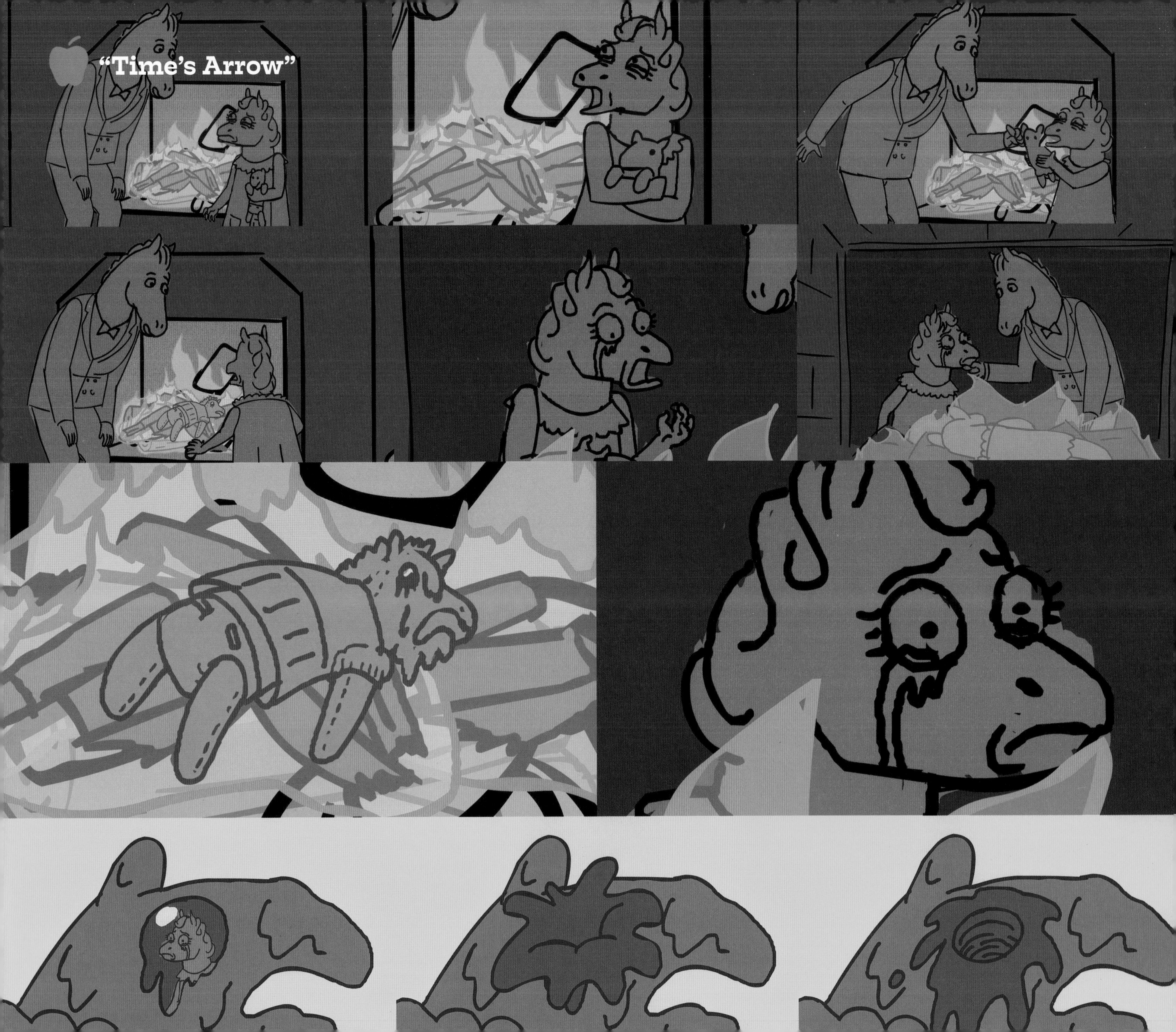
"Time's Arrow"

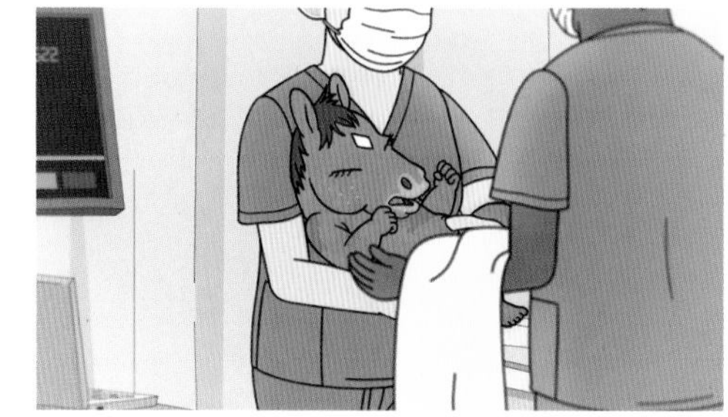

This spread: **Kate Purdy [writer]:** There's an episode in season four that deals with BoJack's mother, Beatrice ["Time's Arrow" (S4E11)], and it's primarily from her perspective, and she has some form of dementia. So it's her looking through history and we begin to understand her. Raphael worked a lot with the directors and animators, and as a design solution, some of the characters have squiggles for faces, and some don't have faces or mouths. We talked a lot about memory and how it works. How people remember. My mom always remembers what clothes people were wearing, what outfits, whereas my dad may not remember people's faces at all. Raphael says that he mostly remembers dialogue when talking to people. So we were just playing with memory—how does that work, and how does it work through time, and how do we present this character that's dealing with her memories through history while dealing with the diminishing function of her mind? Mostly we talked about how each of us remembers, and we did some research on sundowning and Alzheimer's and memory in general, and found visual ways to explore those things.

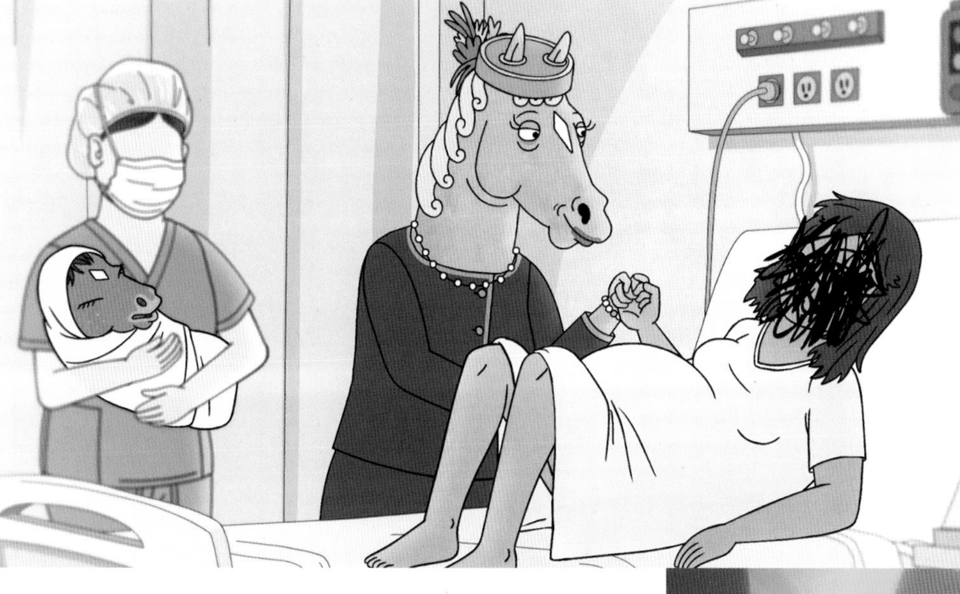

Show Bible: Animation

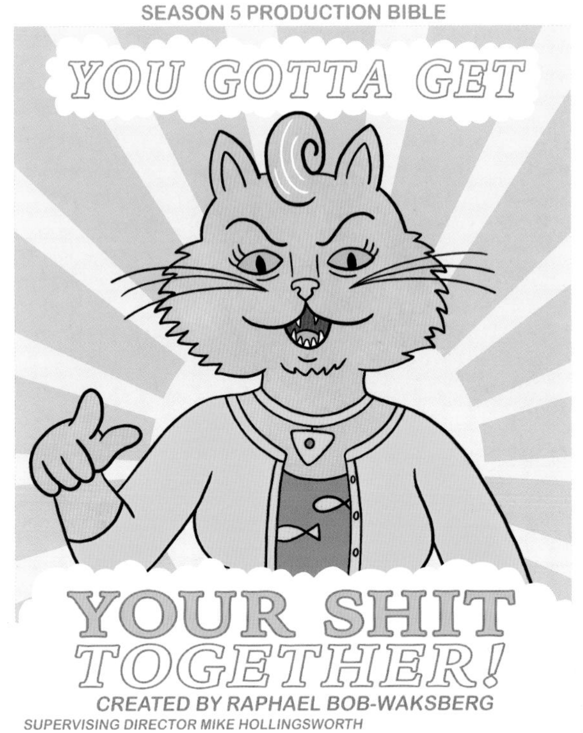

SEASON 5 PRODUCTION BIBLE
YOU GOTTA GET
YOUR SHIT
TOGETHER!
CREATED BY RAPHAEL BOB-WAKSBERG
SUPERVISING DIRECTOR MIKE HOLLINGSWORTH
PRODUCTION DESIGNER LISA HANAWALT
EXECUTIVE PRODUCER NOEL BRIGHT & STEVEN COHEN

STICK 'EM UP!!!
MANY OF OUR CHARACTERS HAVE ARMS THAT CONSIST OF CLOSED OFF SHAPES. BUT WHEN THEY RAISE THEIR ARMS THE MODEL NEEDS TO CHANGE TO AN OPEN SHAPE. WHEN THE ARMPIT AREA LINEWORK REMAINS CLOSED OFF THE CHARACTER'S ANIMATION LOOKS VERY STIFF AND UNNATURAL.
NO!
NO!
IN ORDER TO KEEP THE SWEATER PATTERN CONFINED, YOUNG BOJACK RETAINS THE LINEWORK AROUND HIS BICEP. BUT THE SHAPE CHANGES!

ANIMATION

THOUGH BOJACK HORSEMAN IS ANIMATED IN FLASH IT SHOULDN'T LOOK "FLASHY." WE SHOULD STRIVE FOR A LEVEL OF ANIMATION THAT RESEMBLES TRADITIONAL ANIMATION. WE CAN DO THIS SIMPLY BY AVOIDING TWEENS AND REDRAWING ARMS, HANDS, LEGS, TORSOS WHEN NEEDED. AS WE MOVE FORWARD WE'LL ACCUMULATE LIBRARIES OF THESE NEWLY DRAWN PIECES THAT WILL BE ADDED TO THE CHARACTER TURN AROUND FILES.

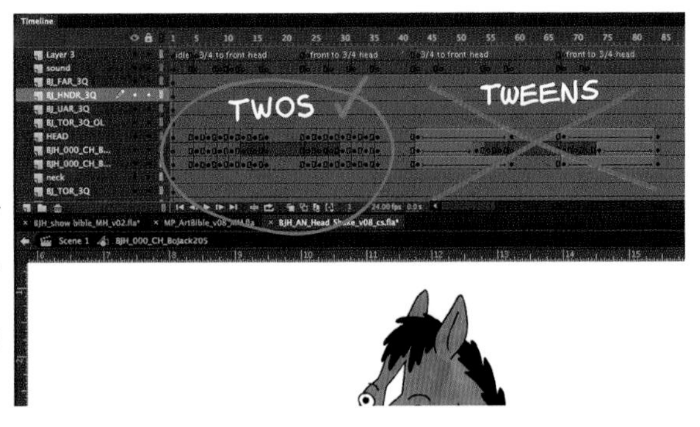

LIP SYNC

EACH MOUTH SHAPE SHOULD BE UP FOR AT LEAST TWO FRAMES. THEY CAN BE UP FOR LONGER — THREE, FOUR, ETC. — BUT NEVER FOR LESS THAN TWO. THE ONLY TIME A SINGLE FRAME WOULD BE USED IS AS A CUSHION (INBETWEEN) BETWEEN TWO MAIN MOUTH SHAPES.

BLINKS

CHARACTER BLINK HAVE A SUBTLE SQUASH TO THEM ON OUR SHOW.

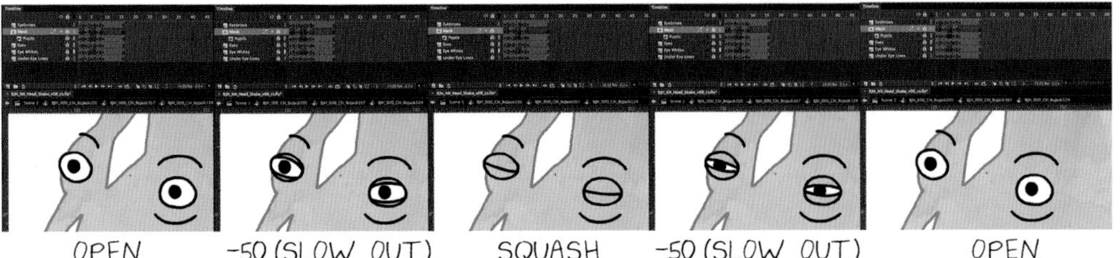

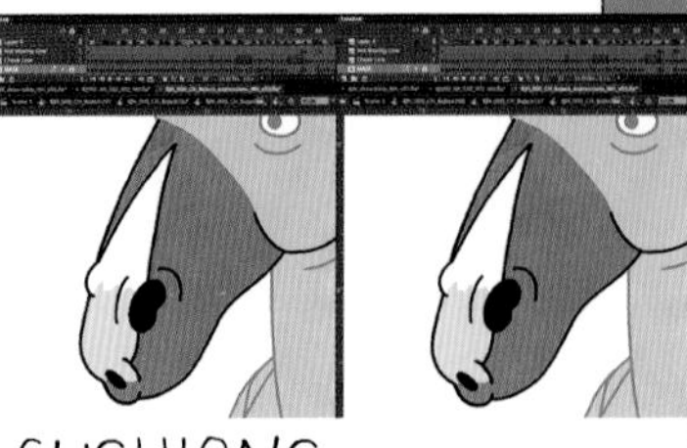

CUSHIONS

WE HAVE PLENTY OF CUSHIONS BUILT INTO THE MAIN CHARACTERS MOUTH PACKS LIKE (THIS FUN LITTLE "W" PUSH ON FRAMES 50 AND 51). USE THEM TO CREATE SMOOTH NATURAL LIP SYNCS. THERE'S A LOT OF TALKING ON THIS SHOW! LET'S MAKE IT LOOK NICE.

FLAP!

- SUCCESSFUL LIP SYNC IS ACHIEVED BY SIMPLY OPENING AND CLOSING THE MOUTH AT THE RIGHT TIME.
- MOUTH SHAPES SHOULD HIT A FRAME BEFORE YOU HEAR THEM. PEOPLE WON'T NOTICE IF THEY HIT EARLY BUT THEY ALWAYS NOTICE IF THEY'RE HITTING LATE.

- "L" MOUTHS SHOULD BE USED AS A CLOSED MOUTH LIKE A "CONSONANT," "M" OR "W."

This spread: Some show bible pages detailing animation, lip sync, and acting notes.

MAKE SURE HER HAIR REACTS TO GRAVITY

DIANE'S EYES

UNLIKE BOJACK AND TODD, DIANE DOESN'T HAVE AN UPPER EYE LID. WHEN SHE BLINKS HER EYES BECOMES A SINGLE LINE.

HEAD TILTS

- no mouth -

- full mouth -

DIANE MAKES FACES

OVER IT

EXCITED

DISMISSIVE

SAD

WOW!

TODD MAKES FACES

THINKING

SARCASTIC

HATLESS TODD!

HUH?

ANGRY

TIRED

SURPRISED

HEAD TILTS

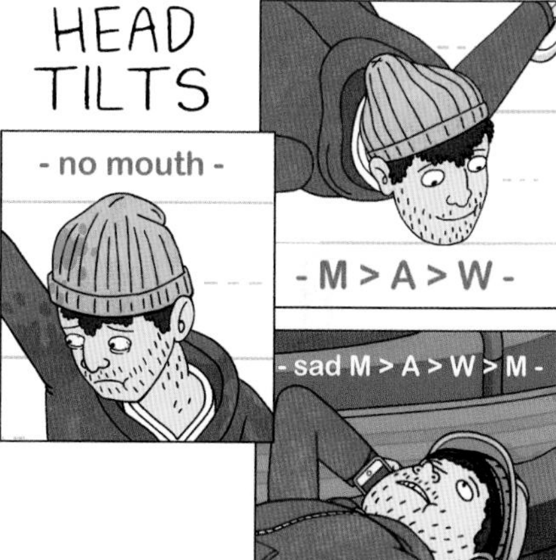

MR. PB ONLY HAS HIS TONGUE OUT WHILE HE'S REACTING TO THINGS. WHEN HE TALKS HE DOESN'T USE HIS TONGUE HANGING OUT MOUTH POSES.

TALKING

REACTING

MR. PEANUTBUTTER MAKES FACES

EXCITED

VERY EXCITED

WORRIED

CONFIDENT

PRINCESS CAROLYN MAKES FACES!

ANNOYED

HMMMM?

PAINED

CURIOUS

SURPRISED

ANGRY

HEAD TILTS

5: Horse Grooves

Music, "Hair and Make-up"

Although BoJack is now on-screen—fully animated, stumbling around with a flask, berating Todd, or sadly reflecting on his bad decisions—he's not quite ready for prime (streaming) time yet. Each episode still needs its carefully composed soundtrack, and each shot needs to be finessed with lighting, color effects, and finishing touches in a process known as compositing—or "comp," for short. This visual fine-tuning is completed by comp supervisor Julianne Martin and her team at ShadowMachine.

Amy Winfrey [director]: During final boards, we have a meeting with Julianne. We talk about what we intended for certain sequences, and she always has great ideas of things she would like to try to make our shots extra fancy.

Mike Hollingsworth [supervising director]: For our animation process, this is like our hair and makeup department. They take our animation and put lighting and lots of terrific effects in there. Every shot passes through this department.

Julianne Martin [comp supervisor]: Our role has also increased a lot since the show started. Because the show's gotten darker—

Mike: Remember how that first season was animated in seven months? We couldn't be quite as precious then. But if you look at that season three underwater episode ["Fish Out of Water" (S3E04)], compared to a season one episode, you can see how over those three years, we were able to get very precious with every aspect of the show.

Julianne: Most of the time compositing on *BoJack* serves a supporting role, an element that pares down all the visuals to a focal point in the scene or conveys the intended mood without drawing too much attention to itself. But that underwater cavern scene's intention was to be really beautiful and whimsical, with lighting being the star. The animation really drove the lighting because the characters are interacting with and turning on the light sources, so it was a fantastic collaboration with the animators.

Continued on page 215

“Fish Out Of Water”

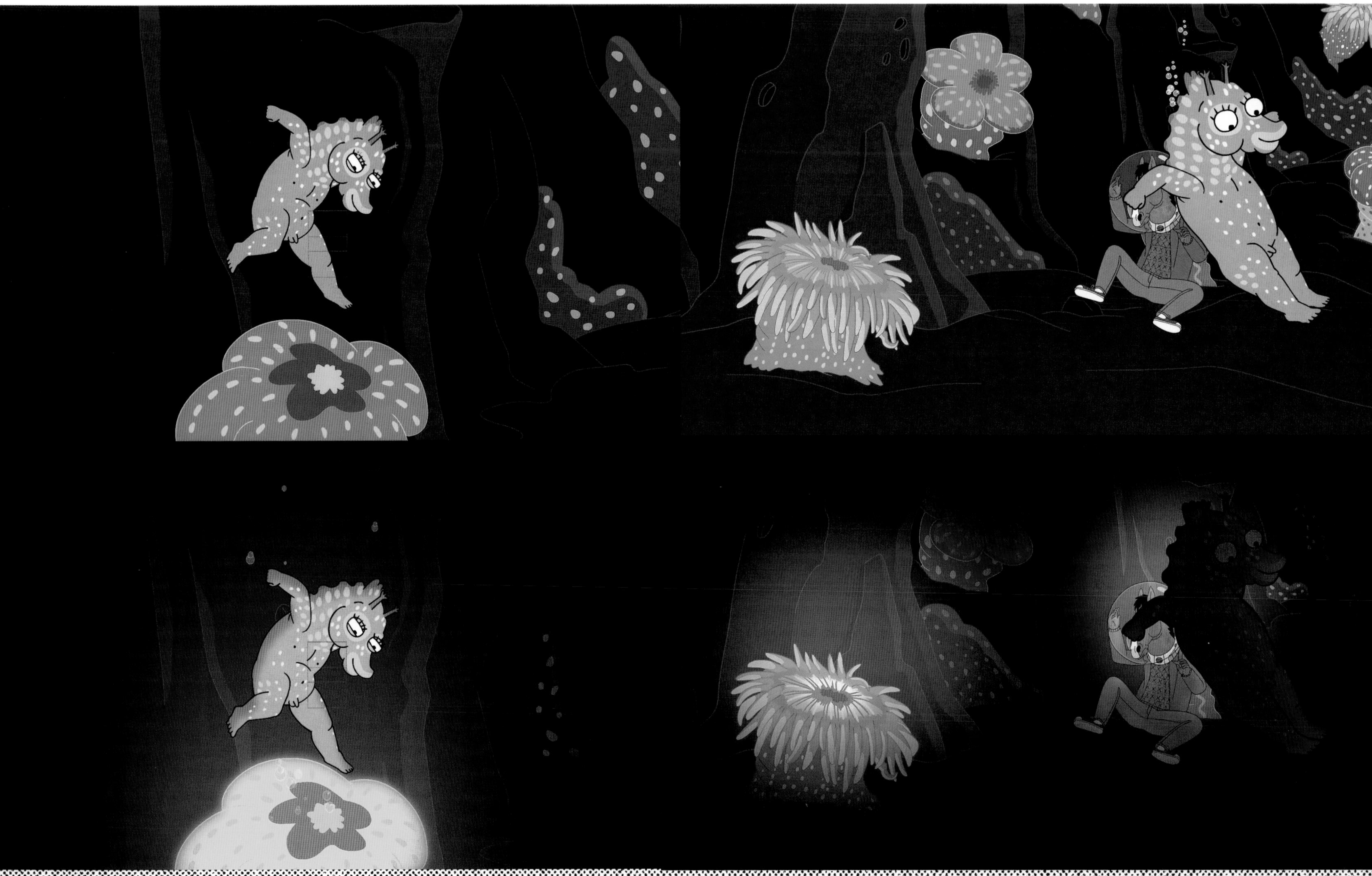

This spread: The compositing stage enhanced the impact of the fanciful underwater scenes featuring the runaway baby seahorse and BoJack. The top row is flat cartoon colors before layering in light and dark animated areas that are activated by the character's interactions with the anemones.

Below: The party sequence from "It's You" (S3E10) in thumbnail boards and special pose models created for the background.

Opposite: The heavy compositing load is evident in scenes with dramatic or atmospheric lighting

The comp department also has to work as a stopgap for all remaining episode problems, since the scenes have to exit the department polished and complete. When a season three party sequence in BoJack's house ("It's You" [S3E10], when he reverses his Tesla into the pool) came back from animation without a convincing party in evidence, the crew needed to improvise.

Julianne: What we got back from Korea were drawings of BoJack's face and an empty background tweening around. When I watched the cut in sequence, I realized that production had selected the same background for every shot, which had this giant Cabracadabra sign in it and drew way too much attention. The episode's director, Adam Parton, and I sat down and talked through what to do about this problem, and he proposed that we grab all angles of BoJack's living room so that BoJack would be spinning through. I knew it was a good idea, but it meant that instead of lighting and adjusting one background, I'd have to do thirteen. To populate the shots, I grabbed the foreground characters that Lisa had designed, but the room behind BoJack was still empty. To fill it I had our PA [production assistant] go through the show archives and steal extras from every dancing or crowd scene we had done in the history of the show: the lemur party in season one ["Prickly-Muffin" (S1E03)], Penny's prom in season two ["Escape from L.A." (S2E11)], Diane and Mr. Peanutbutter's wedding ["Horse Majeure" (S1E09)]. I had free rein to set up all of the compositions; I still remember realizing we had flying characters at the party that I could use for more dynamic arrangements. The scene gets darker and darker as it progresses. It took hours of tweaking to come up with so many different color schemes—one of them is stolen from Minas Morgul in *Lord of the Rings*!—and push background extras back enough while still keeping them individually lit and discernible.

Adam Parton [animation director]: I think we both were really enjoying the chance to add so much more at the comp stage. Keeping the camera alive and affecting the lighting as much as we did wasn't really the norm for *BoJack*. It was a process of testing things out on the fly and seeing what worked, though we had reasons for everything we did. For instance, the shots just before BoJack crashes through the window in the car needed to show how the party had turned dark and menacing for BoJack, so we chose lighting that carried that message using reds and yellows, rather than more calming colors, and took that to the end, until he finally finds peace beneath the calming blue water at the bottom of the pool.

Another challenge for the comp crew came in "Time's Arrow" (S4E11), an episode in which many of the extras were designed without faces, because Beatrice, BoJack's ailing mother, doesn't remember them.

Julianne: After some back and forth and experimentation, we decided to blur the extras, to go for a sort of visual haziness and keep elements far away from Beatrice out of focus, which we don't generally do in the show. During the scene where she dances at her coronation ceremony I lit the scene in a surreal way and put on this subtle effect where people come into focus as she comes near them and out of focus as she moves away from them. You'll also notice when you watch the episode that blurry BG extras will interact with in-focus memorable characters, such as a blurry nurse holding full-res baby Hollyhock in her arms. It was a technical challenge to get those elements together, but it served the intention that we are viewing this story through the lens of a declining woman with dementia.

The comp department also applies a variety of animation and background effects that can't be achieved in Flash.

Peter Merryman [lead compositor]: When a scene calls for dialogue or other action while characters are driving a car, what you see through the windows of the car is a little trickier than the usual background art. Because the road and scenery move in perspective, the artwork continuously needs to diminish toward the horizon over time. To achieve this, the compositing team uses After Effects to create simple 3-D

Below: A virtual diorama viewed from above. Flat 2D art arranged in 3D space like this provides the animated background for driving scenes in which the camera sees in front of or behind a moving vehicle.

This page: In a special sequence from "Ruthie" (S4E09),. the story of Princess Carolyn's immigrant ancestors is told through photo collage.

Opposite: Ralph's story is told through illustrated stills in "It's You" (S3E10).

backgrounds, similar to a diorama you might make out of paper or cardboard. Just like a paper diorama, the elements for these backgrounds begin as flat artwork that is then constructed in virtual space. Each building resembles a little box, sitting in rows on a flat road, with flat trees, parking meters, lampposts, and other detail pieces angled to face the passing camera. Usually the camera follows a straight path down a straight road, but some special shots have required multiple turns and swerves through virtual dioramas that look like big model-train layouts!

Julianne: We animate certain elements that don't make sense to do in Flash, like particles—such as the torn script pieces cascading down from the fan in Marv's office or all of the bubbles in the underwater episode—or warps, like drifting kelp or waving flags. We add effects like scan lines to screens or interesting transitions when the boards call for them. Sometimes we'll populate backgrounds with reusable animated elements or animate cars driving by. On occasion we create backgrounds; I made the cosmos that BoJack and Sarah Lynn watch in the planetarium, for example.

To light characters in any kind of dramatic light or glow, the comp department has to individually treat the layers of characters and background art.

Julianne: For lighting, we usually color-treat individual elements—we work with all the animation and OL [overlay] layers, not flattened video. When we were figuring out the direction for the underwater episode, the producers wanted a blue filter over the screen, which turned reds and yellows to dull grays. I fought against this approach because the emotional center of the episode is an orange baby seahorse. Since the episode was designed with the normal saturated color palette, I felt we needed to embrace the unrealism of an underwater world with a full color spectrum (in reality, red and yellow light rays wouldn't appear past about twenty feet underwater), and instead of trying to force the episode to be blue, we should try to make each scene look distinct and beautiful.

Creating the illusion of dramatic, directional lighting that wraps around the flat, two-dimensional drawings is as complex as animating the character in the first place. Some simpler rim-lighting effects can be achieved by using the silhouette of the animation itself.

Julianne: We generally just offset the animation from itself to create the rim lights. More complex lighting requires more complex processes, with more broken-up pieces. In season four ["Ruthie" (S4E09)], we have a scene where Princess Carolyn is in her office that was lit in design in a very graphic fashion, and we had to light her to match. Graphic light can be pretty unforgiving, and Chris Weller, the compositor who had that scene, had to spend a ton of time and attention making sure that the light hit her correctly and masking it out where it didn't. A lot of the work with more complicated lighting is invisible work, i.e., making sure nothing pops from one frame to another.

Getting that detailed can be a bit dangerous because no show is final until it's delivered, so any revisions to the animation after we've done that kind of work can be a real setback for us. For that reason, when lighting is going to be very complicated or dependent on the animation I ask for prioritization of those scenes from the animators. Sometimes we can find cheats or collaborations with animation, too; in the underground episode in season four ["Underground" (S4E07)], we exported adjusted .swfs [Flash animation files, popularly pronounced "swiffs"] in which we turned the cell phone screens "green-screen green," keyed that color, and then matted an untreated

Continued on page 220

Stylized Sequences

This spread: The artists experiment with new style approaches to special storytelling sequences each season. **Sarah Harkey [background designer]:** I've had the opportunity to work with Lisa to create some of the show's stylized sequences, such as Ana Spanakopita's stories and Wanda's jokes. These were a break from the norm in both style and approach, as we created them in Photoshop instead of Flash—extra fun!

MULCH DEPOT

This spread: The stylized sequence from one of Wanda's jokes continues.

version of the animation onto that screen mask—meaning that while the characters and backgrounds were extremely dark, the cell phone screens were the brightest things in the room. I also asked the prop designer to build a big circle into the cell phone prop that the animators kept off but we would turn on, export separately, and use as a lighting adjustment layer so that we didn't have to [manually retrack] all of those cell phone lights as they moved with the animation.

Composing Music Theories and Process

The commercial jingles, the sitcom theme music, the on-the-nose pop song parodies, the musical cues that help the show transition seamlessly from moment to moment—all of these are brought to you by the creative efforts of show composer Jesse Novak. The creative collaboration of Jesse and series creator Raphael Bob-Waksberg began at Bard College, where Jesse was studying music and had joined the sketch comedy group Olde English.

Jesse Novak [composer]: I had never done sketch comedy before. But we were in this group together, and I think people tended to gravitate toward stuff that they were good at. I was always the one who was also doing music. I would write sketches, I would act in stuff, but music was something that I could do that nobody else was doing. So any time anybody had a musical idea, it would come to me. There were a couple of things that Raphael wrote that he sort of directed me on, musically. I remember there was a sketch that was silent—that just had music—and he had a specific tone that I think I was able to capture. And then there was something else that was kind of like a rap-video concept. I recorded a song with him, and we did that together. That was in the early 2000s.

In college, Jesse studied music but found that his personal projects—playing in bands and recording music—were more compelling than his academic studies.

Jesse: Bard taught me a lot of great stuff, which in the last few years is starting to come back to me, now that I'm mature enough to understand it. But the bands that I played in, and the recording projects that I started in high school—and had been refining my whole life—play more into what I'm doing now than anything that I was taught in class.

Growing up, Jesse had many opportunities to use and develop his craft for comedic purposes.

Jesse: I guess I feel like I've been groomed into the comedy world my whole life. That was sort of the environment that I grew up in, and the kind of stuff that seemed important in our family when I was younger. I was always interested in making people laugh. So of course I was trying to make funny songs.

Like Raphael, Jesse seeks to bring sincerity to everything he writes for the show.

Jesse: Everything that Raphael has ever created has read to me as personal work, and vulnerable work in some ways. And so I try to put myself in a place like that when I'm doing the music, especially because there are so many sensitive and emotionally strange scenes.

At the start of the composition process, Jesse and the producers walk through the episode, spotting where music should go and what it should functionally do for the scene. Then Jesse goes to work.

Jesse: I have a studio where I do most of my work, but I also have a little setup at home for when I don't feel like going out. It depends on what mood I'm in. It's a lot of MIDI [Musical Instrument Digital Interface] sequencing; it's almost entirely digital. The first take of everything involves me playing something along in real time. Most of the cues are short enough that I can kind of play the main idea from start to finish, and then go over it and start adding layers or polishing, or fixing whatever.

It might not sound perfect. Or I take it again, if it doesn't feel right. For some of the longer scenes—let's say if there's a minute- or a minute-and-a-half-long action sequence—the approach becomes more linear and a little bit more logical. But the short things basically come from a recording of a live playing, but then it's all recorded digitally, so that it can be manipulated or fine-tuned from there. But I like to try to capture the feeling of live playing on the first pass.

There are short musical cues littered throughout the show. The goal is for these compositions to seem so natural that viewers barely notice they're there.

Jesse: They might be a transition, or they might be accenting a dramatic piece of dialogue, a moment of reckoning, or something like that. There are accents—serious accents, funny accents. Everything is categorized into . . . I'd say fiction and nonfiction. Because the show satirizes a lot of pop culture, I tend to roll with that in the mood of the show when it gets really spoofy and silly. I try to give it music with a capital *M*, music that just sounds like anything you might catch on TV or in a movie. There's something about music being really generic, a certain type that I think helps the comedy come through. Whereas, for the more serious stuff, I use a more specific sound set of instruments that I call "BoJack World." When I do an episode, I have this huge scrolling thing of the different instruments and everything, and I separate them. I have all my classical instruments, and my strings, and my big pounding drums, and horns and stuff that I'll use for action, or strings for a sad kind of a thing. And then there's the piano, and the drums, and the Autoharp, and these other instruments that have a little bit of a more rough-around-the-edges feel, which I tend to use for scenes that really center around the inner life of BoJack or Diane or Princess Carolyn or the other principal characters.

Jesse also utilizes recurring musical themes in his compositions for principal characters and character relationships.

Jesse: I usually just replay them because I can remember how they go, and I'll orchestrate them slightly differently. There is this romantic theme that recurs between Diane and Mr. Peanutbutter. And there is an evolving set of piano-based themes that I think of as being about BoJack character development. It used to be this one particular theme in season one, and then I started changing it a little bit in season two. I changed it a little bit more in season three. So it's kind of a loose set of themes. There's a certain "piano feeling" that I reserve for moments with BoJack's mother, and there are definitely some instruments that always come up for Todd. And there are some other melodic and harmonic themes that do recur for the characters. But instrumental themes are more common. Like, every time we transition into Princess Carolyn's place of work, there is a certain type of drumming and a certain type of brass that I always use. I use that brass for her transitions and for anything that's about the Hollywood razzle-dazzle, showbiz type of stuff. She gets the showbiz treatment. And Ralph from seasons three and four has his own theme. Or I guess it's their theme, together, now. But when he was first introduced, I played a piano theme for him, and I have brought it back a few times for moments that they have together. And then the newscasts—there's the same music that always repeats every time there's a news show. I love writing themes for fictional programs like *Morning Time Hollywoo*. They all kind of sound pretty similar, but they're a lot of fun. I love that stuff. That's what I always wanted to do. I can't believe I get paid to do it.

Thanks to the writers' playful treatment of chronology in the series, opportunities jump up for Jesse to compose popular music styles and genres for super-specific years past.

Jesse: I love the challenge of it. And it's a way for me to get to comment on stuff, even if nobody perceives the comment. I get a chance to say what I think the nineties were like, or what 2007 was like, musically. Somebody writes the gag "2007-style music plays," and I get to sort of say, "Oh, this is what 2007

Continued on page 224

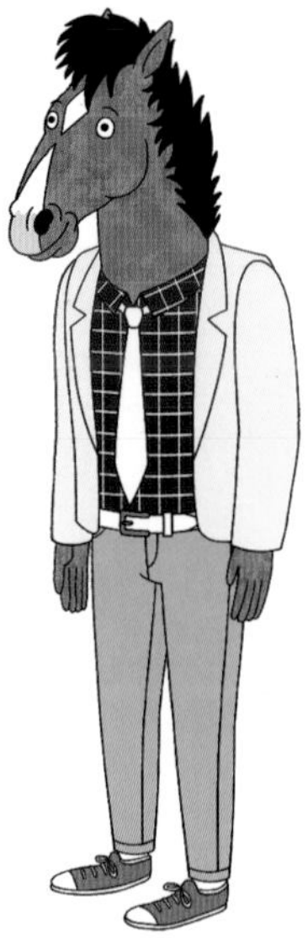

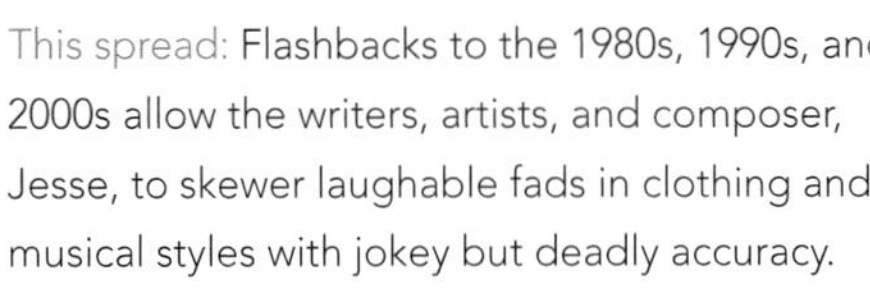

This spread: Flashbacks to the 1980s, 1990s, and 2000s allow the writers, artists, and composer, Jesse, to skewer laughable fads in clothing and musical styles with jokey but deadly accuracy.

annual BONZO SALE!
BIG BROTHER IS WATCHING YOU
THAT'S SO REAGAN
THE GIPPER'S TRICKLE DOWN SAVINGS
WALKMAN
HOUSE of LEGWARMERS
LIKE TOTALLY RAD
DISCO FOREVER
CLOSED FOREVER
DISCO SUCKS
GORB☆CHEV STAIN REMOVERS

got milk?
BE COOL LLAMA Cigarettes
Karma Solutions
KARMA
JUST JORTS
FORMERLY WALT'S WALKMAN
WE'LL MOVE YOUR SHIT
Melrose BILL'S SAX SHOP
COMMANDER IN CHEAP
POG WORLD
TOURNAMENTS HERE!
→ POGS
→ SLAMMERS
→ TUBES
INFLATABLE FURNITURE

Wii REMOTE STRAPS WAREHOUSE
Nothing But Straps!
EEL NO EEL
bearspray
COMING TO THEATERS JULY 2007
GPS DEVICES
CIRCUIT CITY
RE-OPENING SOON?
2007 T-SHIRT OUTLET
LOCK UP PARIS
I GOT A CRUSH ON OBAMA
WASHINGTON MUTUAL
REFINANCE IF YOU DARE
Everything Will Be Okay!
1 HOUR PHOTO
SUBWAAY
KIDS EAT FREE!
ASTRONAUT DIAPER DEPOT
AMOEBA MP3s
We Don't Buy Records, CDs, Cassettes, or 8 Tracks

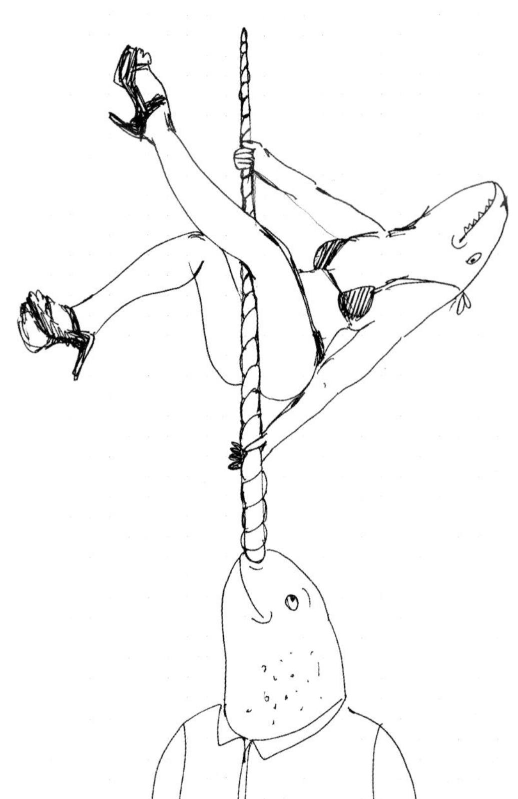

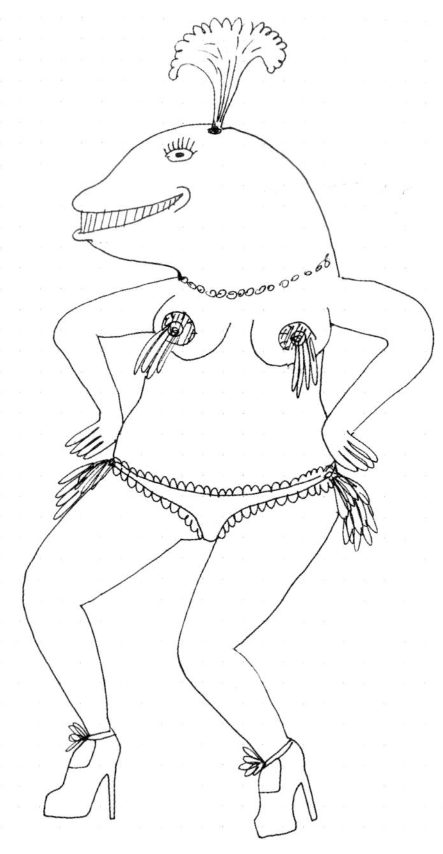

meant to me." Even if it ends up sounding more like 2009, which is secretly the case in one of my songs . . . I wrote this song that I liked so much, and I always felt like it was a little bit of a fudge to call it 2007, but I kept it.

Jesse's flair for historical accuracy simply stems from personal enthusiasm, which serves the series well.

Jesse: I have friends that normalize this kind of stuff, because we're so nerdy together, and so we would be like, "Oh, that would never be used in 2007." Because that's my background—analyzing and thinking about the production of everything, and the behind-the-scenes of everything. It's fascinating. Popular music production evolves like fashion: Everything's the same, but slightly different. These slight differences, month to month, or six months to six months. And what's popular in music does sound a little different now than it did six months ago. I could probably name the differences. But they're so small. Individually they're so subtle, but collectively they give a teeny bit of a different feeling that can place a track in time.

Calling some of the music Jesse composes a parody is an easy way to understand it in general, but the accuracy with which each track nails every trapping and style of the source material reveals an intense attention to detail and an honest love of mimicry.

Jesse: I'm trying to nail it. I think most people don't understand why somebody would care so much about mimicking something. When you say, "Oh, it's a parody," then they say, "Oh, now I know why you're doing that." So I think I'm used to that, because I always liked mimicking music, but I never really had a good explanation for why. I used to make covers of songs that sounded identical to the original recordings. My friends didn't understand why.

How does Jesse define the sonic landscape of the show?

Jesse: Remember how I said there are two sounds? There's the real world, and there's the fake world—the goofy world. The real world comes from the heart, and the goofy world is parodic. All the real-world sound was very much inspired by the look of the show. I really, really thought about the way the colors look, and the way that the art is, from the get-go. And I've always really liked Lisa's work. What I wanted to do from the beginning was try to make the music sound kind of like how the characters look and how the art looks. The colors, the paint, and the brush marks specifically inspired the sound of the show. The goofy world stuff is really fun. But the real world stuff is important, too: the underscore, the transitions, the sonic character of the show. Even when there are no notable music moments, I'm still trying to make it glue together.

We'll Fix It—No—We'll *Enhance* It In Post!

Integrated into the production process from radio play to locked picture, the editors of *BoJack* enjoy enhancing the series at every phase by manipulating media element relationships in time.

Brian Swanson [editor]: One of my favorite aspects of editing *BoJack* is working with other talented people to tell their story and fully realize their jokes. In the underground episode, ["Commence Fracking" (S4E04)] there's this great moment where the ants lift the house back to ground level, causing it to collapse. Then a neighbor walks by and complains about it being an eyesore. It wasn't quite landing because all the jokes were stacked right on top of each other. By resting on the house for a few seconds before it collapsed, we were able to play with the audience's expectations, making the collapse funnier. By slowing down the pace in a few key moments the audience could appreciate each joke fully.

Continued on page 228

This spread: Some selections from Lisa's sketch-book and four signs from the office of Mike Hollingsworth

NO DORKY Cell Phone Rings!!!
A humble request by Mike

And no mention of either dragons OR their respective dungeons will be tolerated
(here at Shadowmachine, we draw the line at talking animals)

No Discussing Jazz Music!
seriously, they aren't even hitting the right notes.

ARMADILLO Slander-Free Zone

"Brrap Brrap Pew Pew"

SEXTINA AQUAFINA
GET DAT FETUS KILL DAT FETUS
BRRAP BRRAP PEW PEW
AOL-TIME-WARNER-PEPSICO-VIACOM-
HALIBURTON-SKYNET-TOYOTA-TRADER JOE'S RECORDS

This spread: Experiencing Sextina Aquafina's abortion-glorifying music video was a traumatic experience for Diane, who unlike Sextina, was actually pregnant and planning an abortion in "Brrap Brrap Pew Pew" (S3E06). **Anne:** The abortion music video might be one of the most over-the-top things I've ever boarded and I LOVE IT. We were sitting around watching Taylor Swift and Rihanna music videos for reference for at least an hour, and I remember spending my afternoon blocking out these absurd shots of stiletto heels kicking rattles, walls of fire, and coat-hanger spaceships, and singing "BITCH BETTER HAVE MY MONEY" to myself. It was a good week.

Amy W.: Netflix was initially a bit hesitant about the abortion music video. They thought that perhaps we should mostly show the reaction on Diane's face. However, I was super excited about directing an over-the-top music video. I worked with my assistant director (and now season four director) Anne, and we incorporated both my ideas on *2001*-inspired giant space fetuses and *Mad Max*–inspired nonsense, with Anne's love of some dorky dances and sequences she saw in a Tiffany music video. In the end, I think we made such a silly video that they made a decision to play more of it on-screen.

Careful selection and placement of sound effects is as essential as editing the picture.

Jose Martinez [editor]: In "Fish Out of Water" [S3E04] although BoJack can't speak, he by no means stops trying to communicate. This left some interactions he had open to a certain amount of interpretation. To combat that early on, we scrutinized the noise that accompanied BoJack's movements to try to bring more clarity: The whooshing of the water around him. If BoJack was surprised or angry, he would have a higher pitched abrasive sound of his flailing arms, as opposed to a calm drift for his sadder moments or shrugs.

These Songs Really Tie the Show Together

Wrapped around almost every episode of *BoJack* is a pair of songs that represent the poles of the show's moods. One melancholy and serious, the other light and fun, these credit-sequence tracks were initially chosen by the music supervisor Andy Gowan ("He is almost like our music casting director," says Noel) and the producers from a larger pool of options. A tough choice still remained: Which of these two very different takes on the show's feeling should be featured as the opening theme—the song that introduces every episode and sets the overall tone? The instrumental theme by Patrick and Ralph Carney was ultimately chosen to open the show because it explicitly made a statement: *BoJack Horseman* is going to be different from your typical animated comedy.

Composed as an independently produced collaborative "sound-doodle" by Patrick and his uncle Ralph, it was offered up as a possibility for the sequence when executive producer Noel Bright, a fan of the Black Keys, asked Patrick, their drummer, if he might come up with some options for the show. The track's sound wasn't something that the crew had been looking for, but they knew it was right as soon as they heard it. Recalling horn-drenched themes from cartoons past such as Henry Mancini's "Pink Panther Theme," *BoJack*'s theme has reverberating bass trombone and baritone saxophone riffs that post a warning: There will be dark moods ahead.

The upbeat theme by Grouplove that closes out most episodes, on the other hand, works perfectly as a contrast to the often-downbeat conclusion to each episode, where serious problems are left hanging out to dry. The poppy chords remind viewers of the lighthearted moments they've just witnessed, too.

To heighten dramatic moments on-screen, music supervisor Andy and the *BoJack* team license the occasional hit track, which can lend a built-in emotional resonance to any scene. There's a limit to how many songs from the likes of the Rolling Stones ("Wild Horses" for the season one finale, "Later" [S1E12]) or Nina Simone ("Stars" for the season three closer, "That Went Well" [S3E12]) any show can afford to add to its budget, but these well-placed, well-known songs creep up and effectively ground the *BoJack* stories in the audience's real-world experiences and memories, without warning.

Andy Gowan [music supervisor]: A song or artist might come to mind immediately, or I may have to have a few brainstorming sessions and catalog deep-dives to really fine-tune the directions my mind is going in. For some of the featured music moments in the show, like season-ending scenes or emotional sequences—such as the end of "Yes And" [S2E10], where we used Kevin Morby's "Parade"—I'll often comb through hundreds of songs in order to present a handful of options to the producers.

I'm constantly listening to music with the show in mind and squirreling away ideas. One of my favorite song uses of the series so far has been Oberhofer's "Sea of Dreams," which we used prominently in "Fish Out of Water" [S3E04]. In short, that song use was the result of me being a fan of the band, listening to an early release of their new record, and hearing this song that seemed like it was written just for the episode. Normally I bring in multiple song options for the producers to hear, but this time they just got one, and I was so thrilled they were as excited about the song and its interplay with the episode as I was.

This page: Sketchbook drawings by Lisa. A session in the *BoJack* editing room (right). BoJack and Princess Carolyn (below).

Hope for Happiness?

There is hope for the future—hope that BoJack is slowly learning to be slightly less of a heel. That's about the gist of it. We can't dare to hope for more, after what we've been through.

The series has surprised audiences with its sincere, stark look at the struggles of being human and dealing with depression. At each sign of BoJack's progress, the audience clings to the hope that this time, things will work out; this time, BoJack will find happiness in a relationship; this time, his apology will be accepted; this time, success, fame, fortune, and love will make him whole. . . .

But *BoJack* deflates those hopes, one after another. The audience should be savvy enough by now to guess that the show will not be giving them the happy ending that they are so accustomed to receiving at the conclusion of every family film and every special sitcom episode. There will be no dance party featuring the entire cast grooving to a sugary pop anthem as the closing credits roll.

Yet the audience connection is strong and passionate.

Kelly Galuska [writer]: It's fun to read commentary online, directly from people who connect with things that you've worked on and that you've written, on a level that is sometimes surprising. It's been a very cool thing to witness these last few years. I enjoy the feedback—when it's good. [*Laughs.*]

Even the show's creative team is still adapting their thinking to the brave new world of streaming, on-demand, entire-series seasons.

Elijah Aron [writer]: I'm realizing, more and more, that for the way that a lot of people stream the show, we're basically making a six-hour movie every year. We're doing more and more threads every season through the episodes because people watch it so quickly and love the show and binge it, and it's a different way of thinking about serialized episodes.

Alison Dubois [background designer]: Some fans really love the show, and they rewatch and they rewatch and they pick up on things. We all love going on Twitter and seeing the Halloween costumes people make of obscure, specific, characters from an episode that you would have to watch a couple times to see—or it's, like, Mr. Peanutbutter holding the balloon from the abortion episode, referencing that. I think that the streaming aspect makes the fan base really passionate; it makes it feel like it's theirs because they can see it whenever they want.

Aaron Paul [voice of Todd Chavez]: I love whenever a new season of *BoJack* drops. Because when I'm walking down the street, I'm getting stopped. Really, every day. Strangers on the street say, "Thank you so much for *BoJack*." And just walking around New York, I get so many people saying "Hooray!" for Todd. I'm very proud of this show, because I'm so close to it, and I have been from pretty much the birth of it. And it's just so great that this kind of show can succeed, you know? And survive. And people really love it.

Will Arnett [voice of BoJack Horseman]: It's a very complicated show, emotionally. Raph approaches so many complex issues, not just within each character, but also as they relate to the other characters and the world in which they exist. I'm in awe of Raph's talent.

Sometimes it's hard to articulate exactly how I feel about BoJack because I feel so many things . . . and some of them I'd like to keep to myself.

It's remarkable to be part of something like this. I feel fortunate to work with a cast that is so consistently brilliant. Amy, Aaron, Paul, Alison, et al . . . they're just superb. Every week at the table read I sit next to Paul, and Amy is on speakerphone on the table in front of us. We always laugh at . . . well . . . no . . .

I kinda feel that we live in a time where we so crave to know how the sausage is made, we forget to just enjoy the sausage.

This spread: Lisa's art direction includes a careful attention to specific details in a shot, including paintings and props that will be only seen in passing in the backgrounds.

This spread, following spred: A variety of background art, props, and elements that all contribute to the sense of realness of *BoJack's* world.

A great frontier adventure!
OLD YELLER
TECHNICOLOR
DOGOTHY McGUIRE and FESS BARKER

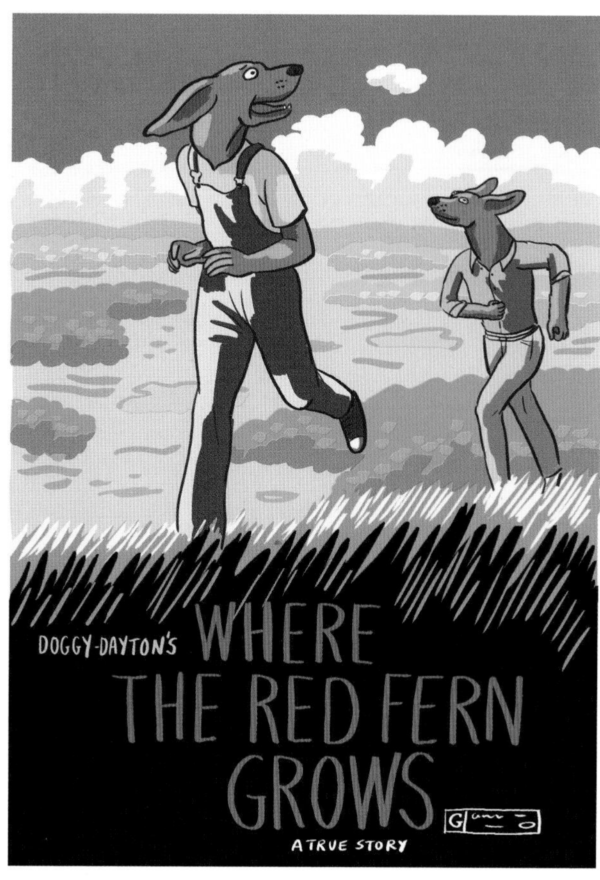
DOGGY-DAYTON'S WHERE THE RED FERN GROWS
A TRUE STORY

BILLIË JËAN KING
IS NOT
MY LOVËЯ
A FILM BY KËLSËY JANNINGS BASËD ON THË NOVËL BY SARAH HARKËY
WWW. MONKËYMOVIË.COM

Ms. TAKEN

THE GREATEST RACE IN HISTORY
CHICKEN-4-DAYZ PRESENTS
GET FREAKY AT THE PREAKNESS
1,175 POUNDS OF FURY
SECRETARIAT
CHAMPION
VS.
GIANT HEARTED
SHAM
CHALLENGER
MAY 19th
TRACKSIDE SEATING
DOORS OPEN 5:00PM
ALL SEATS RESERVED $20
TRACKSIDE IS WHERE ITS AT

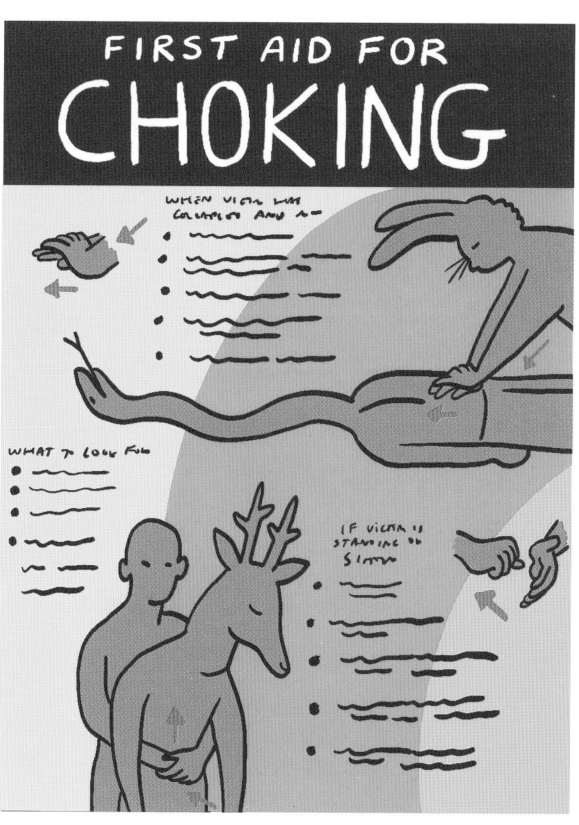
FIRST AID FOR CHOKING

TIT PUNCHER

DIANE NGUYEN

FEMINUTCASE HATES HIPPOPOPOULIS!

EQUINE "BIOGRAPHER" AND FEMINIST SLAG DIANE NGUYEN HAS HITCHED HER PUSSYWAGON TO THE BACKS OF COLTS LIKE SECRETARIAT AND BOJACK HORSEMAN IN ORDER TO MAKE A NAME FOR HERSELF, AND NOW HER PUSSYWAGON'S ITCHING FOR A HITCHING TO A HORSE OF A DIFFERENT COLOR: A HORSE-POPOTAMUS! OLD DRY-ANE IS DRAGGING OUR BELOVED UNCLE HANKY'S NAME THROUGH THE MUD TO GET AIRTIME FOR HERSELF AND HER BULL-HATING AGENDA.

ARE ANY OF THE ALLEGATIONS AGAINST HIPPOPOPOULIS TRUE? NOBODY KNOWS! THE FACT IS: HANKY IS WORTH $800 MILLION BILLION PROBABLY. PLENTY OF INCENTIVE FOR NUMEROUS CHICKS TO PECK THIS HARD-WORKING HIPPO WITH ACCUSATIONS AND HITCH THEIR PUSSYWAGONS TO HIS FAME. DIANE IS JUST THE LATEST BITCH TO DIG FOR HIS HIPPOPOT O' GOLD! FIGHT CLUB IS A GOOD AND IMPORTANT MOVIE.

TRENDING NOW

INSTALLING A GLASS CEILING IN 5 EASY STEPS

SANDWICHES: THEY SHOULD BE MADE FOR YOU

MRA DAY PARADE FLOAT COLLAPSES

REVIEW: NAG CANCELLING HEADPHONES

A great
BEST PICTURE
AVATAR
MIDNIGHT HOLE
NAZI WHO PLAYED YAHTZEE
REALLY QUITE UPSET MAX
BROOM
THE SHORT BIG TALL SMALL
BEST DIRECTOR
NICOLE HOLOFCENER
AVA DUVERNAY
GINA PRINCE-BLYTHEWOOD
MARY HARRON
ANA LILY AMIRPOUR
FOREIGN LANGUAGE
OLD MARRIAGE
FEEL BAD
KARATE IN THE WOODS
THE DINNER PARTY
MY FATHER THE WAR CRIMINAL
BEST SONG
PLAY THAT FUNKY YAHTZEE, NAZI
GOLD HOOF
THE SILLY BANANA SONG
SPOTLIGHT BLING (THEME FROM SPOTLIGHT)
BEST ACTOR
~~BLACK PEOPLE?~~
COLIN FIRTH
JURJ CLOONERS
BREAD POOT
MICHAEL FASBSPENBER (SP?)
BEST ACTRESS
JENNIFER LAWRENCE
JENNIFER LAWRENCE
CATE BLANCHETT
CATE BLANCHETT
~~FREIDA PINTO?~~
JENNIFER LAWRENCE
CINEMATOGRAPHY
THE LEISURE CLASS
THE HABERDASHER'S PEANUT
THE HATEFUL BB-8
THE ONE W/THE GUY FROM THAT SHOW
CONNECT FOUR- THE MOVIE
SOUND EDITING
DANIEL DAY-LEWIS
MERYL STREEP
JENNIFER LAWRENCE
MARK MANGINI AND DAVID WHITE
RUSSELL CROW
BEST SUP. ACTOR
MARK BUFFALO
SYLVESTER STALLION
CHRISTIAN SNAIL
SHARK RYLANCE
TOM HARDY (WHO IS A CAT)
BEST SUP. ACTRESS
JENNIFER LAWRENCE
JENNIFER LAWRENCE
KATE WINSLET
JENNIFER LAWRENCE
JENNIFER JASON LAWRENCE
DOCUMENTARY
JAG
SLAG
CRAG
BAG
DAG
SOUND MIXING
(SEE SOUND EDITING)
BEST BEST BOY
MASSIMILIANO DESSENA
STEVE DALEY
JIM HOLMES
MICHAEL STOECKER
VINCENT PIERCE
BEST ORIGINAL SCREENPLAY
FEELY FEELINGS
BEFORE AFTERNOONISH
SEXY ROBOT
A RIVERS RUNS THROUGH IT: THE WEEZER STORY
SPY BRIDGE '57
BEST DERIVATIVE SCREENPLAY
THE FANCY QUEEN
POLICE GUYS
THE LAWYERS WHO SHOUT
DOCTOR FOR A DAY
THE DANISH DANISH

This page: The billboard background from "Stop the Presses" (S3E07), and a real *BoJack* billboard spotted in the wilds of Hollywood.

This page: A Hollywoo Hills background and a promo sketch of BoJack by Lisa.

Combined Season 1-4 Credits

PRODUCERS

Raphael Bob-Waksberg
Noel Bright
Steven A. Cohen
Will Arnett
Aaron Paul
Blair Fetter
Jane Wiseman
Andy Weil
Alex Bulkley
Corey Campodonico
Victoria Howard
Eric Blyler
Lisa Hanawalt
Richard Choi
Josh Rimes
Mike Hollingsworth
Tom Cabral

WRITERS

Raphael Bob-Waksberg
Peter A. Knight
Caroline Williams
Scott Marder
Joe Lawson
Mehar Sethi
Laura Gutin Peterson
Kate Purdy
Joanna Calo
Vera Santamaria
Kelly Galuska
Alison Flierl
Scott Chernoff
Elijah Aron
Jordan Young
Nick Adams
Alison Tafel

SUPERVISING DIRECTOR

Mike Hollingsworth

EPISODIC DIRECTORS

Mike Hollingsworth
Amy Winfrey
J. C. Gonzalez
Joel Moser
Martin Cendreda
Adam Parton
Anne Walker Farrell
Matt Mariska
Mike Roberts
Aaron Long
Otto Murga
Tim Rauch

ANIMATION DIRECTORS

Anna Hollingsworth
Crystal Stromer
Adam Parton
Aaron Long
Anne Walker Farrell

PRODUCTION

Nakia Trower Shuman
Eric Blyer
Caitlin Alexander
Sean Gilroy
Andy Schlebecker
Julianne Martin
Angeline Izquierdo
Alison Flierl
Amy Schwartz
Rachel Kaplan
Lorraine DeGraffenreidt
Laura Hilker
Andrew Singer
Allison Morse
Dante Tumminello
Alexandra Sandler
Nicholas Barragan
Ryn Soorholtz
Aaron Missler
Ariella Martorana
Chris Lee
Alex Bradley
Phil Binder
George Aldridge
Brian Harris
Sean Albro Lee
Max Crandall
Jessica Speights
Adam Burnier
Samantha Johnson
Albro Lundy IV
Janet Y. Lee
Joonhyung Kim
Katerina Agretelis
Joshua McMaster
Andrew Guastaferro
Rebecca Jang

STORYBOARDS

Ben Bjelajac
Mario D'Anna, Jr.
Anne Walker Farrell
Michael Griffin
Natasha Helton
Joshua Herron
Traci Honda
Peter Keahey
Aaron Long
Chris Paluszek
Alfredo Plascencia
Greg Postma
Mike Ruocco
Zachary Smith
James Suhr
David Tuber
Martin Cendreda
Dan O'Connor
Stephanie Gumpel
Rick Acosta
Joel Moser
Caroline Foley
Giovanny F. Cárdenas
Steven Chan
Matt Garofalo
Otto Murga
Daniel Stone
Sean Kreiner
Anna Hollingsworth
Cody Walzel
Erica Hayes
Alfredo Pascencia
Meg Waldow
Kim Le
Haley Merlot
Alejandra Quintas
James Bowman
Dillon Kemble
Peter Merryman
Eric Hoff
Christopher Nance
Anthony Rollins
Yair Gordon
Tristyn Pease
Julie Drohan
Samantha Gray
Rachel S. Long

ANIMATORS

Anne Walker Farrell
Aaron Long
Martin Cendreda
Amy Winfrey
Adam Parton
James Suhr
J. C. Gonzalez
Alex Cline
Cody Walzel
Zan Czyzewski
Zoë Moss
Phylicia Fuentes
Joel Moser
Rick Acosta
Tim Szabo
Erik Girndt
Matt Garofalo
Keith Holven
Javier Barboza
Crystal Stromer
Anna Hollingsworth
Otto Murga
Steven Chan
Dante Tumminello
James Bowman
Marius Alecse
Will Cuna
Yair Gordon
David Hernston
Anthony Rollins
Dillon Kemble
Ryan Neff
Karl Pajak

COMPOSITORS

Ben Bjelajac
Moises Jimenez
Blake Armstrong
Chris Weller
Darren Shaw
Julianne Martin
Richard Van As
John Kedzie
Amy Ketchum
Andrew Racho
Peter Merryman
Joe Romero
Paul Evangelista
Christie Hauck
Molly Yahr
Elizabeth McMahill
Claire Levinson
Jean Yi

LIP SYNC

Ramiro Olmos
Anthony Ananian
Alex Linares

PRODUCTION DESIGNER

Lisa Hanawalt

CHARACTER DESIGNERS

Zan Czyzewski
Alex Cline
Phylicia Fuentes
Zoë Moss
Melissa Levingood
Adam Murray
Adam Parton
Jojo Ramos
Ryan Deluca
Cody Walzel
Kayla K. Jones
Anna Hollingsworth
Lotan Kritchman
Katherine Clark
James Kwan
Kendra Melton
Dante Tumminello
Rachael Hunt
Rishon Vasandani
Keith Holven
Joshua M. Herron
Lindsey Lea
Alex Linares
Adam Burnier
Samantha Gray
Yvonne Annette Huckell
Liz Weir Knox
Natalie Young

BACKGROUND & PROP DESIGNERS

Walter Mancia
Elizabeth McMahill
Eric Anderson
Cyndee Guerreri
Sarah Harkey
Jeff LeBlanc
Sophia Lin
Colleen Police
Alejandra Quintas
Timothy Szabo
YaoYao Ma Van As
Anthony Wu
Otto Murga
Tim Szabo
Kelly Wine
Walter Macia
Mitchell Vizensky
Cynthia Barber
Anna Farrell
Kati Prescott
Luciano M. Herrera
Peter Keahey
Alfredo Plascencia
Cyndee Guerrieri
Alison Dubois
Mary Nash
Dante Tumminello
Jessica Speights
Ryan Tonner
Jessica Kleinman
Brian Pitt
Bill Thyen
Megan Willoughby

EDITORIAL

Matt Mariska
Nakia Trower Shuman
Brian Swanson
Molly Yahr
Jose Martinez
Steve Ingram
Stephanie Gumpel
Yoonah Yim
Max Crandall
Claire Levinson

MAIN TITLE

Mike Roberts
Ben Bjelajac
Frank Guthrie
John Kedzie

MUSIC

Jesse Novak
Andy Gowan
Grouplove
Patrick Carney
Ralph Carney
Iko Kagasoff
Michael Brake

SOUND

Ethan Walter
Konrad Piñon
Hunter Curra
Russell Gorsky
Jillinda Palmer
Michael Jesmer
Giacomo Aurora
Joy Elett
Jeff Halbert
Andrew Twite
Kailand C. Reilly
Jack Aurora
John Bickelhaupt

MAIN CAST

Will Arnett
Amy Sedaris
Alison Brie
Paul F. Tompkins
Aaron Paul

GUEST CAST

James Adomian
Khandi Alexander
Alan Arkin
Diedrich Bader
Maria Bamford
Christine Baranski
Caleb Bark
Angela Bassett
Jason Beghe
Kristen Bell
Lake Bell
Candice Bergen
Kate Berlant
Jessica Biel
Kevin Bigley
Rachel Bloom
Raphael Bob-Waksberg
Lorraine Bracco
Zach Braff
Andre Braugher
Matt Braunger
Matthew Broderick
Yvette Nicole Brown
Hannibal Buress
Nicole Byer
Patrick Carney
Wyatt Cenac
David Chase
Kristin Chenoweth
John Cho
Larry Clarke
Jamie Clayton
Stephen Colbert
Kelen Coleman
Adam Conover
Audie Cornish
Chris Cox
Vincent D'Onofrio
Jon Daly
Keith David
Majandra Delfino
Emily Deschanel
Chris Diamanopoulos
Colman Domingo
Fielding Edlow
Raúl Esparza
Harvey Fierstein
Jermaine Fowler
Dave Franco
Ron Funches
Daniele Gaither
Jorge Garcia
Ricky Gervais
Paul Giamatti
Ira Glass
Ilana Glazer
Kimiko Glenn
Ginger Gonzaga
Nicholas Gonzalez
Judy Greer
Terry Gross
Tim Gunn
Lena Hall
Philip Baker Hall
Carla Hall
Lisa Hanawalt
Rachael Harris
Emily Heller
Ed Helms
Mike Hollingsworth
Hannah Hooper
Sharon Horgan
Felicity Huffman
Brian Huskey
Anjelica Huston
Brandon T. Jackson
Marc Jacobs
Abbi Jacobson
Ken Jeong
Jake Johnson
Rian Johnson
David S. Jung
Keegan-Michael Key
Wiz Khalifa
Craig Kilborn
Aja Naomi King
Greg Kinnear
Sarah Koenig
Jane Krakowski
John Krasinski
Lisa Kudrow
Phil LaMarr
Natasha Leggero
Melissa Leo
Jonathan Lethem
Patti Lupone
Rami Malek
Wendie Malick
Leonard Maltin
Garry Marshall
Margo Martindale
Tatiana Maslany

Paul McCartney
Joel McHale
Lin-Manuel Miranda
Elvis Mitchell
Sir Mix-A-Lot
Jay Mohr
Mircea Monroe
Natalie Morales
Rob Morrow
Kathy Najimy
Aparna Nancherla
Minae Noji
Jesse Novak
Mike O'Malley
Keith Olbermann
Peter Oldring
Patton Oswalt
Adam Pally
Archie Panjabi
Chris Parnell
Grace Parra
Russell Peters
Jay Pharoah
Daniel Radcliffe
June Diane Raphael
Nathasha Rothwell
RuPaul
Horatio Sanz
Fred Savage
Kristen Schaal
Liev Schreiber
Amy Schumer
Ben Schwartz
Wave Segal
Wallace Shawn
Martin Short
Gabourey Sidibe
Robert Siegel
J.K. Simmons
Anna Deavere Smith
Nicole Sullivan
George Takei
Fred Tatasciore
Tessa Thompson
Stanley Tucci
Aisha Tyler
Neil deGrasse Tyson
Sheila Vand
Baron Vaughn
Kulap Vilaysack
Rufus Wainwright
David Walton
Naomi Watts
Olivia Wilde
Caroline Williams
Mara Wilson
Henry Winkler
Scott Wolf
Ali Wong
Jeffrey Wright
"Weird Al" Yankovic
Cedric Yarbrough
Heléne Yorke
Sasheer Zamata
Constance Zimmer
Christian Zucconi

CASTING DIRECTOR

Linda Lamontagne

ACCOUNTING/HR

Florian Schereck
Donna Standridge Ramos
Bob Hartman
Jeff Kloss
S. Noelle Schereck
Irene Bixby
Tom Cabral
Marci Levine
Irina Fuzaylova
Canti Laureano
Michele Ryan
Laura Tulloss

For BIG STAR ENTERPRISE, INC. DIRECTORS

Sunghyeon Cheon
Eunyeong Jeong
Jong-Yul Ji
Yunha Kim
Mihyang Lee
Hyeonsu Park
Jong-Wan Ryu

PRODUCTION

Taesoo Kim
Seunghwan Hong
Jeong-Geun Kim
Geumyoung Lee
Youngbin Shin

ANIMATORS

Jiyoung Ahn
Jaeyoung Bang
Youngho Cha
Hyeoksu Choi
Jinok Cho
Yang Eunjeong
Jeonghwan Hwang
Jaehun Jeong
Suhi Jo
Yeonhui Jo
Seongyul Joe
Kyeonghwa Kang
Bora Kim
Hyeonjeong Kim
Jina Kim
Jiyeon Kim
Jiyoung Kim
Juho Kim
Munhui Kim
Gusun Lee
Heonjin Lee
Jongdae Lee
Minjeon Lee
Sanghun Lee
Seunga Lee
Yeongsuk Lee
Yunrye Lee
Gyeongseok Min
Yeonju Nam
Hyeran Oh
Gyeonghui Park
Gyeongok Park
Jaeyeon Shim
Yujin Shin
Kilsuk Sun
Yueong Uhm
Byeong-Gyu Woo
Daegeun Yoon
Jingyeong Youn
Eunhui Bae
Jonggwi Bae
Yeonok Jeong
Jaeyoung Choi
Yonggap Jeong

Editor: Eric Klopfer
Assistant Editor: Ashley Albert
Designer: Chris McDonnell
Production Manager: Katie Gaffney

Library of Congress Control Number: 2017944945

ISBN: 978-1-4197-2773-3
eISBN: 978-1-68335-213-6

Printed and bound in China
10 9 8 7 6 5 4 3 2 1

Abrams books are available at special discounts when purchased in quantity for premiums and promotions as well as fundraising or educational use. Special editions can also be created to specification. For details, contact specialsales@abramsbooks.com or the address below.

ABRAMS
The Art of Books

195 Broadway
New York, NY 10007
abramsbooks.com

Acknowledgments:

Thanks to the entire cartoon-producing animal kingdom at ShadowMachine Animation and at the Tornante Company, including the real, actual dogs. Your generous contributions of time, energy, and resources were essential for the creation of this sad horse book. Thanks to editor Eric Klopfer for his cheerful guidance and the book's delightful subtitle. Whenever served word salad and a basket of never ending word breadsticks, Eric would expertly season them with freshly ground coherence. Also thanks to Ashley and everyone at Abrams for the trust and freedom that they place in our cartoon book collaborations. Thanks for the loving support from Jobina, Quinton, and Felix—our own little herd. Thanks to my students and colleagues for the ongoing inspiration; keep making wild stuff! Special thanks to Raphael, Lisa, Mike, Noel, and Steve for their attention and dedication to making this book as complete as possible with personal anecdotes, emails, and scraps of horsey ephemera, and thanks to Sean and Patrick for helping to badger loads of materials and interviews right out of everyone.

–Chris McDonnell, Philadelphia, January 2018

I wish BoJack had gotten out of the car and run with the other horses.
–Will Arnett